EXIT STRATEGY

The Art of Selling a Business

The Vertical Horizontal Selling Method

Recasting & Selling Memorandum

SHELDON MANHEIM

USpublication.com

Copyright © 2009 by Sheldon Manheim
All rights reserved.

No part of this book may be reproduced or transmitted in any form or by any means, electronic or mechanical, including photocopying, recording or by any information storage and retrieval system, without written permission from the author, except for the inclusion of brief quotations in review.

Printed in the United States of America

Published by USpublication.com,
650 Wantagh Avenue
Levittown, NY 11756
(516) 520-2000
www.uspublication.com

The USpublication.com name, logo and colophon are the trademarks of USpublication.com

ISBN 978-1-59594-285-2

First Edition 2009

Library of Congress Control Number 2008944367

Special thanks to WingSpan Press for their work and publishing on this book in behalf of USpublication.com

This book is dedicated to my parents,
Philip and Gussie Manheim,
who set me on the path to success—but didn't live to share it.

CONTRIBUTING AUTHORS

Accounting and Financial Planning
Jay H. Freeberg, CPA, CFP, CMFS, MBA of Janover-Rubenroit
100 Quentin Roosevelt Blvd., Garden City, New York 11530
www.jrfadvisors.com
free@jrllc.com
(516) 445-9898

Insurance Needs
Charles Holzberg of The Charles Holzberg Agency, LLC
275 Madison Avenue, New York, NY 10016
holzagency@elinkisp.com
(212) 279-7500

Legal Advice
Herbert W. Solomon, Esq.,
of Meltzer, Lippe, Goldstein & Breitstone, LLP, PC
190 Willis Avenue, Mineola, New York 11501
hsolomon@meltzerlippe.com
(516) 747-0300 ext. 152

Franchising
Justin M. Klein and David S. Paris of Marks & Klein, LLP
63 Riverside Avenue, Red Bank, NJ 07701
David@Marksklein.com
(732) 747-7100

Financing
Bradley Colehour
of Popular Small Business Capital, Division of Banco Popular, NA
bbcolehour@bpop.com
(847) 671-5666

Guidant Financial Group
www.guidantfinancial.com
(888) 472-4455

Employee Stock Ownership Plans (ESOP)
Jerry Shapiro of RJ Group
RJGroupbbn@aol.com
(732) 462-1859

Professional Practice Sales
The professional staff of Manheim Business Brokers
650 Wantagh Avenue
Levittown, NY 11756
drstu@professionalpracticebrokers.com
(516) 520-1000 Extension 406

CONTENTS

FOREWORD xi

CHAPTER ONE
EXIT STRATEGY 1

    All Businesses Need an Exit Strategy

    Fourteen Different Ways of Exiting a Business

    Motivations For Selling a Company

    Ten Basic Steps to Building an Exit Strategy

    Other Factors in Planning an Exit Strategy

CHAPTER TWO
THE VERTICAL HORIZONTAL SELLING METHOD 15

    The Proven, Simple, Effective Method of Selling a Business

    Putting The Vertical Horizontal Selling Method to Work For You

    Being Selective in the Way That You Find a Buyer

    The Pitfalls of Advertising Your Business For Sale

    Utilizing the Expertise of a Business Broker or Merger and Acquisition Specialist

CHAPTER THREE
THE ART OF SUCCESSFULLY SELLING YOUR BUSINESS 29

    Examine How Much Money You Really Earn From Your Business

    Gathering Records

    The Effective Way to Sell

    Confidentiality is a Must

    Choosing the Very Best Legal and Financial Advisors

    Bringing in the Strongest Business Broker

    Losing Money? No Profit? No Problem!

CHAPTER FOUR
RECASTING & THE SELLING MEMORANDUM 39
- Recasting
- Recasting: Its Meaning, How it Works, and What it Can Do For You
- How To Recast Your Financials
- Selling Memorandum

CHAPTER FIVE
EBITDA 55
- Interest and Taxes Do Cost a Company Cash
- Depreciation and Amortization are Tools to Save Taxes
- EBITDA is an Aggressive Accounting Tool
- Factors Affecting the Multiple Of EBITDA

CHAPTER SIX
WHAT IS YOUR BUSINESS WORTH? 61
- Recasting is Important
- Separate Your Assets
- Setting a Value
- Raising the Worth of Your Business and its Ability to be Sold Profitably Before it Comes Time to Sell
- The Price of a Business is Right if the Business Can Pay For Itself
- Cash Flow
- Getting Expert Advice
- The Role of the Business Broker or Merger and Acquisition Specialist
- Choosing a Merger and Acquisition Specialist or Business Broker

Determine Method of Valuation
Rules of Thumb to Estimate Selling Price of a Business
Tax Consequences of a Sale
Always Check the Tax Consequences of a Sale With a Trusted Advisor
The Importance of Expert Professional Advice

CHAPTER SEVEN
APPRAISALS 77
BizComps
Pratt's Stats

CHAPTER EIGHT
OUTSOURCING: TODAY'S BUSINESS-BUILDING NECESSITY 95

CHAPTER NINE
MERGERS AND ACQUISITIONS 105
Motives Behind M&A
Definitions
Experience Counts!
Understanding Acquisitions
Mergers
Creating Synergy
Horizontal and Vertical Mergers
Pitfalls to be Aware of When Creating a Merger
Create a Win/Win Situation

CHAPTER TEN
PROJECTING AN IMAGE 119
The Value of Brand Imaging

CHAPTER ELEVEN
GENERAL ACCOUNTING ADVICE 125

    Anticipate Tax Consequences

    Types of Deals Involved in the Sale of a Business

    Always Check the Tax Consequences of a Sale with a Trusted Advisor

CHAPTER TWELVE
INSURANCE NEEDS OF SELLERS AND BUYERS 133

    Insurance Needs of the Seller

    Health Insurance

    Disability Insurance

    Life Insurance

    Pension Plan

    Estate Planning

    Insurance Needs When Starting a Business

    The Role of an Insurance Broker

    Property and Casualty Insurance

    Other Protection Needs

    Protection Related to Death or Departure of an Owner

    Other Policies

    Who Should Own the Policies?

    Summary

    Top Ten Do's and Don'ts

CHAPTER THIRTEEN
LEGAL ASPECTS OF BUSINESS SALES 145

    Due Diligence

    Accounting and Financial Information

    Legal Information

    General Due Diligence

CHAPTER FOURTEEN
FRANCHISES 157
Considerations in Buying (or Selling) a Franchise

What is a Franchise?

Before Selecting a Franchise System

CHAPTER FIFTEEN
FINANCING THE DEAL 177
Financing Alternatives

Cash from Buyer

Seller Financing

Lender Financing

Lender Financing—What They Look For

Transaction Structure

Buyer Qualifications

SBA Financing

Alternative Methods of Financing

Making a Graceful Exit

CHAPTER SIXTEEN
EMPLOYEE STOCK OWNERSHIP PLANS (ESOP) 195
Unlock the Hidden Value of Your Business

What's the Magic About an ESOP?

What Makes a Good ESOP Candidate?

The Challenge

CHAPTER SEVENTEEN
THE ART OF CLOSING A DEAL 205
The Importance of Speed in Closing a Deal

Negotiations

Letter of Intent

Examination of Documents
Financing
Closing the Deal
Philosophical Advice
Beware of Hourly Fees if Possible
Problems and Solutions

CHAPTER EIGHTEEN
WHAT THE BUYER WANTS TO KNOW 219
Does the Buyer Really Want to Own a Business?
What Sort of Business Does He Want to Own?
Is the Buyer Ready to Buy a Business?
Buying a Business or a Franchise?
Questions Sellers Will Be Asked
Other Important Considerations
What the Buyer Will Need to See
To Prospective Buyers: Do You Sincerely Want to Own a Business?

CHAPTER NINETEEN
PROFESSIONAL PRACTICE SALES 231
Foreword

19A Selling a Professional Practice 240
Are You Ready to Sell?
Special Circumstances Affecting Medical Practice Valuation
This is No Job for an Amateur!
Thinking "Outside The Box"
Can You Sell Your Own Practice?
What is a Practice Worth?
The Vertical Horizontal Selling Method for Professional Practices

  Notifying Your Patients
  Is There Life After Practice?
19B Buying a Professional Practice 250
  To Buy or Not To Buy?
  Practice Philosophy
  Demography
  Questions to Ask When Considering Buying a Practice
  Tax Ramifications
  Why Does a Good Practice Not Sell?
  Summary
19C Professional Mergers 258

CHAPTER TWENTY
AFTER THE SALE 261

APPENDIX I
BUSINESS BROKER TRAINING MANUAL 265
 Training Manual 267
 The Process of Business Brokerage: From Beginning to End 278

APPENDIX II
FORMS 305
 Commission Agreement For a Professional Practice
 Sample Confidentiality Agreement
 Buyer Registration
 Medical Practice Questionnaire
 Sample Letter to Patients
 Practice Appraisals

GLOSSARY OF TERMS 315

FOREWORD

The shining dream of success.

Goals, dedication, productive hours, and years of experience.

What do these superior qualities have to do with winning?

Everything.

These time-tested ways to succeed in business can be found along two paths—hard work and knowledge.

Hard work may be the foundation, but you also need to build on that base with knowledge of your field, the proper tools, the know-how required to run the company, and business acumen.

While diligence and commitment make up hard work, the most intricate part of success is the learning curve. All roads lead to the future, but some require a mentor, a guide, with the experience to achieve your goals, to help you stay on the path. The road to success is easiest to travel when the way has been paved for you by those who have developed proven business strategies.

You've seen many good books about starting a business and keeping it running, but few written guidelines exist that deal with how to successfully, speedily, and profitably sell a business.

Until now.

Our forty years of experience in brokering mergers and acquisitions, as well as consummating lucrative business brokerage deals both small and huge, have led to the concepts outlined in this book.

We want you to profit from our experience and our proven success strategy: The ***Vertical Horizontal Method*** of selling a business!

Into the life of most businesses comes a time when the owner or owners are ready for a change. They may want to merge with another company, to the benefit of all. They may want to be acquired by an appropriate buyer, take their profits, and move on to other endeavors or to retirement.

To emerge a winner in merging or selling a business, you must prepare for that eventuality. All businesses, from their inception, must have, in effect, a competent EXIT STRATEGY before they need or want it.

Through our years as a top merger, acquisition, and business brokerage firm, both in the New York metropolitan area and nationally, we have created a novel and successful approach to helping buyers and sellers of all kinds of businesses. Our Vertical Horizontal Selling Method of linking buyers and sellers expands potential contacts, and greatly increases the market share possibilities, to everyone's benefit. Knowledge of the fundamentals involved in mergers and acquisitions adds to the basis for a satisfactory transition.

Before sellers reach the stage at which they can apply the Vertical Horizontal Selling Method, however, they must properly prepare for their exit. This book will demonstrate the best methods for a profitable and rewarding EXIT STRATEGY!

Sellers must know how to *RECAST* earnings to present their businesses in the most accurate way in order to entice a successor. Even if they are losing money on the books, recasting their financials will substantially increase the actual, as well as the perceived, value of a business. Sellers must also be aware of the intricacies of EBITDA: *Earnings Before Interest, Taxes, Depreciation and Amortization.* EBITDA and Recasting are aggressive accounting tools, the multiples of which can actually increase the selling price of a business.

We are proud of our expertise in the field of business brokerage and as merger and acquisition specialists, but, just as any seller should do, we have further enlisted the assistance of acknowledged experts in formulating this guide to a profitable EXIT STRATEGY. We have included the valuable insight and advice of top professionals in the fields of accounting, law, franchising, insurance, appraisals, graphic design, and financial and retirement planning, to assist in presenting as comprehensive a guide as possible to a prosperous exit strategy.

Note particularly the keys ⚷ at the beginning of each chapter. They serve as both introduction and review aids and are expanded upon within each section.

FOREWORD

In addition, this book has two special components:
- *What A Buyer Wants To Know*
- *Professional Practice Sales*

By being aware of potential questions that may arise, a forewarned seller can be forearmed with answers and better prepared for a rapid and profitable sale. You need to be ready as we will remind you in the chapter on *The Art of the Sale*. Time kills deals!

And, as you will note in the *Professional Practice Sales* chapter, even doctors, dentists and other professionals are businessmen, although self-admittedly, most are not very good at it. This chapter was written to guide both buying and selling professionals through the often-difficult business transition process.

Exit Strategy and the contents thereof are in no way to be considered a substitute for good, experienced legal and accounting advice. Rather, this book is to be used as an important guide, and a path, to properly and economically utilize expert advice. The services of a good business broker or mergers and acquisitions specialist, as well as other experts as indicated, are highly recommended.

Good reading and good luck in achieving a rewarding Exit Strategy and departure from your business!

Sheldon Manheim, CEO

www.BusinessBrokers.com
www.MergerAcquisition.com
www.BuyRentLease.com
www.PR.com
www.ManheimRealty.com
www.eBusinessForSaleByOwner.com
www.FranchiseMe.com
www.ManheimRealty.com
www.ProfessionalPracticeBrokers.com
www.MedicalDentalHealthCare.com
www.eRestaurantBrokers.com

CHAPTER ONE
EXIT STRATEGY

 **KEY POINTS**

All Businesses Need an Exit Strategy

Fourteen Different Ways of Exiting a Business

Alternatives to Selling

Continue to Run Your Business as if You Will Be Doing So Forever

Choosing a Successor

Maintain Confidentiality

The Importance of Competent, Experienced, Expert Advice

No Business Should Have to Die Due to Attrition or Neglect

CHAPTER ONE
EXIT STRATEGY

ALL BUSINESSES NEED AN EXIT STRATEGY
There comes a time when a business has reached a point where the owners want to realize their profits and move on, whether to other endeavors or to retirement.

THERE ARE 14 DIFFERENT WAYS OF EXITING A BUSINESS:
Here are 14 various ways to run a business until the end, with the assurance that a beneficial successor will be put in place:

1. Pass the business on to a family member
Although some sources state that 70% of family owned businesses do not survive to the second generation, you should still plan ahead. Consider yourself the Monarch of your Domain, one who must establish an heir to the throne. Perhaps there is a next generation of leadership right before your eyes. Family members are good starting points when looking for potential successors, and they may just be waiting to become the new Captain of the ship. It is important to know that a "functional" family must be a given, in this situation. To consider family in an exit strategy, you must be prepared to confront and resolve intra-familial jealousies and rivalry. Petty differences and in-fighting will undermine any smooth transition, and ensure the eventual (sooner rather than later) demise of the company. Don't just look toward your son or daughter for a successor—many successful businesses were taken over by nephews, nieces, cousins, and even fathers and mothers.

2. Sell the business to a partner

This may require the seller's financing of the deal, to some extent, or "taking paper," but, when available, usually makes the most sense. A partner knows the business best, and will most likely continue to ensure the concern and nurturing needed to assist in its continued success.

3. Sell the business to a trusted employee

Current employees or managers know the business, and the customers usually know them. The buyer, if a trusted employee, is more likely to preserve what is important to the owner about the business. If management buys the business, they have a commitment to making it work. This may require the seller to "take paper," which means that you take a down payment from the buyer and receive the balance as a monthly "note," plus interest, so that the buyer can pay for the business over time. In preparation for such an event, more than 11,000 companies have an ESOP, Employee Stock Ownership Plan, covering some nine million employees. You can start selling shares in your company whenever you wish, and in any amount you choose. One advantage would be that, if you sell shares—even majority shares—you can still run the company as long as you desire. There are tax advantages as well, since, if you sell at least 30%, you can defer capital gains taxes, sometimes indefinitely. And you can sell up to 100%, taking out as much cash as you wish.

4. Merge with another company

Rather than sell your business outright, there always exists the possibility for a lucrative merge with another company in the same business, using a Horizontal approach. You can also merge your business Vertically with a supplier or user of your product, or with someone in a related business. Our firm has found that selling a business using the Vertical Method has resulted in the highest amount of profit.
(See Chapters on Mergers and Acquisitions and *the Vertical Horizontal Selling Method*)

5. Take the company public

Going Public may be one alternative to selling off the firm. Offering company stock to the public on an open market can raise capital, especially if you have a good product and a market-driven reason to attract new capital. Exploring partnership with an underwriter may be an out, although it will mean a significant loss of control. You will be accountable to your investors, who care more about their return rather than sharing your passion for your company and its product. Some forms of corporation—S-corporations, for example—need reorganization before going public. This can take an inordinate amount of the owner's time—time better spent in running the company than in trying to sell it. In addition, there are strict Securities and Exchange Commission regulations and record-reporting rules, allowing once-confidential company information to become a matter of public record. Furthermore, there are significant costs to going public. It is also important to note that about 30% of companies that go public succeed over a 5-year period.

6. Sell the business to a competitor
Selling to a rival may sound agonizing, but, when you are ready to put your business on the market, people in the same industry are the most likely buyers. This is what we call a Horizontal sales method approach. It is amazing, but true, that so many businessmen spend years building up a business, only to undo that effort at the end by selling to the wrong person. You must have help in choosing carefully, especially if selling to a competitor.

7. Sell to a qualified buyer
Having a fully qualified buyer—either one who is new to the business, or one who has had employment or managerial experience and seeks ownership—is essential to a successful sale. A good Merger & Acquisitions Specialist or Business Broker can be invaluable in this effort.

8. Give the business to a charity and take a tax write-off
Depending upon your personal needs, or the needs of your heirs, you may derive a greater degree of personal satisfaction, or satisfy your need for a tax deduction, by giving the business to a favorite charity. Obviously, you need expert financial planning advice to be certain there are is no potential for negative fallout in the future.

9. Pursue other avenues available to Public companies
If a business is already a Public company, and you own the majority

share, the business can continue to operate and the company can run on its own upon your exit. But if the seller is the CEO, and it is unlikely the company will survive without him, his choice is to sell his shares, or, in consideration of the company and its employees, pursue and force a merger. A merger or acquisition that allows the owner to stay on in an advisory capacity, perhaps as senior advisor or CEO emeritus, can offer both your company and you a way to move smoothly through a difficult transition. New owners often value the benefit of retaining a veteran advisor. Advisory roles also offer a reluctant company owner a way to exit gracefully when it's time to retire, or if stricken with a sudden illness.

10. Selling company assets

Another alternative may be the selling off of company assets. If your company has been over-extending itself, cutting back or restructuring into a smaller division of a field may be the best alternative to selling the business outright. A good outside financial advisor must be called in to appraise your assets and determine a fair market price for each of the divisions you're considering selling, and help you choose which assets to divest.

11. Selling to a trusted friend

You might want to consider selling your business to an old and trusted friend. After all, much like a member of the family, he or she has known you for years and can appreciate the time, effort and hard work you have put into the company. A trusted friend will value what you have built and would like to see it "live on" and grow as much as you do.

12. Sell your business to your lawyer or accountant

Over the years we have been involved in many deals where lawyers or accountants have referred the business to their clients. Your lawyer and accountant are already well aware of the assets and true facts about the company and can put together a fair deal. Of course, it might be wise to seek an outside legal advisor who is not a direct party to the business sale to assist you in this matter and avoid any conflict of interest.

13. Go bankrupt and/or reorganize the company

In some cases it might actually make the most sense to go bankrupt and take a loss on your investment, or reorganize and then try to sell the business (although this last method may cause you to have problems with unions).

14. Run the business until your death

Should you decide to do this, you are not so much planning an Exit Strategy as you are letting fate decide when you should quit—without planning for either your company's future or, perhaps more important, for your family's well being. If you plan on running the business until your death, you should at the very least develop a benefit plan that will assist with the departure of each partner in case of death, disability, or retirement. Have a plan in effect from the start of the business. You should spare family and partners from the friction and squabbles that will ensue if a proper plan is not in place. If you are not business savvy enough to create an Exit Strategy, at the minimum, the Company should take out and pay for the largest life insurance policy possible. If you get this insurance policy, you would now have a terrific Exit Strategy.

As we will repeatedly advise you in this book, your company can be successfully sold or passed on using the techniques revealed to you throughout this book.

NEVER simply close the doors and walk away

NEVER let your company die by attrition

REMEMBER: EVEN IF YOU ARE LOSING MONEY, YOU CAN SELL YOUR BUSINESS AND MAKE A PROFIT!

> To suddenly realize you are at the point of wanting to exit your business, without preparing for it years before, is a huge mistake.

ALL businesses, from day one, must have in effect a competent EXIT STRATEGY! Some wise entrepreneurs start planning an exit strategy the day they start their business. They choose their business carefully, knowing that, someday, they will want to sell that business at a profit.

You must know the industry you choose to do business in, inside and out, in order to run it—and sell it—successfully.

As a simple example, let's look at a small business sale our firm handled 30 years ago. We had a businessman come into our office who was unsure whether to start up a local hardware store or a card store. The initial cost of the two businesses would have been about the same, although the hardware store would have given a greater immediate return. But this investor was looking to build a business, and then sell it for a profit. In our area at that time, a card store doing the same dollar amount in gross income would sell for nearly twice the selling price of a hardware store. So, in that instance, knowing the mechanics of the industries involved, and what the values were, enabled the businessman to make a judgment as to which enterprise suited his immediate and long-term needs.

This knowledge enabled him to choose to purchase the card store AND plan his exit strategy at the time of his initial investment, an ideal situation.

Not everyone is so prescient (although, after reading this book, we hope you will be). In most scenarios, you build a company or profession to a certain point, and then, somewhere down the line, decide when and how you will exit. A knowledgeable businessman, though, having been prepared, can decide if he wants to sell the company in a finite period—perhaps one, two, three, five or ten years. He might decide to pass it on to family, or a trusted employee. He might want to run it "forever," or for as long as he can. Even then, he needs an EXIT STRATEGY.

MOTIVATIONS FOR SELLING A COMPANY

Let's begin at the beginning.

Every owner must decide, at some time, when he wants to let go of the business. With the proper Exit Strategy on hand the owner can, at the appropriate time, decide how to successfully accomplish this.

Why are you thinking of selling? If the reasons are not valid, you will not be committed to the sale, and will be wasting a great deal of time, effort and money. As well as risking your reputation!

If you attempt to sell your business without the genuine motivation needed to successfully see the deal through, you may very well turn down good, strong offers. When you turn down a legitimate offer, it creates a domino effect of negativity. It turns off all associates around you, such as the brokers, your lawyer, and your accountants. Furthermore, your industry may discover you are selling. If you back out, and then decide to really go ahead and sell two years later, the industry thinks you have been trying to sell, and unsuccessfully so, for two years. What's more, the associates you brought on to help you sell the first time may not help you the second time around! So DO NOT PUT YOUR BUSINESS UP FOR SALE UNTIL YOU ARE TRULY READY TO SELL.

The decision to sell your company can be generated by a laundry list of motivating factors. Do you find yourself in any of these situations?

- Selling a company while it's "hot" is the best time for owners to sell their businesses. The business will sell much faster, with better terms, and for a much higher price. What better time to sell than when earnings are above average and performance is optimal? A successful company always sells for more money, and it is most beneficial to sell when an owner is guaranteed a greater price for his money-generating business. Most owners of companies will not sell when they are earning large profits. That is a mistake if your short term idea is to sell. For the highest profit on the sale of your company, sell when your earnings are high.

- When the general market has taken a downturn, and cash is not as readily available to be spent, you may want to assess your business to ensure it will survive the bear market. The earlier you sell in that type of economy, the more you will receive for your company. That might mean dividing the company up differently or lowering the price; but sometimes it is better to go while the going is good. If you think business is going to get much worse in the short term, sell quickly.

- The daily routines called for in business ownership become the boredom-bearers that make many entrepreneurs sell their businesses. In this case, selling could provide the finances needed to start up a brand new business, or pave the way to a life of financial leisure that includes travel and hobbies.

- Advances in technology can bring a once-profitable business to its knees. If you find that current trends are making your business obsolete, it may be time to liquidate your assets and sell before your organization becomes a dinosaur. An example of this is how the internet is destroying many retail businesses.

Once you actually determine that the decision to exit the business is the right one, this book will guide you through your decision-making process for results that are on-track, profitable and successful for ALL parties involved.

TEN BASIC STEPS TO BUILDING AN EXIT STRATEGY

STEP 1: Make certain the decision to exit your business is the RIGHT decision

Often, the decision to sell or merge is more difficult than the decision you made to start your business in the first place. When selling your business, there are important questions to be answered first:

- Do you need the proceeds from the sale of your business to finance your retirement?
- Are there partners or shareholders who need to be involved in this decision?
- Are there any major loans outstanding, or vendors that have to be contacted?
- Are you willing to wait for as long as it may take to find a buyer? If you are rushing, you will end up selling for less money.
- Is now the most opportune time to sell, based on what is happening in your market?
- Is there someone within the company who can take over, and is willing to do so?
- Is there an opportunity for an employee buyout?

STEP 2: Make your business transferable

Can goodwill be transferred, or are you the business? This is especially true for professional practices, as we will discuss in a future chapter. If the business depends on your presence and visibility, you must work on making key employees more visible and more responsible, so that goodwill can be a significant part of any future exit transition from your business or practice. You may also find yourself having to work with the new buyers longer than you would in a traditional sale—sometimes for one to two years after the sale. This all takes time, but it can be well worth it to all parties concerned!

STEP 3: Prepare your business to be sold

Accurate record-keeping implies a well-run and organized business. Determine the strengths and weaknesses of your business. Improve on the weaknesses and work on your strengths to build the business even further. There are also ways to shed positive light on your business' finances to make it appear more tempting to the buyer. See the chapters in this book on *Recasting* and *EBITDA* for details on how to go about this.

STEP 4: Seriously consider the amount you would like to receive from the sale of the business

A proper appraisal expert or experienced business broker can help. It is vitally important to choose a trustworthy Business Broker or Real Estate Broker. Many brokers will tell you your property is worth much more than it really is, simply to get your listing. Furthermore, almost all sellers themselves think their business is worth more than it is. If you have the opportunity to do so, go with a larger and more well-established Business Broker or Mergers & Acquisition company to determine THE REAL VALUE OF YOUR BUSINESS. It is very important to have a realistic selling price when you are deciding your Exit Strategy.

STEP 5: Research the competition to determine where you fit

This will further determine how saleable your business may be, and at what price point. By knowing if a similar business has sold easily and quickly, or if it took a long time to sell, you will get an idea as to whether you have a sellable company. By knowing how much a similar company fetched, perhaps as a multiple of its earnings, you can decide what your asking price should be in order to expedite the sale.

STEP 6: The only people who should be aware of the sale of your business are the buyer, the broker, the accountant and the lawyer

In general, we can say that in nearly 100% of cases **confidentiality is a must!** There are ways to protect yourself from both outsiders and insiders finding out that your business is for sale. You will read more interesting details about this below.

STEP 7: Choose an expert to help you sell your business

This may be a lawyer, accountant, merger & acquisitions specialist or business broker. An expert will ensure confidentiality and bring years of experience to work for you. Of the specialists that can assist you, most often a merger & acquisitions professional will bring maximal knowledge of your industry and expertise to the process, while bringing in more contacts than an individual owner or other professional might possibly reach.

STEP 8: If you decide to sell the business yourself, prepare a list of possible buyers

Using the Vertical-Horizontal approach we will detail later in the book, your list may include competitors, complementary businesses, suppliers looking for sector integration or diversification, employees of the company, and many others. Be sure to have each potential buyer sign a non-disclosure agreement, or leave it to your business broker or attorney to do so. A clause restricting potential buyers from using information gleaned through examining your business from profiting in any way is essential. You do not want someone opening a competing business in your area because he knows you are selling your business.

STEP 9: Properly market your business-for-sale

You must reach as many people as possible in the right target market. The problem is that advertising your business for sale can be expensive and time consuming, and will hinder your goal of maintaining confidentiality, which is always a priority. You can place a non-identifying ad in a newspaper, trade magazine, or online. And of course, choosing a skilled business broker to place properly worded ads for you, and to get the "word" out in other professional and secrecy-maintaining methods, is always a smart decision.

STEP 10: Respond to prospective buyer inquiries in a timely manner

You may be too busy to do this yourself, which is another reason why hiring an expert is the way to go. A professional whose job it is to sell your business will always keep on top of inquiries. He can market your business, and identify and reach out to qualified buyers, while you keep your mind on running your company smoothly and profitably.

Two general matters to keep in mind to make a sale go through quickly: First, have your attorney draw up a contract even before a buyer becomes interested. Second, make sure your accountant has a minimum of three years of your business tax returns and your final paperwork ready before you even start your exit strategy.

Selling the company outright is certainly not always the only way out. It is important, when planning an Exit Strategy, to choose a successor that is most beneficial to you. There are a number of choices available to business owners, including reducing their active role without necessarily leaving the business completely.

OTHER FACTORS IN PLANNING AN EXIT STRATEGY

These may seem obvious, but, in the interest of completeness, the questions that follow need reaffirming. You must look at many aspects of your personal life, including:

- Is your estate planning in order?
- Are you thinking about timing and phasing?
- Can you afford to retire?
- Are there liability issues you should handle before you involve any assistance in exiting your business?
- Are there recapitalization strategies which will allow you to unlock a portion of your wealth without giving up control?
- Is your insurance adequate, both personal and health?
- Do your previous financial plans and insurance coverage reflect today's reality?
- Finally, do you have other interests you already enjoy, or do you have some you want to explore? Think about what you will do AFTER the sale.

CHAPTER TWO
THE VERTICAL HORIZONTAL SELLING METHOD

 **KEY POINTS**

The Vertical Horizontal Selling Method is an Extremely Simple, Yet Extraordinarily Effective, Means of Selling a Business

The Vertical Horizontal Selling Method
- Companies in the Same Business
- Companies in an Ancillary Business
- Companies in a Related Business

Finding a Buyer

Advertising, Personal Contacts, Networking

You Cannot Sell a Multimillion Dollar Business With an Ad in the Newspaper!

Some of the Best Businesses May Never Be Advertised

Utilizing the Important Services of Business Brokers

CHAPTER TWO
THE VERTICAL HORIZONTAL SELLING METHOD

THE PROVEN, SIMPLE, EFFECTIVE METHOD OF SELLING A BUSINESS

We have developed a method in which the number of prospective buyers for a business is greatly increased.

This expanded manner of finding a buyer involves looking not only at prospective buyers in the same business—that is, horizontally—but looking "outside the box" to multiple peripherally related companies as well—that is, vertically.

PUTTING THE VERTICAL HORIZONTAL SELLING METHOD TO WORK FOR YOU

The traditional approach to linking buyers and sellers can be hit-or-miss, to say the least. Many business brokers and sellers merely throw advertisements up into the wind, seeking buyers in a disorganized and inefficient manner. For the last 60 years 52% of all businesses sold were sold in this "old-fashioned" way. A Broker or Seller would place an ad that goes something like this: Manufacturing Plant for sale. Asking 3.4 million, net profit $374,000/yr. Florida area. Call Steve, (516) 520-2000. Then, the long wait. Although many businesses have been sold the "old way," the results take too much time and the outcome of the sale is not generally good for the seller.

In order to rectify this haphazard system, and sell a business faster and more profitably, we have created the Vertical Horizontal Selling

Method, a successful solution that identifies and appropriately links sellers or merger candidates to buyers.

The powerful Vertical Horizontal Selling Method is a highly targeted, pinpoint approach to finding buyers who have the expertise and financial wherewithal to successfully complete a merger or acquisition in a shorter amount of time.

The definition of our Method is quite simple. And quite effective!

The Horizontal approach to selling a business identifies companies or potential buyers in the same or similar fields, who have experience in the designated field.

The Vertical approach identifies companies in peripheral areas, related by virtue of being suppliers or users, or through their involvement in similar products, labor or services.

The following charts illustrate examples of how we use the Vertical Horizontal Selling Method.

CHART 1
Let's begin with an alarm company, for example:

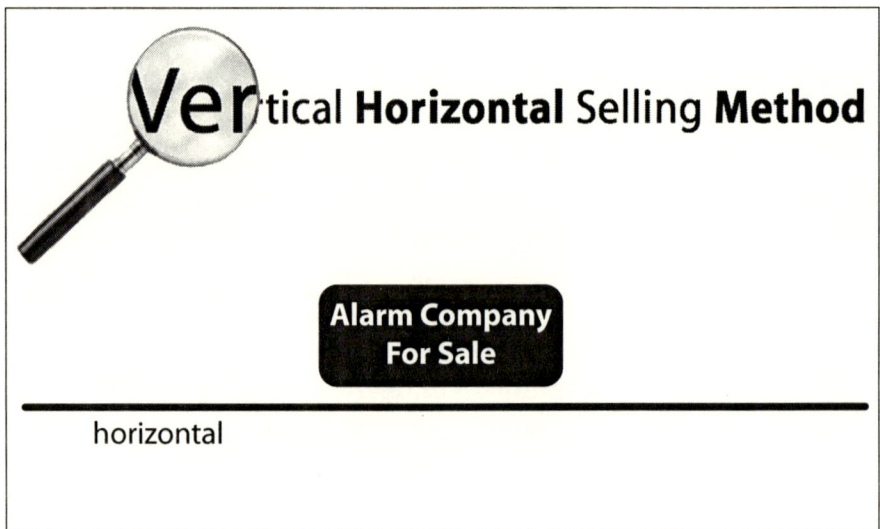

CHART 2

In the example given below for an alarm company wishing to sell, the broker or agent contacts potential buyers *in the same type of business*. This would be along the horizontal line. Of course, this would be done without divulging the name of the company that is for sale, maintaining confidentiality.

A purchase or merger may make very good sense to the buyers along the horizontal line. That is because the result would be elimination of a competitor, which would increase the buyer's company market share. It would also cut overhead (rent, staff, utilities, etc.) and add to the company's gross and net. The gross income of the business purchased may become fairly close to net for the buyer, with the elimination of all duplicate expenses, as market share is increased.

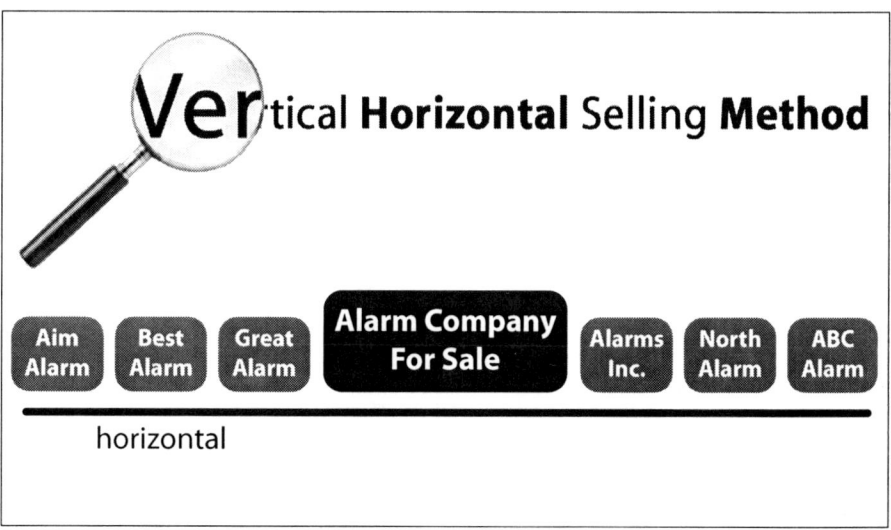

CHART 3

The broker may also proceed vertically, as shown in Chart 3, contacting ancillary services that impact upon the seller's business.

To illustrate an example of a solid vertical sale, I once sold a glass wholesale company for $4,500,000 to a construction company that was showing a yearly profit of $680,000. The construction company was purchasing over $700,000 in glass every year from other glass companies. After the vertical purchase of the glass company, the construction company began saving over $300,000 a year in their purchase of glass. What's more, the construction company owned an 85,000 square foot building, of which 15,000 square feet was now being used to house the glass company, merging two companies into one building. Here is a breakdown of the profit-increasing Vertical Plan for the construction company:

$680.000.00   (Glass company's profit in last year of ownership)
$300,000.00   (Amount saved by Construction company on purchase of glass per year)
$280,000.00   (Amount saved by moving Glass company into Construction company's building; includes savings on rent, sales force, human resources, utilities)
$350,000.00   (Amount saved on cutting salaries, Controller, etc.)
$1,610,000.00

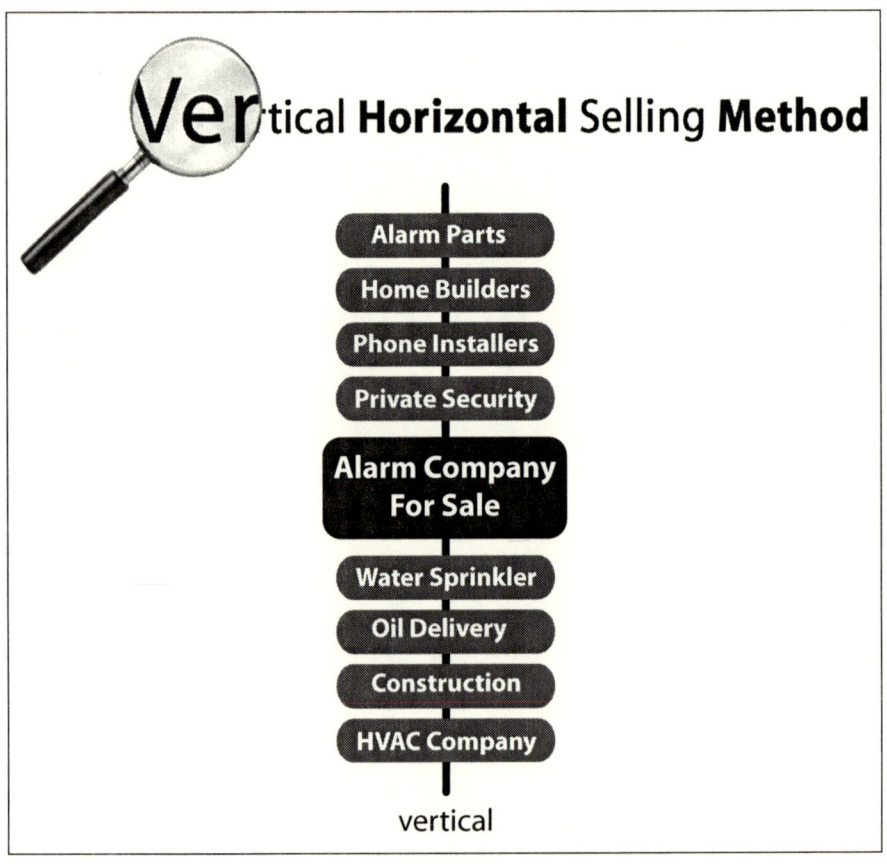

Look at the magic of this Vertical move. Overnight, a company that was showing a profit of $680,000 per year is now AUTOMATICALLY taking in over $1,600,000.00 a year thanks to the purchase of a "vertical" company! And the figures above only show the profit increases by saving on expenses. In that same merger, sales also increased greatly. In most cases, the relationship between buyers and sellers in a good one. In the merger between the construction company and glass company, the construction company—which had 1,500 loyal customers—took on the 2,700 loyal customers of the glass company. The newly merged company now enjoys a loyal customer base of 4,200! Sales increased in a very short time; in this case, 22% in the very first year.

Going back to our alarm company on the vertical chart, above, the alarm company would be a natural target for takeover by an oil company, a bottled water supplier, a construction company, phone installers, home builders, private security firms or even alarm parts manufacturers. This vertical sale would increase the customer base as both companies merge, enabling them to combine the sales forces of both companies. Again, the cost of doing business is lowered, and the buyer increases product line, brand recognition and profits.

As yet another example of utilizing the Vertical Horizontal Selling Method, a Title Company for sale might be sold to competitors in the same field—the horizontal line—in a merger and acquisition agreement. Or, a buyer may come from the vertical column—perhaps a large law firm, an appraiser, an insurer or an underwriter.

CHART 4

The beauty of the Vertical Horizontal Selling Method, as shown below, is that the list of potential buyers increases geometrically. The more qualified potential buyers you have,

(a) the faster the business will sell, and

(b) the potential final selling price may be greater as a bidding war (or "auction") occurs.

Brainstorming is a valuable tool that we use to further enhance the Vertical Horizontal Selling Method.

EXIT STRATEGY

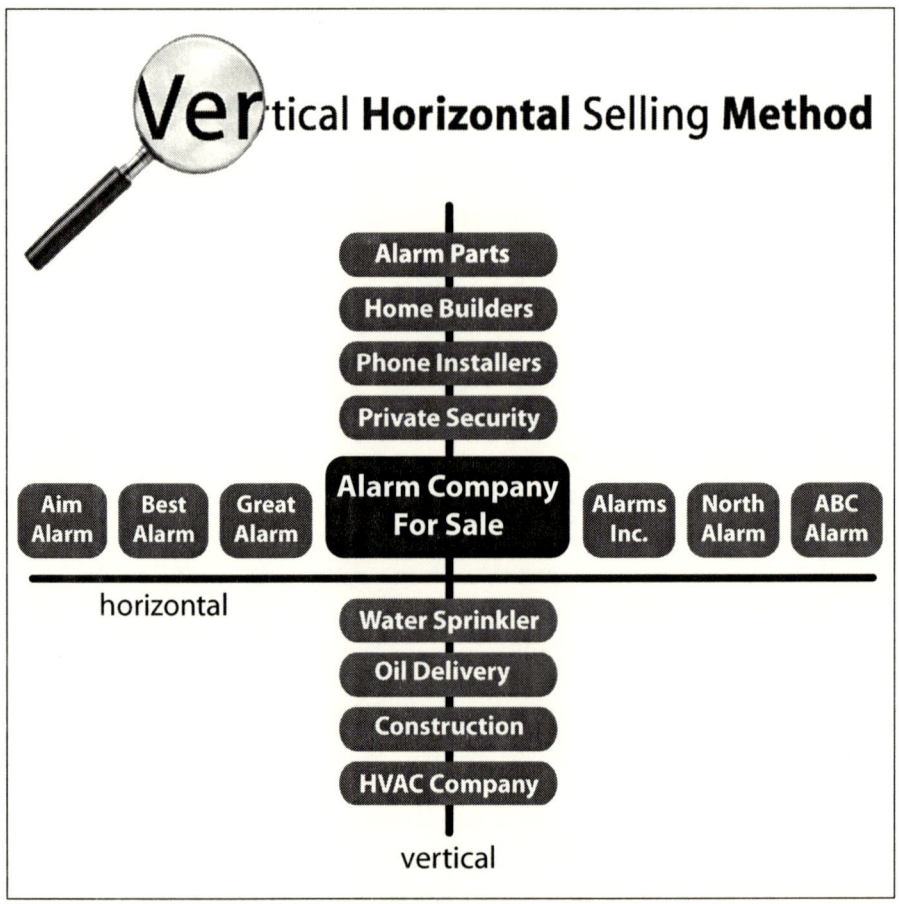

When you have thirty or more experienced business brokers sitting around a conference table throwing out suggestions about businesses to target along the vertical and horizontal lines, as we do, the results are incredible.

At a recent meeting, one broker in our firm brought in a nine million dollar landscaping company that services municipal locations. It was thrown out to our group for a Vertical Horizontal Selling Method discussion.

Potential horizontal buyers included other municipal landscapers, of course, but also general, residential and commercial landscapers, as well as the alumni of landscape architecture schools.

Potential vertical buyers mentioned were trucking companies, fertilizer distributors, construction companies (especially those involved with building schools and municipal buildings), tree service and sprinkler companies, fencing manufacturers, sod suppliers, builders of playground equipment—the list went on.

The selling broker then linked up with three other vertical sales experts in our office, brought all of the ideas together, and started contacting potential buyers identified through our Vertical Horizontal Selling Method brainstorming session. He hit the jackpot with a wealthy alumnus of a landscape architecture and design school who was looking for just such an investment!

Whether it's for the sale of a small business or a large one, the Vertical Horizontal Selling Method works.

As an example of a large business entity seeking to buy other companies, we recently had a huge vitamin manufacturer as a client. We linked them, successfully, with a 34 store retail vitamin chain. Rather than effect an acquisition, we wound up orchestrating a most successful merger using the Vertical Horizontal approach.

On a smaller scale, we've had hundreds of potential buyers who already own small businesses come to our office intending to buy one type of business, who then wound up buying a totally unrelated company. For example, buyers have come to us seeking card stores. We would not be doing our job if we did not show them other businesses, either vertically or horizontally related, such as gift shops or convenience stores. A motivated buyer who wants a business in which to invest, so that he may earn a good return on his investment, might have the savvy to grasp an unrelated opportunity if properly presented. This is a well-planned alternative, using the Vertical Horizontal approach, and years of experience, to successfully link a buyer with a suitable seller. In this manner, a business broker familiar with the Vertical Horizontal Selling Method, can expand a seller's potential buyer list to include those who did not know they might be interested in such a business.

BEING SELECTIVE IN THE WAY THAT YOU FIND A BUYER

Being selective in the manner in which you find a buyer for your business is vital to the sale—and continued success!—of your business. There are various ways to seek out a qualified buyer. Whichever option you choose, we strongly advise you to set up a third-party contact to keep your sales intent confidential. Your competition may read the same listing services and note that you are for sale. This gives them a reason to move against your market share at a time when you need to be at optimal market strength at the time of your sale.

Personal Contacts

Everyone knows someone, and that person knows other people. If you are not concerned with confidentiality (which you most definitely should be!), networking might be an effective means of locating possible buyers. But you must be wary of to whom you talk, and be selective in the way you let the information about your potential sale get out.

That is because once the word is out that you are thinking of selling, several things can happen:

- Employees begin to feel fearful about their security. They may start looking for positions in other companies, rather than risk getting a new employer who may be unwilling or unable to keep them on.
- Customers may start looking for other suppliers they know, rather than have to deal with an unknown entity.
- Competition will let the word out, and they will most likely go after your current customer base by letting them know your company is going out of business.

As a result, sales may start to fall, leading to a lower bottom line, and thus a lower valuation for the business when it is sold.

That is why an intermediary, such as a mergers and acquisitions specialist or experienced business broker, is—as mentioned before—the best way to go.

THE PITFALLS OF ADVERTISING YOUR BUSINESS FOR SALE

Newspapers, the Internet, and of course, word-of mouth, are strong advertising tools. However, the desire for privacy, again, is a deterrent. Confidentiality when you are selling a business is paramount.

Some of the best businesses are *never* listed. At Manheim Business Brokers, 40% of the businesses we sell are never advertised in the newspapers or on the internet.

Many sellers do not want to advertise their businesses to the general public because they are concerned about confidentiality. They quite correctly do not want competitors, employees, and vendors to know that they are for sale. The answer, again, is to use an intermediary. In addition, mergers and acquisitions specialists often hear about businesses that are not "officially" for sale, but in which the owner is willing to speak to a potential buyer. These opportunities are often the most attractive and desirable, but buyers never hear about them if they rely solely upon database searches.

An Ad Alone Will Never Sell a Multi-Million Dollar Business

You simply cannot sell a multi-million dollar business with just an ad! These buyers must be pursued. A merger and acquisition firm or business broker knows how to make the phone calls needed to find potential buyers. The owner of the business for sale usually does not. What's more, a good broker using the Vertical Horizontal Selling Method is not limited to just organizing a sale. He can also put together a powerful merger. The Vertical Horizontal Selling Method really works.

When seeking buyers vertically, we would ordinarily approach larger rather than smaller companies. A small company is only interested in how acquiring the seller's business will put more money in its pocket today. A large company can afford to spend money for a business that will lead to diversification, and increase its gross, without affecting the bottom line for some time to come, if at all.

In fact, it is often wise to consider a merger rather than a sale, as the cost of doing business, almost always, is lower with a successful, well-planned merger. It may mean the seller giving up some control, but it can be a profitable move that can keep the owner involved in a business he has nurtured.

Keep in mind that purchases of suppliers or customers by a strong company, resulting in the knocking out of competition, may attract anti-trust regulators. Expert legal advice must be sought when such a problem is even a possibility.

UTILIZING THE EXPERTISE OF A BUSINESS BROKER OR MERGER AND ACQUISITION SPECIALIST

The sale of a business, then, is rarely accomplished without the services of a qualified intermediary.

To say that even more strongly, IT IS VIRTUALLY IMPOSSIBLE FOR A COMPANY TO REPRESENT ITSELF IN A SALE AND GET THE BEST DEAL FOR ITSELF! When discussing the art of closing the deal in a subsequent Chapter, you will discover the reasons for this in more detail.

Most sellers of businesses, and many inexperienced business brokers, use a haphazard approach to finding a buyer. They are essentially fishermen, throwing bait into the water (fishermen call it "chumming") hoping the fish will gather and one will bite on their line.

I will let you in on a better way. In our organization of experienced brokers, we apply the following lead generators to the Vertical Horizontal Selling Method in order to seek out qualified buyers for our clients:
- Drop Notes
- Direct Mail
- Telephone
- Advertising
- Internet Leads
- Organizations
- Trade Shows and Trade Publications
- FSBOs (For Sale By Owners)
- In-Person "Cold Calls"

THE VERTICAL HORIZONTAL SELLING METHOD

Although knowledge of such approaches is common, in our firm, this list is gone through in a very specific and methodical way. Business brokers know who is looking to buy a business in a given area, and can help match you with a buyer that fits your industry and experience. Most important of all, a specialist will carefully take every step needed to sell your business while maintaining complete confidentiality.

What about the commission? From a financial point of view, it is most often found that a broker will increase the net purchase price to the seller, above and beyond what the seller might be able to do by himself. This is because a good broker will often get several buyers involved, creating a bidding war or auction, and thus increasing the price to the point at which the commission will be paid, and then some. In fact, the National Association of Realtors reports that a real estate broker's handling of a home sale increases the selling price by an average of 16%. We have found that similar numbers apply to the sale of a business, especially when the Vertical Horizontal approach is used.

There are many ways in which a good business broker can work for you. A business broker can advertise—the right way. Ambiguous ads, strategically placed, can generate many responses, especially if the brokerage has a large internet presence. Confidentiality is preserved, casual callers are weeded out, potential buyers are pre-qualified, and time and money are saved. It is even more likely that, using a good merger and acquisition firm or broker that incorporates the Vertical Horizontal approach and other techniques outlined in this book, including recasting, a seller will command a much better price for the business.

A merger and acquisition specialist can also reach out to his vast contacts in the legal and accounting professions, tapping into their knowledge of clients who might wish to acquire, merge or otherwise be involved with a business, while giving them only a brief idea as to the nature and location of the business for sale.

The result—especially when combined with the Vertical Horizontal Selling Method—is that confidentiality is always preserved and horizons are widely broadened.

CHAPTER THREE
THE ART OF SUCCESSFULLY SELLING YOUR BUSINESS

 **KEY POINTS**

Examine How Much Money You **Really** Earn From Your Business
Gathering Records
The Effective Way to Sell
Confidentiality is a MUST
Honesty is the Best Policy
Choosing the Very Best Legal and Financial Advisors
Losing Money? No Profit? No Problem!

CHAPTER THREE
THE ART OF SUCCESSFULLY SELLING YOUR BUSINESS

EXAMINE HOW MUCH MONEY YOU REALLY EARN FROM YOUR BUSINESS

I once had a seller come into my office who told me he was losing money and had to sell his business. It turned out that, upon examination of his finances, he was earning more than he thought. While he believed that he was making only $175,000 a year in profit, he was actually earning over $450,000.00 a year. That's because he was taking out so much money from the business for personal expenses—cell phones, insurance, cars, pool maintenance, family entertainment, clothes, mortgages, and so on—that he was not taking into account the ENTIRE income that his business was really generating. This is where Recasting comes in, which is discussed in a following chapter.

GATHERING RECORDS

Sooner, rather than later, you must begin preparing valid financial records. It is never too soon to do this! The earlier you start to collect the necessary statements, the more time you give yourself to correct any aspects of the paperwork that don't seem to add up.

In gathering records, I recommend having at least three to five years' pertinent papers available, should the potential buyer request them. These include, of course, financial statements, tax returns, and fixed inventory purchases and service records. If there are buy-sell agreements, leases and vendor or wholesaler agreements, they should be available as well.

If there have been any legal or financial problems, such as pending law suits or unsatisfied liens, there is nothing to be gained from hiding them. They *will* be discovered, and the fact that they were originally hidden may destroy otherwise potentially fruitful negotiations. Governor Ann Richards of Texas, who made the inaugural address at a political convention, said, "You can't put lipstick on a pig!" She meant that an ugly situation does not get better, even if you try to dress it up. (This quotation was used, as well, in the 2008 presidential primaries.) Recasting will help you show a good business off, in order to attain a better advantage. However, in business, camouflage will not cover up a disaster in a way that will make someone want to buy it.

You must approach the problem, solve it and correct it before you try to sell. Failing to accomplish this, you must be forthright and honest to potential buyers in disclosing the problems. Honesty breeds trust, while attempts to hide problems breed distrust and kill deals.

THE EFFECTIVE WAY TO SELL

Keeping a business in ready-to-sell condition will enable an owner to sell when market conditions are right and a buyer appears. Once you decide to sell, you must decide HOW you will do so. Will you want to, or be able to, sell it yourself? Or should you use an intermediary—an accountant, an attorney, merger and acquisitions specialist or a business broker? *A word about using a broker.* A good business broker knows the industry, can help you evaluate your business' worth, can put together impressive proposals and can refer you to legal and financial consultants with whom he has worked before, and in whom he has confidence.

Even when you have decided to sell, you must keep running your business as if it will be yours forever. You must try to increase your profits in the year(s) before the sale. Try and improve your bottom line by outsourcing, cutting expenses, and increasing sales. This is, of course, to increase the selling price, but it is also to protect your reputation. This will also protect your investment in case a deal does not go through. If there is a payout plan, it will improve the likelihood that the buyer will be able to pay the notes.

CONFIDENTIALITY IS A MUST

Confidentiality is an absolute must! It is vitally important to keep the likelihood that you are going to sell the business away from your employees, suppliers, and of course your customers. Confidentiality can be complicated, but has to be maintained as closely as possible.

We once sold a large and very well known restaurant. My team cautioned the owner, a rather public figure in the area, to not let anyone know that he was selling. "But how can you sell if you can't let anyone *know* we are selling?" the owner exclaimed.

The answer? The story must be gotten out in such a way that confidentiality is maintained, and the highest discretion used. This is one instance, among many in the sale of a business, when an experienced business broker is needed to accomplish a most difficult task.

When speaking of maintaining confidentiality, it all boils down to two choices:

1. DO NOT TELL ANYONE.

2. Tell a modified truth. Tell your employees that you want the company to grow. You can intimate (for it may turn out to be true) that you or the CEO are planning to stay and merge with a much larger company. The implication is that every employee will do better with the merger.

The importance of confidentiality cannot be overemphasized. Colleagues and staff should not be told about the transfer of ownership until you have a deal going through. This is to retain current quality staff, prevent an employee from opening up in the area to capture the customers who are familiar with him or her, and to keep competitors from capitalizing on an impending sale by wooing your customers.

On the other hand, possible loss of key employees, whose feelings may have been hurt by not being told of a possible sale, can kill a deal at the last minute. These key employees should be told, before they find out from a third party, that a transaction is imminent, and that you are relying upon them to guide your company through the transition as an integral part thereof.

Furthermore, if the wrong people find out your business is for sale, the damage can be incredible. Such a revelation can affect relationships with your customers, employees, suppliers, competitors or even your bankers. It can make your customers worry whether their orders will be filled, or if you will stand behind your work. Employees will question their job security. Suppliers will wonder if they will be paid, or if they should extend you credit. Your bankers may wonder if you will meet your obligation. They may even fail to renew your line of credit or call in your outstanding loans. So, to reiterate: Confidentiality is crucial!

HONESTY IS THE BEST POLICY
BUSINESS (AND PERSONAL) INTEGRITY ARE PARAMOUNT

TELLING PROSPECTIVE BUYERS EVERYTHING IN ADVANCE BREEDS TRUST.

HOLDING BACK IMPORTANT INFORMATION KILLS DEALS!

Just as you must protect yourself by maintaining confidentiality, the most important responsibility you have to the prospective buyer, as a seller, is complete honesty.

Fraud has no place in the selling of a business, and even the mere suspicion of it—understatement of expenses, overstatement of income, failure to divulge known hazards or impending problems—can break your deal and even lead to legal action. As a matter of personal integrity, any adverse information must be divulged. Are there liens on the property or against the owner? Is there a problem with the lease? Are there structural problems with the building of which you are aware? NOW is the time to tell all, not at or near closing.

Way back in 1968, when I was starting in the business brokerage and mergers and acquisitions field, I was helping a client sell a large piece of property that was perfect for a major department store to build upon. When walking around the property, I noticed an area that had a significant amount of water. Being young and foolish, and wanting this major deal to go through, I did not tell the prospective buyer what I had found. Needless to say, the buyer did find out. Suspecting that I knew about the water situation and failed to share the information up front, or thinking that I SHOULD have known about it as a professional in the business, the buyers feared I might be holding back on—or simply was not aware of—other potential problems. They backed out.

I cannot stress enough how important that lesson was to me, and should be to any seller or business broker reading these words. I am so fortunate I learned it early, and have never made that same error in judgment again. A follow up to this tale: Learning from this, I immediately told the next prospect everything—good and bad—about this same property, and the deal went through smoothly. The lesson: *Telling prospective buyers everything in advance breeds trust. Holding back important information destroys trust and kills deals.*

A similar experience with an optical store that was part of a large franchise brings up the importance of due diligence and full disclosure for both the buyer and the seller. Just before closing the buyer found out that, within the next two years, each franchisee would be required to refurbish its store to match the company model, at an anticipated cost of $150,000. This led to a bitter confrontation with the seller, who did not know in advance about this requirement, and thought he had a sale. The sale, of course, broke up. The seller should have known more about his franchise, and informed the buyer and the broker of this requirement. When the next buyer came to the table, there was full disclosure, and the deal went through without a hitch.

CHOOSING THE VERY BEST LEGAL AND FINANCIAL ADVISORS

There is no substitute for good legal and financial advice. This is one area in which you cannot scrimp on costs.

Use contacts you have known for years if you have confidence in them. However, just because someone is a fine CPA does not mean he is a good financial advisor or manager for your business. In fact, many CPA's are novices when it comes to business acquisitions, sales and mergers. Even a good attorney may not be an expert in all aspects of selling a business. You will need help in appraising the business. A good mergers and acquisitions specialist will have recommendations based on years of practice. You must choose one who has excellent negotiating skill and experience, and is able to work, if necessary, with other, perhaps even larger, mergers and acquisitions specialists.

Three important things your accountant and your lawyer MUST have:
1. The means to legally protect you
2. The ability to work very fast
3. They must be "deal makers," not "deal breakers!"

BRINGING IN THE STRONGEST BUSINESS BROKER:

A good negotiator should be able to fight for the highest price, and set up a valuable auction or bidding war. An auction, of course, involves having two or more prospective buyers competing to push the sale price higher.

An experienced business broker, for example, has the knowledge to evaluate and interpret information you provide, and present your business in the most favorable way to pre-qualified buyers. Many can arrange financing. They are able to mediate the transaction, and close the deal. *And they maintain confidentiality throughout the deal.* No one is better trained to negotiate an auction or bidding war than a Business Broker or Merger and Acquisition firm. How do you find one?

It is important to go on the basis of personal recommendation from others in your field, if possible. Failing that possibility, interview more than one business broker.

Many business brokers are small firms with a handful of brokers. While they may get good results, simple statistics show that a firm with many brokers, each of whom is actively engaged in pursuing clients, will stand a better chance of selling your business more quickly and profitably. Our firm, in business for nearly 40 years, has over 50 full-time Business and Merger and Acquisition Brokers. We use a team approach. We assign at least four individual brokers to sell a listed business, with a manager and facilitator overseeing the process. We also have a full time legal and accounting staff to expedite deals when they are created. While bigger is not always better, it is a factor to be considered in choosing a business broker or mergers and acquisitions specialist.

On the other side of the coin, beware of a Business Brokerage that values quantity over quality. This is when experience is most valuable. A good, experienced broker will not accept listings that are inappropriately priced, or are of known inferior quality. Ask a broker about his firm's experience in selling businesses in your field. Our firm was approached to list a dental office in Massachusetts that had over three million dollars in revenue annually. Needless to say, the prospects of a hefty commission made our eyes cross. Then we did our own due diligence, and discovered the owner was facing a jail sentence for Medicaid fraud, and had a history of scams in other fields. We immediately withdrew the listing. Very often, the adage, "Anything that seems too good to be true probably is!" is absolutely correct. A good broker will protect the interests of sellers and buyers. His integrity and reputation depend on that.

LOSING MONEY? NO PROFIT? NO PROBLEM!
Planning an exit strategy, using techniques we will discuss below such as RECASTING and EBITDA (Earnings Before Interest, Taxes, Depreciation and Amortization), can help any business, even one that shows no profit, become attractive to the right purchaser, while maintaining strict honest and legal principles.

As a stopgap, for example, a seller planning an exit strategy, but strapped for cash, might consider accounts receivable financing. Accounts receivable financing involves the purchase of accounts receivable from a business at a discount. Some small business owners or professionals will include accounts receivable in the selling price, to help the buyer get off to a good start by providing an initial steady flow of cash. Those who decide not to do so may wish to be finished with all aspects of the business the minute they close on a sale, and may then involve an accounts receivable funding company to help them "take the money and run." The fact is that any business that is not "cash & carry" (like a hair salon or dry cleaner) can benefit from accounts receivable funding, as long as an invoice is generated and a verifiable product or service is delivered. Accounts receivable funding can benefit an owner planning an exit strategy by offering immediate access to working capital, strengthening the business to make it more saleable, or as an alternative to just closing the doors or filing for bankruptcy.

From a potential buyer's standpoint, there are times when buyers of small to mid-sized businesses or professional practices need funding that is unavailable through traditional sources such as banks. Many businesses must depend at the start on alternative forms of financing to provide capital for start-up and operating expenses and purchases of equipment. It is sometimes necessary, therefore, to consider the use of a financial mediator to provide a bridge to capital and access to alternative forms of financing.

Throughout this book, we will provide ideas and concepts to help sellers plan and execute an easy and profitable departure. The important lesson here is that no business need die of attrition or neglect. Numerous businesses that show yearly losses are sold for large profits every day.

CHAPTER FOUR
RECASTING & THE SELLING MEMORANDUM

 **KEY POINTS**

RECASTING

"Recast" Financials Substantially Increase the Actual and Perceived Value of Your Business

A Significant Number of Businesses Fail to Show a Profit. This Does Not Mean They Make No Money!

Businesses Go Out of Business Because They Do Not Know They Have a Business to Sell

A Small Adjustment (Recasting) May Result in a Huge Increase in Value!

Recasting Honestly Reflects How the Business Should Look to a Buyer

Tax Returns are Not Prepared to Help a Buyer Evaluate the True Worth of a Business

To Recast Earnings:
    Deduct the Owner's Salary and Bonuses
      • Add Back Replacement Manager's Salary

- Deduct Owner's Car Payments and Insurance
- Deduct Owner's Retirement Plan Contributions
- Adjust For Family Leaseback Arrangements
- Deduct Any Other "Perks"
- Deduct Surplus Staffing
- Deduct Extraordinary Accounting Fees
- Deduct Extraordinary Legal Fees
- Deduct One-Time Product Development Costs
- Write Off Any Loans the Company Made to You
- Remove Debt Buyer Will Not Be Assuming
- Remove Expenses Not Expected to Persist

SO MANY BUSINESSES GO UNDER SIMPLY BECAUSE THE OWNERS ARE UNAWARE THAT THEY CAN SELL, EVEN IF THEY ARE LOSING MONEY!

SELLING MEMORANDUM

A Selling Memorandum should be honest, easy to read, and should create marketing excitement

A Selling Memorandum includes:
- An Overview of Your Company
- A Personal Viewpoint
- Asking Price and Terms
- About Your Industry, Competition and Products
- What is Needed For Service vs. Product Industries
- Who Are Your Customers?
- Key Personnel
- Hard Assets, Buildings and Equipment
- Projection of the Company's Future and Long-Term Plan
- Financials
- Graphics
- Executive Summary
- Appendix

CHAPTER FOUR
RECASTING & THE SELLING MEMORANDUM

RECASTING

Losing Money? No Profits? No Problem! The Magic of Recasting.

The business is making no profit. It is losing money on the books. Actually, this is all quite common! In fact, the Small Business Association reports that 80% of small businesses fail in the first 10 years, and 53% fail in the first 5 years.

A large number of small businesses go under because they fail to keep adequate records. Poor record keeping is often associated with poor management. If record keeping is poor, a business is much more difficult to sell at a desired price. It will take some expert reconstruction of financial records and recasting to get a borderline business saleable.

The good news is that most small business owners do make a living. They just fail to show a profit on the books. If you are in that group, all is not lost. You just need competent, experienced help (something you will read in this book time and time again).

In fact, there are, in general, too many buyers looking for too few good deals. But to sell a business for the right price, you must do everything you can to make the deal look as good as it possibly can.

An experienced business broker works with the seller and his accountant to appraise the business using EBITDA (discussed in the next chapter) and Recasting. It is important to show the *true* bottom line, and to make the company appear as profitable as possible in the eyes of a prospective buyer.

Even if a business is losing money according to tax returns or financial statements, with proper recasting it CAN and WILL be sold.

You are not being deceptive here. You are selling a business that may be minimally profitable (at least based on tax returns) and giving someone who may be younger, perhaps more creative, and may have a better idea of how to manage your business, the opportunity to take a losing company and make it profitable. Recasting allows a seller to point out to the buyer that, while he took $500,000 salary out of a business that grossed $1,000,000, the new owner might be content with a $250,000 salary to start, putting the difference back into the company to build it up.

RECASTING: ITS MEANING, HOW IT WORKS, AND WHAT IT CAN DO FOR YOU

The period before a sale is the time that savvy business owners "dress up" their historical financial statements by recasting—the process wherein several years' financials are restated, in order to more accurately reflect the true profit of a business, and to show how the business would look with a new owner

"Recasting" financials, from as many as the previous five years of a business, substantially increases the actual and perceived value of that business.

Legitimate deductions lower taxes, but they negatively impact the bottom line. Recasting "removes" these deductions, and demonstrates the true value of a business.

Adjustments during recasting can be made by restructuring:
- Income Statements
- Balance Sheets
- A change from a cash to an accrual basis
- The amount of excess cash retained in the company
- Salaries/benefits/bonuses in excess of market
- Undervalued/overvalued securities and investments
- Salaries/benefits below market

- Debt owned to/by shareholders and related parties
- Relatives on the payroll
- Unrecorded retirement benefits
- Excessive perks (e.g., company cars)
- Unrecorded bonuses and commissions
- Favorable or unfavorable leases
- Vacations
- Favorable or unfavorable interest on debt
- Tax loss carry-forwards
- Management fees/related party transactions
- Contingent liabilities
- Accelerated depreciation
- Non-recurring expenses (litigation, relocation, casualty losses, etc.)
- A move of revenues and expenses between fiscal periods for tax purposes
- Charitable contributions
- Any other expense that would be different if the company were no longer a stand-alone entity

When a business is being sold, due diligence requires that tax returns be provided. Sellers also provide, on request, three years of financial statements signed by accountants. These reports, however, do not always accurately portray the true profit and loss situation. Small business owners, especially solo proprietors, may be casual about their bookkeeping. They may have taken legitimate deductions, deductions which could easily have been considered more personal than business in nature. While that may have helped them in the short run, tax-wise, those deductions will negatively impact the bottom line. Tax returns are prepared as a report of taxable income, in order to determine related taxes to be paid to the government. It has been reported that a significant majority of businesses in this country do not report a profit, or report very little profit, on their tax returns, although they may be making a great deal of money. *Remember, tax returns are not prepared as a means to help a buyer make decisions about whether or not to buy a business!*

Tax Returns are Not Prepared as a Means to Help a Buyer Make a Decision Whether or Not to Buy a Business!

In fact, many small businesses have only a single owner, who has full discretion over how he compensates himself, what purchases to make, and what income the business will wind up reporting and being taxed on. This makes it impossible to make a purchase decision based only upon the net income of a small business.

Financial statements of small businesses must be restated to determine the Seller's Discretionary Cash Flow (SDCF). Recasting is the process by which this is done.

Even in large businesses, some owners actually bleed the company dry daily, paying themselves huge salaries and bonuses, or issuing a special privately held class of shares which give off dividends far in excess of those given to other shareholders. Even large publicly held companies have gotten away with this in the recent past (until they were caught after ruining many employees' and shareholders' lives). But in smaller, privately held companies, this may be a matter of routine. Rather than reinvesting money in the business, many owners take out sizeable chunks. Money taken out is money not invested in the business. A potential buyer must be educated into realizing that, with more appropriate management, a "losing" business can be a goldmine! Recasting is the tool used to do this.

The process of recasting, as we will describe it, sounds simple, but, in reality, it is a time consuming job, and a difficult endeavor to perform properly. What you are doing, basically, is taking the past three to five years of your company's financial reports and re-analyzing them to fit the needs (and excite the imagination) of a potential buyer for your company. If a specific buyer is not in the present picture, the analyst must, nonetheless, recast earnings, to make the business attractive to any potential buyer, as we will describe below.

The analyst must be completely aware of the operation of your company, its core business, expenses, profits, and all the "perks." When there is a known likely buyer, the analyst must then must discover the same information about the company interested in purchasing yours. He will be able to see the duplication of expenses, such as in advertising, management, sales force, computer systems, accounting and legal structure. The analyst then can demonstrate the profit potential inherent in combining the two as an acquisition, or perhaps even a merger. In either event, recasting is the key. In this chapter, you will find a complete plan to guide you in recasting your company's financial statements in order to portray your company's true earning power, and thus increase its value.

It has been a basic tenet of our nation's economy, as stated by our Founding Fathers, that no citizen should be obligated to pay more than his true share of taxation. Major corporations spend small fortunes in accounting and legal fees to find ways of avoiding excess taxation, through expensing items which may be considered personal. Small business owners do the same. They "expense" personal items, often justifying this by pointing out how such items contribute to the company's welfare and prestige. The problem is that if you, as an owner, legitimately find ways to have these personal expenses paid by the business, you have a two-edged sword. You may reduce taxes, but your profit and loss statement suffers. When you are contemplating a sale of that business, you must accurately convey, to the buyer, the information as to what you have taken from the business, and how it impacted your bottom line. You must point out any inefficiencies in your accounting practices as well, thus "recasting" your company's earnings to reflect true cash flow. The "recast" financials will substantially increase the actual and perceived value of your business.

What an owner will do is have an accountant recast past income statements to reflect what would have happened, had he removed the owner's salary and perks, and those of family members not expected to remain with the company, along with any expenses or income that would not be expected to recur or continue after the sale. This might include, for example, income or expenses associated with discontinued products, or gains or losses from the sale of any business assets. When recasting, he will remove any investment or other non-operating expenses or income, and remove interest payments on any business loans, since such liabilities will be removed from the balance sheet.

The accountant must then take these recast financials and use them to project how future statements are likely to look for the next five years, making reasonable assumptions about future growth or decline in income, expenses, value of assets, etc. In doing so, it is reasonable to assume that trends established in the past few years, such as a certain percentage increase in revenue each year, will continue. A buyer, looking at this projection, will likely increase the rate in his calculations, since most buyers believe they can do a much better job than the seller, and thus have an even better rate of growth. This method overcomes a buyer's resistance to put a dollar value on "potential" in a sale, especially if accompanied by the current owner's suggestions for a marketing plan.

Recast historical financial statements determine the Seller's Discretionary Cash Flow, and serve as a basis for five-year pro formas of income statements, cash flow statements and balance sheets, all of which will show the true financial operating potential of the company. The result? A much higher price for the sale of the business.

HOW TO RECAST YOUR FINANCIALS

To recast your company's earnings, you must do the following:

- Deduct from expenses the owner's salary, bonuses and other direct payments by the company to the owner(s).
- Remove the salary and perks of family members who are not expected to remain with the company.
- Add to expenses a reasonable replacement manager's salary.
- Deduct owner's car payments, gas and insurance.
- Deduct profit sharing or retirement plan contributions on owner's behalf.
- Adjust for leaseback arrangements between your company and you or your family.
- Deduct any other "perks" such as home-office expenses, automobile leases and expenses, including insurance and any other expenses you can enumerate and value honestly. Some accountants also try to deduct boats, airplanes, motorcycles, swimming pools, and the like because, of course, these all show as additional income.
- Deduct surplus staffing. Some employees who are lingering on

RECASTING & THE SELLING MEMORANDUM

the payroll may be considered expendable by the buyer. Deduct their salaries.
- Deduct extraordinary accounting or legal fees incurred in preparation for the sale.
- Deduct one-time or extraordinary product development costs.
- Remove any debt that the buyer will not be assuming, and the interest payments they engendered. Note that this is one of the most important items on this list. Paying back loans and expelling interest really means more profit to a company when recasting.
- Remove any expenses that will not be expected to persist after the sale, such as discontinued products, or losses associated with the sale of assets.
- Have your accountant determine if some costs you have declared may have been capitalized.

Furthermore, the accountant can adjust past balance sheets to:
- Remove any assets that will not be sold with the company.
- Remove any obsolete or slow-moving inventory.
- Value the remaining inventory at current replacement cost.
- Value remaining balance-sheet assets at current fair market value.
- Write off any accounts receivable that are uncollectable.
- Write off any loans the company made to the owner.
- Remove other debt that will not be assumed by the buyer.
- Remove expensed costs that could have been capitalized.

Look at each item on your profit and loss statement for opportunities to recast. Be sure to list everything that fits into this niche, and include comments to justify why they are there. Whatever you do in the way of recasting your financials, make sure that any changes to your historical statements are carefully documented on the face of the statements, so that the buyer knows you are not trying to cover up anything.

If you value your business as a multiple of earnings, every dollar increase you show by recasting will add a multiple of that in dollars to your selling price.

A Small Adjustment (Recasting) May Result in a Huge Increase in Value!
Let's take a simple example. A business owner with a wife, 4 children and an ailing mother gives each one a cell phone, costing the business $60 per month each. This expense of $420/month becomes $5,040 a year. Since the value of a business is often determined as a multiple (usually between two times and ten times earnings) of net income, this dramatically affects the potential selling price. Using a multiple of 10 times profits, the $5,040 becomes $50,400 in added value to the business. That's just a few cell phones. Imagine! Putting back into the equation $60,000 in "perks" that may make a difference of $600,000 or more in the final selling price. Recasting works!

Label Recast Earnings as Such. These Must Not Be Submitted to a Lender!
IMPORTANT: Be careful to label recast financials as such. You will still be providing non-recast financials to the buyer. That set of financials accurately depicts the net income after taking legitimate deductions. Everyone appreciates the concept that no one should ever be paying a cent more in taxes than he or she must. But you must know exactly what your bottom line is when you figure in the perks you receive, because that will greatly affect the selling price of your business. Hence, a second set of figures, prepared for such a purpose and clearly labeled "Recast Earnings," is most helpful. While these may legitimately be presented to the lender, they are ***not*** a substitute for filed tax returns. Assuming money is being borrowed from a bank or other financial institution, recast earnings must never be submitted to such institutions. Lenders ***always*** will present the forms they receive for verification to the Internal Revenue Service. If the IRS sees a discrepancy between stated recast earnings and tax forms filed, they ***will*** spot this "red flag" and, without hesitation, go after the seller, seeking back taxes plus penalties. They may even file criminal charges for failing to file accurate returns.

A lending institution need not necessarily be involved. An alternative to having a Small Business Association or other commercial lender review the recast earnings, ignore them and reject a loan, might be to have the owner self-finance the sale, with all parties being fully aware of the true value of the business.

SELLING MEMORANDUM

Preparation of a middle-market company for sale almost always begins with a Recasting or Selling Memorandum. It may also be called recasting, an offering memorandum, a business plan, a confidential descriptive memorandum, the book or selling book. Regardless of what you call it, its function is to encourage prospective buyers to take an in depth look at the company. A good Selling Memorandum must perform two tasks:

1. **A Selling Memorandum must present completely factual information.**
2. **A Selling Memorandum must create marketing excitement.**

While it may take months to complete, a well-prepared Selling Memorandum will pay off many times over. You cannot first start creating one when prospective buyers ask for it! Ideally, all the groundwork should be done way before the first buyer arrives. Spend the time needed to put together an excellent Selling Memorandum. If you utilize the services of a good merger acquisition/business brokerage firm, they often will prepare this document for you. You should use a CPA firm, your attorney and/or a merger acquisition/business broker to help create your Selling Memorandum at a reasonable price. **A word of warning: There are companies that charge up-front fees from $10,000 to $60,000 to create a Selling Memorandum. This should not be necessary. In my opinion, a merger acquisition or business brokerage firm that tells you they can sell your business should do everything possible** *to sell your business.* **For them to charge an additional and exorbitant up-front fee of up to $60,000 is unconscionable.**

As a point of fact, all business owners already should have a clear understanding of the operation and financial situation of their business. When they set this information to print, it becomes a business plan, chronicling the past and present, and projecting the future operation of the business. A Selling Memorandum is essentially the same as a business plan, but in reverse. It is written to present your company's financial and market information in the best possible light. It is a marketing tool, in which you must explain why your company is a great investment for the prospective buyer. It must tell a story in such a way that it excites prospective buyers, and encourages them to further evaluate the company. It should, of course, only be shown to a serious buyer who has signed a confidentiality agreement. And it should not include confidential company information or reveal trade secrets.

Incidentally, another benefit in preparing a Selling Memorandum is that it causes the seller to reevaluate his company. It may look so good that he realizes he does not want to sell. Or he may decide there are things that must be done to improve the situation before he even tries to sell the company.

The following information will provide you with a format for discussion with your accountant regarding establishing the true value of your practice. Follow the instructions below in preparing a Selling Memorandum, and you will save time, effort and money. You will sell your business more rapidly, and more profitably, than you would ever do without it.

As we have repeatedly pointed out, your tax returns do not present the most accurate and timely information prospective buyers need in order to properly value your business. A Selling Memorandum states the major strengths of your business, plus all the material, including recast financials, that you and your advisors need in order to establish an asking price that is fair to both seller and buyer.

A Selling Memorandum includes:
1. An overview of your company
When I give a speech, or teach other brokers what I have learned about selling and buying a business, I break the speech down to three parts. I tell them what I am going to say, I say it, then I tell them what I have said. A Selling Memorandum should ideally do the same. In the introduction, you must highlight the most important points you want a buyer to know. Whet his appetite.

2. A personal viewpoint
You should detail when and why you bought or started the business, how it is set up (sole proprietorship, partnership, corporation, etc.), what you have achieved to create a successful and growing company, and, carefully phrased, your reasons for selling at this time. The latter

is very important. It is among the first questions a broker is asked, and the answer should be brief, honest, and encouraging, not discouraging, to a prospective buyer.

3. Asking price and terms

While this is important to both seller and buyer, what is more important is a description of how you came to that price. Terms of the sale are not discussed here. The paperwork you used to come up with the valuation, and/or a report from a professional appraiser (see the Appraisal chapter in this book, along with the chapter on how to value a business), should be provided clearly so the buyer's advisors can understand and appreciate it. Make sure the asking price is justified. If you ask for 50% more than you are willing to settle for, your prospective buyer will stop reading right there, and leave. This is not the place to autocratically say, "This is what I want!" or "This is what I need!" The buyer will realize there may be room for negotiation, but items in your valuation that are non-negotiable should be highlighted.

4. About your industry, competition and products

Provide an overview of the industry, although, hopefully the buyer will already understand that. The Selling Memorandum is used to assist skeptical accountants, buyers, investors and attorneys in their evaluation. Provide a description of your market share, and some idea as to the nature and amount of competition. Include current trends and industry growth potential.

5. What is needed for service vs. product industries

In a service industry, your personal views are most important. How is the service provided? What supervision and controls, and user feedback, are in place? In a product-based industry, you must list and explain the products produced and their contribution to the top and bottom line. This is also the place to discuss patents, trademarks and royalty arrangements. Point out the channels of distribution and marketing methods. What products are in the pipeline, what is being done, and how soon can release be expected? And be certain the buyer knows that the entire company is for sale. He cannot pick and choose the portions he wants.

6. Who are your customers?

Definitely do not list your customers' names, but you should give some demographics. Where do your customers come from? Are they primarily users or retailers of your product. If both, give some percentages.

7. Key personnel

Who are the major players in running your company? Again, you need not give their names at this time, but merely their titles. Do they know about an impending sale? Will they stay on for a new owner? For how long? Do they have any restrictive covenants to prevent their competing after the sale. If there is a hierarchy, it should be noted and even charted for ease of understanding. If there are many divisions, a breakdown in each division is required.

8. Hard assets, buildings and equipment

The buyer will have to know the purchase date and condition of all major hard assets, along with warranty information. You may omit the depreciated value at this time (see the chapter on EBITDA, Earnings before Interest, Taxes, depreciation and Amortization). Details of leases, if any, must be provided. Photographs might be included. But do not risk losing the reader's attention. Actual lists may be put in an appendix, and the hard assets can be summarized in this section. The Selling Memorandum should be readable. The appendix can also include relevant corporate and/or product brochures.

9. Projection of the company's future and long-term plan

Detail the 5-year goals for the company. A seller may have ideas for future plans he has not yet initiated. This is the time to share them with the buyer. Most large companies have in place a three to five-year plan, which will include goals and the strategies and resources you would need to use to achieve those goals. If you do not have a plan, it would be an excellent idea for you to formulate one, not only to help the buyer, but, should the sale not go through, to enable you to grow your business. In the plan, you should detail the company's goals, and how you plan to reach those goals. Be optimistic, but also be realistic.

10. Financials

While your accountant will provide all the needed tax forms and profit and loss statements, along with accounts payable and receivable, this is the place to explain anything that might be used to provide a clear picture of your company's financial position. You would ideally include at least a three-year history of earnings broken down by quarters, and a three-year forecast if possible.

11. Graphics

Any forms, charts, diagrams or photographs used to provide a clearer picture of your company may be included here. The services of a graphic designer or your business broker (see chapter on Projecting an Image) can be useful.

12. Executive Summary

Now that you have told the buyer what you were going to provide, and have provided it, this is the place to tell the buyer what you have said. While the Selling Memorandum may be as lengthy as is needed, an Executive Summary should be prepared that describes the entire offering in brief. It too, is a selling tool, whose purpose is to generate interest and excitement. Summarize the company's strengths, its markets, and any potential risks and how they may be handled. Provide reasons you believe buying your business will be a wonderful investment for the buyer.

13. Appendix

This is the section in which to put product literature, detailed asset lists, appraisals, photos, maps, drawings, articles from magazines, newspapers, TV, radio, web site links, and anything else that would disrupt the reading flow if it were in the body of the memorandum. The Selling Memorandum will not include copies of actual financial statements, those can wait until later as long as the summaries provided sufficient information.

Make up a strong Selling Memorandum

Don't oversell! Make sure your Selling Memorandum is written in such a way that the company sells itself. If you are uncomfortable writing such an important document, enlist the assistance of your business broker, merger acquisition firm, attorney or other trusted

advisor. You will still need to provide the data, but an expert can put it together for you.

And be honest. As we explain elsewhere in this book, honesty is not only the best policy but it is the **only** policy. Impending lawsuits or structural flaws, for example, must be disclosed. Hiding anything will come back to haunt you later in the sale process, perhaps even on the day of the closing!

Most important: A Selling Memorandum should be honest, easy to read, and should create marketing excitement.

CHAPTER FIVE
EBITDA

 **KEY POINTS**

EBITDA: Earnings Before Interest, Taxes, Depreciation and Amortization

The Earnings of a Business After Eliminating Non-Cash Expenses For Depreciation and Amortization, and After Eliminating Expense of Interest on Debt

Interest and Taxes Do Cost a Company Cash, While Depreciation and Amortization are Tools to Save Taxes

EBITDA is an Aggressive Accounting Tool Used to Analyze Profitability, and to Create a Picture More Indicative of the Company's Value

A Multiple of EBITDA Can Determine Selling Price

CHAPTER FIVE
EBITDA

EBITDA = Earnings before interest, taxes, depreciation and amortization.

Definition: The earnings of a business after eliminating non-cash expenses for depreciation and amortization, and after eliminating expense of interest on debt.

As discussed in the chapter on Recasting, an important concept any businessman must grasp is the importance of increasing the value of your business before you are ready to sell or merge it.

Creative accounting, which is perfectly legal, may have produced financials which did not clearly show the profit being made. Like recasting, EBITDA, an acronym for Earnings Before Interest, Taxes, Depreciation and Amortization, is a well established, though aggressive, accounting procedure, used to demonstrate the true profitability of a company. Though it is often used on its own, it is sometimes used in recasting, as well.

EBITDA is a good measure to use in evaluating core profit trends. EBITDA can be used to evaluate the profit potential between companies and industries because it eliminates some of the extraneous factors, and allows a more "apples-to-apples" comparison.

The utilization of EBITDA has spread to a wide range of businesses. Champions of the process claim that EBITDA offers a clearer reflection of operations by stripping out expenses that can obscure how the company is truly performing. Interest, which in most part is due to management's choice of financing, is not taken into account. Taxes are left out because they can vary widely depending on acquisitions and losses in previous years. And EBITDA removes the subjective judgments that can go into calculating depreciation and amortization, such as useful lives, residual values and various depreciation methods. This makes EBITDA an easier tool to use in comparing the financial health of various companies, while giving investors a better sense of how much money a young or restructured company might generate, before it has to hand over payments to creditors or the government.

There are many formulae used by professionals to appraise a business. Value is determined based on what a seller is willing to take, and what a buyer is willing to pay. Sellers must realize that the price paid must allow the buyer to cover the debt service, and compensate him or her for the financial investment, and for the effort needed to run the business.

Of course, if time is an important factor in the sale, the better the deal is for the buyer, the faster the business will sell. The seller may make financing easier for the buyer by holding some paper himself (self financing). There may be tax advantages to the seller for doing so, and it would give the buyer the good feeling that the seller is confident he will do well in continuing the business. As a point of fact, it is very likely that a new buyer will increase the business' revenue. New blood often brings creative energy and innovations. There is a hunger for success, which the previous owner, set in his ways, may no longer have had. Smart buyers often take the better profit-increasing ideas developed by the seller and add fresh ideas to make a really profit-building business.

Appraisal of a company's value to a buyer will depend largely on EBITDA.

EBITDA helps a business to shine by revealing the earnings of the business, after eliminating non-cash expenses for depreciation and amortization, and after eliminating expense of interest on debt. EBITDA can be used to analyze profitability, but it does not represent earnings or cash flow. It can, however be used as a substitute for cash flow, and it is often advantageous to the seller to attempt to do so. Good accounting advice is essential in this determination.

INTEREST AND TAXES DO COST A COMPANY CASH

Two of the four items listed in the acronym EBITDA, interest and taxes, can and do cost a company cash. While debt holders do, indeed, have a claim on a company's assets, some of the debt may disappear as earnings are recast. Taxes are inevitable, but will be present for the new owner as well, so there can be an argument for or against removing them from the calculations needed to reach a selling price.

DEPRECIATION AND AMORTIZATION ARE TOOLS TO SAVE TAXES

Depreciation and amortization are often tools used to save taxes. An important consideration for the buyer would be whether depreciated equipment nearing the end of its term, tax wise, may also indicate the possible need for new or replacement equipment.

EBITDA IS AN AGGRESSIVE ACCOUNTING TOOL

EBITDA can be utilized as an aggressive accounting tool, to create a picture the management considers more truly indicative of the company's value than cash flow. It is most useful in evaluating firms in the same industry with widely divergent capital structures, tax rates and depreciation policies.

Both parties to a deal must remember that EBITDA is just a tool. There is so much more to consider, especially free cash flow and other important items of recasting.

IMPORTANT! You must have a qualified and knowledgeable accountant work out all the details of EBITDA. *Exit Strategy* was written and developed as an aid in helping you sell a business. It will give you the information and guidance needed to properly execute the successful sale of your business, but it is not a substitute for the personal attention and skill of a good accountant.

FACTORS AFFECTING THE MULTIPLE OF EBITDA:
Positive Factors
- Location
- Retention of key personnel
- A diverse customer base

- Strong management and weak competition
- Strong established products and/or a strong pipeline of new products
- A good lease
- The ability of the firm to continue to grow in the current location

Negative Factors
- Products that are readily available elsewhere
- A customer base heavily weighted with only a few customers, any of which may stop buying and hurt the business
- Soon-to-be-outdated equipment

There are many factors influencing the multiple of EBITDA used in valuing a business. A common multiplier would be between 2 and 10 times the EBITDA, most often 2.5 to 6 times that amount.

If a business has a strong concept, if it is a traditional type of business, if it has a good market share, if key personnel are staying on, and if there is strong management and weak competition, then the multiplier will be higher. If, on the other hand, the customer base is heavily weighted with only a few customers, any of whom may stop buying and hurt the business, and/or there is outdated equipment, the multiplier will be lower.

To reiterate, EBITDA is a powerful tool, and must be used properly to honestly portray the profitability of a business.

CHAPTER SIX

WHAT IS YOUR BUSINESS WORTH?

 **KEY POINTS**

Raise the Value of the Business Before Selling

Using the Services of a Promotional Services Company to Increase Your Bottom Line

Outsourcing

Bring the Expenses to Within Industry Norms

Separate Your Assets

70% of Small Businesses Do Not Sell Without Experienced Help

Setting a Value For Your Business
- Determining the Value of a Business is Not a Do-It-Yourself Project
- Recasting
- EBITDA
- Ability to Generate Sales
- Cash Flow
- Adjusted Net Income
- Net Assets Method—Tangible/Intangible

- Excess Earnings Method
- Economic or Capitalization Rate Method
- Market Comparison Approach

Evaluation of "Goodwill"

Always Check the Tax Consequences of a Sale With a Trusted Advisor

The Importance of Expert Professional Advice

CHAPTER SIX
WHAT IS YOUR BUSINESS WORTH?

Here is something that should NEVER happen: you are evaluating the worth of your business for the first time because you are thinking of selling.

Any owner should periodically determine the business' value throughout the life of the business! Before you even entertain the thought of selling, do your homework. That is what *Exit Strategy* is all about.

Some of the most important times to determine business worth are when you are considering expansion, thinking of bringing in new blood, getting a loan or line of credit, determining estate tax strategy, settling a divorce, or buying out a partner. And of course, the owner should certainly have thought about the value of the business when buying it or starting one in the first place!

When planning an exit strategy, knowing what your business is worth is an absolute must. There are many ways to determine this value. And as the reader will learn throughout the content of this book, there are always professional ways to handle the often-found fact that an owner does not like what the business computations show.

Without a doubt, determining the value of a business is not a do-it-yourself project. We will present some tools to help the owner collect and analyze information about the company, and get a rough estimate of the business' worth, before getting the recommended professional help. Once the necessary records are available, a good accountant, working with a business broker or other qualified intermediary, can determine how capitals or EBITDA will present the business in the most favorable manner.

As a general rule, the price of a business is right if the purchase price for the business can be paid for over a reasonable period of time.

RECASTING IS IMPORTANT

We always advise potential sellers to omit nothing in their calculations that pertain to the business. This thoroughness and honesty may lead to some unpleasant surprises, and the owner should be ready for them. Only if you are brutally honest when accumulating data can a professional guide you in presenting everything in the best light, and in getting the best price.

There are many things a professional can do. That's why recasting is vitally important when a sale is imminent. When recasting your business financials, an expert will beam the brightest light on your bottom line.

SEPARATE YOUR ASSETS

Separating assets can be done simply enough, and it must be anticipated before you put a value on your business.

Is the building in which the business is housed owned or rented? The disciplines of real estate appraisal and business valuation are very different and quite specialized.

Does the business own other buildings or assets that will not be included in the sale? Separate them out before they become a matter of contention.

A professional can also help with an "income approach" to separating real estate from other assets. This involves isolating the property from intangibles such as business trade names, franchise agreements, trademarks, existing workforce, licenses, customer lists and key employees.

SETTING A VALUE

Just as a buyer wants to avoid overpaying for a business, as a business owner, you want to avoid selling for less than the enterprise is worth.

While your accountant, or the business broker representing you, can provide an appraisal, buyers rarely accept that appraisal on faith. An independent appraiser may have to be hired. Even if you are years away from selling a business, it's always a good idea to have the business appraised at some point so you can plan accordingly (see Chapter 10 on Appraisals).

When we help evaluate the value of a small business, we look at two key factors:

1. The company's ability to generate sales, cash flow and/or profits, taking into account ALL expenses.
2. The company's assets, both tangible and intangible.

RAISING THE WORTH OF YOUR BUSINESS AND ITS ABILITY TO BE SOLD PROFITABLY BEFORE IT COMES TIME TO SELL

If the expectations of business worth are far from met, there are things that can be suggested to increase the bottom line, even if it takes a few years. In fact, it might save time in the long run to raise the value of the business by owning it a bit longer, so that it will sell more quickly and at a higher price.

Here are some significant ways you can increase the value of your business in the period before you sell:

Ability to Generate Sales

When we determine a likely selling price, we often use a multiplier of a firm's annual sales. If a business has low fixed costs, few assets and little retained earnings, the sales multiplier technique may be appropriate. This is often utilized for the sale of a professional practice or other service related company.

But whether you own a business that is large or small, and no matter what the goods or services provided, its ability to generate cash flow is integral to the life—and eventual sale—of the entity.

Bring The Expenses To Within Industry Norms—The Use Of Employee Outsourcing

Want to show even more profits when selling-time comes? One resource not often considered when building up a business for sale is outsourcing.

I am not speaking of sending business to India, Pakistan or China, although that sometimes is necessary. Full time employees drawing large salaries often perform work that can be done by a part time bookkeeper, for example, or by a stay-at-home mom working in sales or doing secretarial work from a computer at home. In fact, at-home workers are an excellent resource. They are often highly educated, or even over-qualified were you to attempt to hire them full time, but are delighted to earn money and keep their minds active working from home. They have no travel time, and no lunch hours or coffee breaks. You are helping your company, and you are also helping people, domestically, who really need the income. It can be a win-win situation.

Companies have been created that offer you centralized, off-site switchboard/receptionist functions at a minimal cost, eliminating the need for on-site operators. One company we worked with had two switchboard operators, with the second one only used as a back-up when the first was busy. This cost the company $60,000 a year. They are now using a service and paying just $250 a week. Net saving? $48,000 annually!

In my firm, we had a bookkeeper for many years who was earning $80,000 per year. She retired after 26 years. We replaced her with an outsourced bookkeeping service for $15,000 per year. Other examples abound. For more details on the benefits of outsourcing, see the chapter titled "Outsourcing: Today's Business-Building Necessity."

THE PRICE OF A BUSINESS IS RIGHT IF THE BUSINESS CAN PAY FOR ITSELF

This cannot be stated often enough: The price of a business is right if the business can pay for itself over a reasonable period of time. If it cannot, the price must be looked at again by both buyer and seller.

CASH FLOW

When we use cash flow (sales less expenses) or profits, we help the seller project the flow of cash over five or more years to calculate the worth of the business. We determine the likely projected money generating power of the business over five years, giving everyone a starting point. In doing this, we would ideally rely on recast earnings, since it would more accurately reflect true cash flow, and it would definitely increase the sale price for the business.

As mentioned in the chapter above, a common multiplier would be between 2 and 10 times the EBITDA, most often 2.5 to 6 times that amount.

When a business has little in the way of profits or cash flow, and a sale is planned, the only way a decent price may be set might be the company's assets.

Tangible assets like a plant, equipment and inventory may set a minimum selling price.

Intangible assets like goodwill, customer lists, trademarks, patents, leases, permits and contracts may be factored into raising the selling price.

An appraiser may be important when the price of a business will be based on assets rather than cash flow.

GETTING EXPERT ADVICE

You may have used a particular CPA or lawyer for decades, but if this otherwise trusted expert is inexperienced in business sale matters, having him guide you in evaluating the worth of your business may be a costly error. For example, income statements may need to be adjusted to market or industry standards, something an accountant outside the industry may not realize.

Ideally, you need an accountant, attorney and financial advisor who are all experienced and knowledgeable in EBITDA and recasting principles. A good business broker can most likely steer you to one, or to all three. A business appraiser familiar with your industry can also be a very good investment. Once you have interviewed each, and hired them to evaluate the worth of your business, you must be honest and open.

Never leave negative financial disclosures for someone else to find at the time of closing! This will lead to a terrible waste of time, money and status.

By the same token, be forthright and demanding of your consultants. Don't be intimidated by them. You want to know the tax ramifications of what you are doing, the documents that need to be reviewed and prepared, and exactly what it will cost. Bring up the subject of recasting, and see if that will add to your bottom line and hence the selling price. Be prepared with your exit strategy firmly in place, and you can look forward to an easy and profitable sale.

THE ROLE OF THE BUSINESS BROKER OR MERGER AND ACQUISITION SPECIALIST

As we point out repeatedly in this book, there are numerous ways in which an experienced business broker or merger and acquisition specialist can be an asset. It has been our experience, in fact, that it is virtually impossible for a company to represent itself in a sale and still gain the best terms of sale and the greatest profits!

Visualize yourself trying to sell a car. A potential buyer comes, looks at it, and says he'll get back to you with an offer. He doesn't call, so you call him and leave a message. When he doesn't call you, you call again, and then again the next day. By the time he does return your call, he knows he has you over a barrel, and will lowball the offering price. You have shown him you are desperate.

If you had an intermediary, (a broker, of sorts), whose job it is to sell the car for you, that intermediary can call dozens of times. He is just doing his job. It does not alter your bargaining power. A broker can call, badger, negotiate—even hassle a buyer. It's his job. A business owner's job is to keep making the business as profitable—therefore, as easy to sell—as possible. An impartial intermediary is essential to a sale at an appropriate price.

The merger and acquisition specialist or business broker assists the seller with preparation, such as establishing the transaction objective, and preparing marketing materials like an offering memorandum or a financial model, using the Vertical Horizontal Selling Method to target buyers.

The merger and acquisition specialist or business broker assists the seller with marketing, such as finding and contacting prospective buyers, setting up meetings, and receiving proposals. The broker also will assist in evaluating alternative offers and proposals, negotiating a letter of intent, setting a time table for due diligence, and expediting the deal.

The merger and acquisition specialist or business broker also assists the seller with providing material for the necessary due diligence by ensuring all required documents are available, and by referring the proper experienced legal and accounting help that is needed.

Finally, a good agent can assist the seller with closing the deal. This agent will negotiate and finalize the purchase agreement and close the transaction.

CHOOSING A MERGER AND ACQUISITION SPECIALIST OR BUSINESS BROKER

Know what you want and convey those expectations to a broker you interview. Hopefully, your people skills will enable you to gauge his honesty and integrity.

A broker with a sincere, likeable and enthusiastic personality will most likely sell your business more rapidly than someone dull. You will be able to see if the communications will be open and direct. Will the broker return your calls promptly? If the broker has no time to talk to you, he will have no time to work on your deal. Time kills deals. You need a broker who will be responsive.

Ask the broker how he will get the word out about your business. Will confidentiality be maintained? It must be! Internet capability is a must these days. What budget is allocated for advertising? Who will be paying for it?

If possible, check the broker's record. How many deals has the broker done in the past month? Past year? Past five years? Have they ever sold your type of business? When and for how much?

Now, here's a surprise for you. If the broker gives you TOO much information on a business he has sold, with specific names and amounts, this should be a warning to you. He is not going to respect your confidentiality either. Walk away.

Nationally, according to the Small Business Association, 70% of small businesses never sell. That's because the owners may not realize they have a saleable commodity. They may think they are not making money, and that the business has no value, not realizing that a buyer may welcome the opportunity to turn around such a business. Owners may put too high a price on the business for the current marketplace, or have unrealistic terms and conditions. Odds of a successful sale are much, much better with the advice of a good merger and acquisition specialist.

As an aside, we are proud to point out that the Manheim Business Brokers and Merger and Acquisition firm has over 50 certified real estate sales persons fulfilling continuing education requirements to assist them in the sale of businesses and increase their productivity. While only 14% of our business sales involve real estate, it is nonetheless important to have a well rounded staff, benefiting both buyers and sellers. We would urge sellers to find a firm similar to ours, with adequate and well-trained staff who are capable of helping you find the greatest number of qualified buyers in the shortest amount of time.

Make sure the broker you select is comfortable and well-versed in selling your type, location and size of business. This is not the time to just pick a broker out of the Yellow Pages.

Does the broker participate in continuing education courses? Even better, does the broker teach the subject, or has he written articles for the trade publications or a book on the subject? Is the broker familiar with your field? This is of crucial import in professional practice sales. Get references from buyers, sellers, accountants, attorneys or bankers. Then ask them for other references. Selecting the right broker will greatly increase the likelihood of a quick and appropriate sale.

The listing time should be spelled out. It is best to give a broker an exclusive contract. The broker is more likely, in most instances, to put himself out more, in both time and investment of resources, when he has the exclusive. Unfortunately, many sellers believe that when they have their business-for-sale presented as an open listing, using several brokers to sell the business will make the sale happen faster. This is not the case. Open listings generally go to the bottom of a broker's list of things to sell. With an exclusive listing and a 10% to 12% commission, a business broker or merger and acquisition specialist will have the incentive to sell your business fast, and sell it for the highest possible profit.

DETERMINE METHOD OF VALUATION

You need not decide on a single manner of evaluation at this time. As a matter of fact, when the time comes, we recommend that you use at least two. And, as always, unless you are eminently qualified to make the decision, let the experts choose for you.

An independent appraiser may be quite advantageously enlisted in this stage—the earlier the better.

Remember: Many deals never happen because an owner values his business unrealistically high.

And, many businesses sell for too little because an owner does not realize its actual value.

If you are thinking about evaluating your business yourself, the methods used include net assets, excess earnings, economic/capitalization rate, and market comparison. (If you have not already done so, read the Chapters titled *EBITDA* and *RECASTING*).

1. NET ASSET APPROACH:

The assets of a business include tangible assets such as fixtures, inventory, and accounts receivable. Intangible assets include primarily that oh-so-difficult-to-put-a-dollar-sign-next-to factor, goodwill. Owners tend to overestimate the value of goodwill, while buyers are often reluctant to pay for it.

The net asset method is usually used only when a business must be disposed of quickly. When used, it rarely reflects the true value of a business. The book value of hard assets is an illusion. The equipment may have been depreciated to far below its value, or may be so obsolete that it has no value. With the net asset method, the net worth of the business is adjusted for bad debt, obsolete inventory, and value of fixtures and equipment, then a small amount is added on for goodwill. Some experts use a five year average of net income to determine "goodwill." More about this below.

Adjusted net income, on the other hand, includes the profits of the company, plus the owner's salary and all the cash related benefits enjoyed by the principals of a small business. These 'perks' include a company car, health, life and automobile insurance, and personal expenditures tucked into Travel and Entertainment, subscriptions, etc. Depreciation and amortization also detract from the reported bottom line, but add to the value of the business. This is another reason why the use of EBITDA and Recasting is best put to use.

2. EXCESS EARNINGS METHOD

Use of this method forces the seller to look at the business from a buyer's viewpoint. As detailed in the Business Valuation Bluebook, it incorporates risk factors into the picture. The seller must look at:

- a. The financial picture
  - Five year revenue trend
  - Capital structure
  - Leverage
  - Earnings
  - Cash flow
- b. Management control
  - Employee turnover
  - Employee compensation
  - Market penetration
  - Potential for litigation
- c. Marketing plans
- d. Company brand identification
- e. Market differentiation
- f. Sales training and incentives
- g. Type of merchandise sold
- h. Production factors
  - Inventory management and obsolescence

i. Service history
   - Customer satisfaction
   - Employee recognition
j. Intellectual capital
   - The knowledge the owner has of the market and the competition
   - His vision for the business
   - Development of key personnel
   - Employee motivation

When all these factors are evaluated, each is given a score between zero and five, with zero being the highest risk, and five given to a business that is well managed, profitable and growing. This gives a risk/price ratio, which is the average of those scores. When excess earnings are multiplied by risk/price ratio, you get a number, which represents true excess earnings. You factor in a reasonable return on that amount, perhaps 10%, then add in tangible assets and reach a value for the practice. If this sounds oversimplified, that's because it is. This is one more reason why this is not a "do-it-yourself" project.

Earnings based valuations take into account historical financial figures, including debt payments, cash flow (past, present and projected) and revenues. Earnings-based valuations are often combined with asset-based valuations for a more inclusive appraisal.

3. ECONOMIC/CAPITALIZATION RATE

A buyer, when push comes to shove, wants to know only one thing. Will he make money on the investment, and how much? In evaluating this, you must know the net income from the business, and bring the expenses to within industry norms. If the owner has been taking a lower salary for tax purposes, recasting is imperative to show what a new owner can hope to earn. Every industry has a known capitalization rate, which can project the new owner's potential future return on his investment. Obviously, the lower the investment (i.e., the purchase price), the higher the return will be.

4. THE MARKET COMPARISON APPROACH

The market approach takes into account the way other businesses in the same local market and the same industry are valued. This approach requires an in-depth awareness of your local economy, and of your business' place in it. It only works for large businesses, since small businesses are difficult to compare with each other due to differences in management, accounting procedures, capital structure and market dynamics. If it can be used (and only an expert would know), it would result in a much higher valuation for most businesses.

5. EVALUATION OF "GOODWILL"

As mentioned above, goodwill is often overestimated in value by the seller, and unappreciated by the buyer. To help put a number on this elusive factor, one can just assume that the net income is due to goodwill. All the things that make clients or buyers happy—the attentive personnel, nice surroundings, fair prices and solid reputation—lead to a healthy bottom line. Therefore, a simple way of factoring goodwill is to take a five year average of net income.

Another method to determine goodwill is to compare your business' bottom line with the industry's average net income. Any difference above industry norms can be considered goodwill.

A less simple method to assess goodwill relies on the excess earnings evaluation noted above. Calculate the fair market value of tangible assets, add in the safe rate of return and net cash flow, and you have excess earnings, which can be used as the dollar value of goodwill.

RULES OF THUMB TO ESTIMATE SELLING PRICE OF A BUSINESS

1. The Seller should always get a third party appraisal. An experienced business broker will be able to offer a Seller a list of appraisal companies. See the Chapter on Appraisals for further information.

2. A good and experienced business broker will have access to "Field Formulas." He will know the selling price of other businesses

similar to yours, and can guide you in setting a reasonable price that will enable you to sell quickly.

TAX CONSEQUENCES OF A SALE

As soon as you consider the possibility of selling a business, an owner must consider the tax consequences. It is a given that Buyers and Sellers are on opposite poles when it comes to evaluation and costs, but they always will agree on one thing: "How can we minimize the amount we have to pay in taxes?" In evaluating the sale of a business for taxation purposes, the IRS is concerned only with who is going to pay, and how much they can get. This depends on how the business is structured. Here again, we recommend expert advice. Tax avoidance strategies may be quite efficient—or may lead to unanticipated disasters. The importance of expert advice cannot be overstated. If you plan wisely, you can minimize your tax liability.

For the seller, the objective must be to receive as much as possible for the company. Only then should tax considerations come into play. In general, a business sale should be structured to show as much of the sale as a capital gain as possible. Deferring income to a year or years down the line when anticipated income is lower, and tax bracket may be lower, sometimes works, and is often a good reason for the seller to take paper. On the other hand, the deal may be structured so that the seller does not pay any tax on the gain until all installments are paid or stock shares received. And your tax advisor must do all possible to avoid double taxation.

ALWAYS CHECK THE TAX CONSEQUENCES OF A SALE WITH A TRUSTED ADVISOR

When stock is sold, gains or losses are treated as capital gains or losses. Goodwill, most real property gains and any appreciation over original equipment cost are also usually treated as capital gains. But when you sell individual assets of the business, such as equipment or inventory, this is ordinary income. In the case of equipment, the ordinary income might be based on the depreciated cost of that equipment, some of which may have been depreciated down to a zero cost through the years, while maintaining a sale dollar value.

Most businesses are individually owned, or are set up as S corporations, C corporations, or Limited Liability Corporations (LLCs). Taxes are assessed differently for each.

As a general rule, C Corporations generate capital gains taxes, while the others generate individual income taxes or taxes on dividends. C Corporations are governed by the most complicated tax rules, generating corporate revenue and incurring taxation at corporate rates. Owners and stockholders, of course, pay taxes on income, dividends and capital gains.

S corporations pass income through to owners or stockholders, who pay taxes at personal rates. Only individuals own stock, and there can be a maximum of 75 shareholders. They pay no taxes as corporations. While this is in no way to be considered accounting advice, the benefits of being an S corporation are well known. Please see the Chapter on anticipating the tax consequences of a sale, and get expert help!

THE IMPORTANCE OF EXPERT PROFESSIONAL ADVICE

Despite the tax implications, it can be quite costly and difficult to change corporate structures at the last minute. Here again, the importance of having an expert's advice cannot be overstated. Now would be good time to read the Chapter on Accounting.

CHAPTER SEVEN
APPRAISALS

 **KEY POINTS**

The Importance of Independent Appraisals
- Buying a Business
- Selling a Business
- Marketing a Business
- Planning the Exit Strategy

Using Data Bases

BizComps
- Pratt's Stats
- The Database of the Institute of Business Appraisers (IBA)

Calculating SDE (Seller's Discretionary Earnings)

CHAPTER SEVEN
APPRAISALS

In buying or selling a business, it is always wise to attempt to get a professional appraiser's opinion of value. The preparation of an appraisal involves research into appropriate market areas, the assembly and analysis of information pertinent to a business or a property, and, of course, the knowledge, experience and professional judgment of the appraiser. The appraiser's role is to provide objective, impartial and unbiased opinions about the value of a business and, if relevant, of real property.

While all the discussions in previous chapters may make you a more knowledgeable seller with regard to an optimal asking price for your business, there is no substitute for hiring an expert who can keep you from selling too low or asking too high. Owners who sell without getting an independent third party appraisal of their business' value are likely to get lower offers, and eventually sell for a lot less than they should. Statistics show that appraised businesses sell for 20% or more than equivalent businesses that have not had that advantage.

The appraisal is a tool used in marketing a business and negotiating a sale. It justifies the asking price leaving less room for downward negotiation. It points out the anticipated return on the buyer's investment better than any single set of figures. This is only true, though, if the appraisal is done by an independent, experienced, qualified appraiser who is familiar with the seller's industry. An appraisal by your accountant or broker holds no such power.

A good appraiser will interview the company's principals, do an on-site survey, and do a comparison study within the industry. He or she might work with the accountant and other advisors to recast financial statements and prepare a business profile. Armed with this information, the business broker can do an even better job of marketing the business successfully.

As an aside, even if you are in the early stages of planning your Exit Strategy, and not planning to sell for a few years, an appraisal can be of great value. An owner can see what factors influence a company's value, and plan accordingly to create a greater value at the time of the sale.

It would be nice if there were a simple way to appraise a business—a standard formula that would be exact and would apply to all businesses, large and small. Unfortunately, there is none, but there are simple things one can do to get a rough estimate of the value of a business before calling in the experts. One can use comparable data from businesses that have sold. In its aggregate form, this does offer surprisingly close information. As a guideline, even a novice can use one of the three major databases: BizComps, Pratt's Stats, and the database of the Institute of Business Appraisers (IBA). The business sales they contain are fairly reliable barometers for business valuations. From these sales, earnings multiples are derived. The data provided lead to a multiple of cash flow to the owner, an expression of earnings that is labeled SDE or Seller's Discretionary Earnings. SDE is calculated by taking EBITDA and adding the owner's salary. SDE also calls for the adding back of all non-cash, non-operating and non-recurring expenses, as well as income taxes paid, hence the need for RECASTING. However, for most small businesses, seller's cash flow is thought to be a more appropriate measure of earnings. EBITDA is used mostly to measure earnings of the so-called mid market businesses that have professional management separate from ownership.

Historical sales figures show that small businesses tend to sell for between 1.5 and 3.5 times historical SDE, not including inventory and/or real estate. This multiple is only a general guideline. It does provide a good starting point for an asking price. We then add in the business' furniture, fixtures, equipment, and all other tangible assets. Intangible assets such as "goodwill" must be added in. Real estate, when part of the sale, and inventory must then be added, usually at the lesser of either cost or wholesale market price. As an aside, when calculating EBITDA, the databases use the most recent reporting period. In actual practice, however, buyer prospects are usually thinking ahead of what the future will hold for them. What the current owner did last year is not as important as what is happening now, and what estimates the buyer makes of future cash flows. Accounts receivable are usually retained by sellers, and collected in the transition period following a sale. Occasionally, they are included in the sale to provide a cushion for the purchaser. This formula assumes a debt-free business. Existing business debt obviously must be settled or subtracted from the value estimate to arrive at a net figure for the seller. If a buyer assumes debt when buying, it is counted as part of the purchase price.

This simplified method for appraising most businesses has major exceptions. It does not apply to larger businesses with sales over, say, $5 million. It doesn't apply to businesses like motels, hotels, campgrounds and marinas, where real estate values are such major elements.

BIZCOMPS

BIZCOMPS® provides almost 8,000 comparable sales transactions, over a 10 year period, for businesses that have sold for under one million dollars. The built-in Market Data Appraisal Module automatically generates a 10+ page appraisal report in under 30 minutes.

A sample report is available from their web site, www.cpa2biz.com or by going directly to http://www.cpa2biz.com/AST/Main/CPA2BIZ_Primary/BusinessValuationandLitigationServices/BusinessValuation/PRDOVR~PC-016160HS/PC-016160HS.jsp

The following is adapted from their web site:

> BIZCOMPS provides small company sales comparables, which is valuable for anyone interested in determining the value of a small company. BIZCOMPS can be used by itself or in conjunction with ValuSource's business valuation applications ValuSource Pro and Express Business Valuation. BIZCOMPS also contains a Market Data Appraisal module that generates a 10 page Market Data Appraisal report.

The BIZCOMPS studies of small business sales were initiated in 1990 to investigate and report financial information about small business transactions in the marketplace. The individual transactions are supplied by Certified Business Intermediaries. Historically, market data on small business transfers has been virtually nonexistent, leaving the appraiser, investor, and advisor to speculate about the fair market value of the enterprise. The BIZCOMPS studies remove the marketplace uncertainty and provides the user with detailed, meaningful financial information about real world transactions. Since its inception, BIZCOMPS has accumulated and reported data on almost 8,000 transactions in the United States.

The BIZCOMPS Report Writer automatically generates a fully customizable seven page Market Data Appraisal Report in Microsoft® Word in 60 seconds.

PRATT'S STATS

Pratt's Stats can be accessed at http://www.bvmarketdata.com/defaulttextonly.asp?f=PS%20Faqs. The following is abstracted from their web site:

The legend for Pratt's Stats® Transaction details the following:

Term	Definition
Broker Name	The name of the business broker or business intermediary that was involved with the sale of the business. This intermediary provided the sale details to Pratt's Stats®.
Public Buyer Name	The name of the public acquiring company.
CIK	The Central Index Key (CIK) is a unique SEC identifier for the public acquiring company.
8-K Date	The date of the public buyer's Current Report discussing the acquisition.
8-K/A Date	The date of the public buyer's Amended Current Report discussing the acquisition.
Other Filing Type	Type of other SEC filing that reports information regarding the acquisition.

APPRAISALS

Other Filing Date	The date of the other filing type.
Broker Firm Name	The name of the firm with whom the business broker or business intermediary works. This is not the name of the acquirer.
SIC	The four-digit Standard Industrial Classification (SIC) code associated with the description of the sold business. Go to http://www.osha.gov/oshstats/sicser.html to search for an SIC code.
NAICS	The North American Industry Classification System (NAICS) code associated with the description of the sold business. Go to http://www.naics.com/search.htm to search for a NAICS code.
Business Description	The description of the sold business.
Target Name	The name of the sold business.
Sale Location	The geographic location of the sold business.
Years in Business	The number of years the sold business has been in operation.
Number of Employees	The number of employees working in the sold business.

This is the legend for Pratt's Stats® Income data:

Term	Definition
Data is "Latest Full Year" Reported	Indicates that the Income data reflects the latest reported full year financial statement.
Data is Restated	Indicates that Income data is reported without non-recurring and exceptional items that will not affect future financial statements. (e.g. Items not transferred with the sale of the business.) The Pratt's Stats® notes field may contain further details pertaining to the restatements.
Income Statement Date	Date of the last filed Income Statement.
Net Sales	Annual Gross sales, net of returns and discounts allowed, if any.

COGS	(Cost of Goods Sold) the cost of the inventory items sold during the year. Net of any discounts, returns or write-offs.
Gross Profit	Net Sales minus COGS.
Yearly Rent	Annual cost of occupying all space necessary for operation of the business.
Owner's Comp	Annual income, salary or wage paid to one business owner plus any incidental payment, benefit, privilege or advantage over and above the income, salary or wage.
Other Operating Expense	All selling and general and administrative expenses, excluding Rent, Owner's Compensation and Non Cash Charges.
Non Cash Charges	Annual decrease in value due to wear and tear, decay or decline in the price of a tangible and/or intangible fixed assets (Depreciation and Amortization).
Total Operating Expenses	Sum of Yearly Rent plus Owner's Compensation plus Non Cash Charges plus Other Operating Expenses.
Operating Profit	Gross Profit minus Total Operating Expenses.
Interest Expense	Cost of borrowing expressed as an annual dollar amount. (Does not include interest earnings. If the company had interest earnings, you will find information on it in the notes field.)
EBT (Earnings Before Taxes)	Operating Profit minus Interest Expense.
Tax Expense	Annual value of tax expense. This figure only includes income taxes and does not include sales taxes, property taxes, payroll taxes, etc. (Does not include an income tax benefit. If the company had a tax benefit, you will find information on it in the notes field.)
Net Income	EBT minus Tax Expense.

APPRAISALS

This is the legend for Pratt's Stats® Asset data:

Term	Definition
Data is "Latest Reported"	Indicates the data is from the latest Balance Sheet. (See Balance Sheet Date)
Data is "Purchase Price Allocation" agreed upon by "Buyer and Seller"	Asset Data reflects the agreed upon allocation price between buyer and seller.
Balance Sheet Date	Date of most recent balance sheet reported.
Cash and Equivalents	All cash, marketable securities, and other near-cash items. Excludes sinking funds. Cash equivalents (NOW accounts and money market funds) must be available upon demand in order to justify inclusion.
Trade Receivables	All accounts from trade, net of allowance for doubtful accounts, that will result in the collection of cash.
Inventory	Anything constituting inventory for the firm including raw material, work in progress and finished goods. Those items of tangible property which are held for sale in the normal course of business, are in the process of being produced for such purposes, or are to be used in the production of such items.
Other Current Assets	Any other current assets, excluding Cash and Equivalents, Trade Receivables and Inventory.
Total Current Assets	Cash and Equivalents plus Trade Receivables plus Inventory plus Other Current Assets.
Fixed Assets	All property, plant, leasehold improvements and equipment, net of accumulated depreciation or depletion.
Real Estate	Dollar value placed on any real estate associated with the sale of the business. The real estate value is not included in the MVIC.

Intangibles	Assets with uncertain or hard-to-measure benefits such as brand names, trademarks, patents or copyrights, a trained workforce, special know-how, and customer or supplier relationships, that make the company a viable competitor and give it earning power. These values are net of accumulated amortization.
Other Noncurrent Assets	Any other non-current asset, excluding Real Estate, Fixed Assets, Intangibles, a Noncompete Agreement and an Employment/Consulting Agreement.
Total Assets	Total Current Assets plus Real Estate plus Fixed Assets plus Intangibles plus Other Noncurrent Assets.
Long-term Liabilities	Any monies owed that are not payable on demand within one year. The current portion of long-term debt is a current liability, as distinguished from a long-term liability.
Total Liabilities	Current Liabilities plus Long-term Liabilities.
Stockholder's Equity	Paid-in capital, donated capital, and retained earnings less the liabilities of the company. (Stockholder's Equity = Total Assets - Total Liabilities)

Regarding the legend for Pratt's Stats® other data:

Term	Definition
Date Sale Initiated	Date business was listed for sale.
Date of Sale	Date sale of business was closed.
Asking Price	Price desired by seller at time of listing.

MVIC (Market Value of Invested Capital)	Also known as the selling price, the MVIC is the total consideration paid to the seller and includes any cash, notes and/or securities that were used as a form of payment plus any interest-bearing liabilities assumed by the buyer. The MVIC price includes the noncompete value and the assumption of interest-bearing liabilities and excludes (1) the real estate value and (2) any earnouts (because they have not yet been earned, and they may not be earned) and (3) the employment/consulting agreement values. In an Asset Sale, the assumption is that all or substantially all operating assets are transferred in the sale. In an Asset Sale, the MVIC may or may not include all current assets, noncurrent assets and current liabilities (liabilities are typically not transferred in an asset sale). Asset Data labeled as a "Purchase Price Allocation" will provide definitive information as to what was included in the asset sale. If the Asset Data is labeled "Latest Reported," the appraiser can look to the Additional Notes field to see if a purchase price allocation is presented there. If the Asset Data section is marked as "Latest Reported," and there is no purchase price allocation in the Additional Notes field, the appraiser needs to use his/her experience and knowledge in the field and the buyer's/seller's knowledge and experience with his/her business to determine what is customarily transferred in an asset sale in that industry.
Debt Assumed	Those interest-bearing financial liabilities that the buyer assumes upon the purchase of the company.

Employment/ Consulting Agreement	Dollar value placed on an agreement between the buyer and seller for the seller's personal services to be provided to the buyer either as an employee or consultant after the sale of the business. The Employment/Consulting Agreement is not included in the MVIC.
Noncompete Agreement	Dollar value placed on an agreement with the selling party not to compete with the purchaser, usually for a certain period of time and usually in a specified geographic area. The Noncompete Agreement value is included in the MVIC.
Amount Down	Dollar value of consideration given as a down payment.

Again, this is not a "Do-it-yourself" project! These are all important factors in appraising a business.

There are four business types:

Term	Definition
C Corp	A corporation acting as a separate entity, for income tax purposes.
S Corp	A corporation with restrictions on equity ownership.
LLC	A Limited Liability Company is one wherein the members have limited legal liability and may participate in the management of the organization.
Partnership	A business comprised of two entities, either created as a general partnership or limited partnership.

The following is taken directly from their web site and is written by Nancy Fannon, ASA, CPA, ABV, MCBA:

> In the Pratt's Stats database, the MVIC price for asset sales and stock sales are being reported correctly. You will never add the value of unassumed interest-bearing liabilities to the reported price. Doing so will overstate the price and create over-inflated

multiples. A user of the database will also not want to convert the given MVIC price to an Equity Price—applying equity multiples assumes the same capital structure and proportion of debt between the subject company and the comparable. Often this is not the case. It is advisable to apply an MVIC multiple to the subject and then subtract the subject's interest-bearing liabilities (note that the user will next need to look at what transferred in the comparable sale and make adjustments accordingly to the subject's final value).

Here is an example of why you would not add the unassumed debt: Company X buys Company Y for $20M in cash. Company Y has $10M in debt on their books, but Company X does not assume this debt. Because this debt is not assumed, Company Y uses the proceeds of the cash sale to pay off their debt of $10M. The MVIC price for this acquisition is $20M not $30M—adding the unassumed debt of $10M would overstate the price paid for the assets of the company and would cause an over-inflated MVIC price. The MVIC price will only include those interest-bearing liabilities that are assumed, not those that are retained by the seller.

In its data collection process, Pratt's Stats® uses the following:
- The selling price has to be clear (i.e. if restricted stock is part of the consideration, the value of the restricted stock issued in the transaction must be given, etc.).
- Earn outs (or contingency payments) cannot be included in the selling price; if the earn outs cannot be removed from the given selling price then the transaction will not be included.
- Product/Service description of the seller must be disclosed.
- Latest full year Income Statement must be given in US dollars.
- Company type must be disclosed (C or S Corp, LLC, LLP, Sole Prop. etc.).
- The type of transaction must be disclosed; either a stock or asset sale.
- The transaction must not be a reverse acquisition, reorganization, recapitalization etc.
- Must be 100% acquisition (no partial transactions).

There is a difference between stock versus asset sales. In asset sales, what transfers are the following:

Usually transfer
- Inventory (if applicable to industry, e.g. a CPA firm may not possess any inventory while a convenience store may)
- Fixed assets
- Leasehold improvements (if any)
- Intangibles (such as trade name, customer lists, etc.)
- Goodwill

Rarely transfer
- Cash and equivalents
- Trade receivables
- Real estate (this value will not be included in the Pratt's Stats MVIC price if transferred, but will be noted in the Additional Notes field)

Gary Trugman (*Understanding Business Valuation: A Practical Guide to Valuing Small to Medium-Sized Businesses, 2nd Edition.* New York: American Institute of Certified Public Accountants, Inc., 2002. p. 223) writes:

> "Small businesses typically are sold as asset sales as opposed to stock sales. An asset sale is a transaction where only certain assets (and maybe liabilities) are transferred to a new owner who will effectively become the new owner of the business. More often than not, only the operating assets of the business are transferred to the buyer. This type of transaction is common for smaller businesses. It is also very different from a stock sale, which is typical of larger business transactions. In a stock sale, the stock (all assets and liabilities) is transferred to the buyer. This transfer represents the entire equity of the company."

Scott Gabehart and Richard J. Brinkley (Gabehart, Scott and Richard J. Brinkley. *The Business Valuation Book: Proven Strategies for Measuring a Company's Value.* New York: AMACOM a division of American Management Association, 2002. pp. 198-199.) write:

"The main point is that because of the greater risk of buying a company's stock rather than assets, the purchase price reflects this risk in the form of a lower value.

Generally speaking, the sale of stock is treated primarily as a capital gain, whereas the sale of assets generates a substantial gain (typically) that is taxed in large part as ordinary income. Ordinary income tax rates can be as much as twice as high as the current capital gains tax rate."

For the sake of clarity and understanding, review the following major differences between an asset sale and a stock sale.

Asset Sale

- Seller keeps cash and receivables but delivers company free of any debt.
- Seller keeps corporate entity to later dissolve or use for new endeavor.
- Seller pays combination of capital gains tax and ordinary income.
- Buyer and seller agree to allocation of purchase price between IRS asset categories.
- Buyer may redepreciate fixed assets based on allocation.
- Buyer avoids assuming both known and unknown liabilities.
- If price is greater than identifiable, tangible assets, the excess is allocated to one or more intangible assets (written off over fifteen years for tax purposes and up to forty-two for book purposes).

Stock Sale

- Seller pays primarily capital gains tax rather than higher ordinary income tax rate.
- Seller endorses stock certificates over to new owner.
- Buyer assumes all assets and liabilities unless specifically excluded.
- Buyer takes on risk associated with unknown liabilities.

- Buyer inherits tax depreciation schedules as they are (for better or mostly worse).
- Buyer may inherit tax loss carryforwards to shield future income.
- There is no allocation of purchase prices or goodwill related to transaction.

There is a relation between Market Multiples and Capitalization Rates:

1. Market multiples and capitalization rates are the inverse of each other. For example, if the P/E ratio is 20 times last year's earnings, then last year's earnings are capitalized at 5%: 1/20 = .05 = 5%
2. Conversely, if the capitalization rate is 5%, then the market multiple for that variable is 20: 1/5% = 1/.05 = 20X
3. Any market multiple can be converted to a capitalization rate, and vice versa. The capitalization rate form of presentation is commonly used in the income approach to valuation. It is more common to use the market multiple form of presentation in the market approach.

There are differences between BIZCOMPS® and Pratt's Stats®? BIZCOMPS® mainly covers main street businesses. The median selling price in all of the 8,740 transactions in BIZCOMPS® is $135,000. BIZCOMPS® data includes up to 21 data fields. Pratt's Stats® covers both main street businesses and larger M&A transactions. 46% of the 8,606 deals in the Pratt's Stats® database are businesses that sold for $1,000,000 or less. 53% of the 8,606 deals in the Pratt's Stats® database are businesses that sold for between $1,000,001 and $500,000,000. The median selling price in Pratt's Stats® is $1,500,000. Pratt's Stats® data includes up to 81 data fields. BIZCOMPS® and Pratt's Stats® should be looked at since there is little overlap of information from BIZCOMPS® and Pratt's Stats®. In addition, BIZCOMPS® and Pratt's Stats® do not calculate transaction multiples the same way.

The key difference between the two databases is that BIZCOMPS® sales are all asset sales and the selling price does not include the cash, accounts receivable, accounts payable and inventory. Pratt's Stats® sales can be either an asset sale or stock sale. For an asset sale, the

APPRAISALS

Pratt's Stats® selling price generally includes inventory and generally excludes cash, accounts receivable and accounts payable. The appraiser may determine what assets transferred in the Pratt's Stats® sale by looking at the Asset Data. If the Asset Data is reported as a Purchase Price Allocation, or a Purchase Price Allocation is available in the Pratt's Stats® the Additional Notes field, the appraiser can make a definitive determination as to what assets transferred. If the Asset Data is reported as Latest Reported, the assumption is that the inventory transferred with the sale and that cash, accounts receivable and accounts payable did not transfer with the sale. For a stock sale, the Pratt's Stats® selling price generally includes all operating assets and liabilities. Therefore, when comparing multiples that use the selling price from Pratt's Stats® and BIZCOMPS®, the above should be taken into consideration and any necessary adjustments should be made.

A business' "selling price" in each database at BVMarketData.com uses different terminology. This is what the "selling price" means in each database:

Below, we show the term used for the "selling price" in each BVMarketData.com database and its respective definition:

Pratt's Stats® uses the term MVIC (Market Value of Invested Capital) for the "selling price." The MVIC is the overall consideration in the business sale and includes any cash, notes and/or securities that were used as a form of payment plus any interest-bearing liabilities assumed by the buyer.

The Mergerstat®/BVR Control Premium Study™ also uses two terms for the "selling price"; the Target Invested Capital (TIC) and Price. The TIC is the target company's implied total invested capital based on the sum of the implied market value of equity plus the face value of total interest bearing debt and the book value of preferred stock outstanding prior to the announcement date. The Price is the implied market value of equity.

BIZCOMPS® uses one term for the "selling price": Sale Price. Sale Price is the actual sale price ($000's) where inventory has been deducted, if it was included in the sale price.

Public Stats™ uses the term MVIC (Market Value of Invested Capital) for the "selling price." The MVIC is the overall consideration in the business sale and includes any cash, notes and/or securities that were used as a form of payment plus any interest-bearing liabilities assumed by the buyer.

The FMV Restricted Stock Study™ does not report details on the sale of either a portion of a company or an entire company and therefore does not contain a selling price field. Instead, this database reports the details related to transactions in restricted stock. This database does report a Market Value (in $000s) which is the market value of the firm determined on a pre-deal basis. The market value is calculated by multiplying the shares outstanding before the private placement with the high-low average market price for the stock for the month prior to the transaction. The market value is not the selling price, per se, but a calculation of the value of the total equity on the date of the restricted stock transaction.

The Valuation Advisors' Lack of Marketability Discount Study™ does not report details on the sale of either a portion of a company or an entire company and therefore does not contain a selling price field. Instead, this database reports the details related to transactions in common stocks, stock options or convertible preferred stocks prior to an initial public offering, and the relationship of these prices to the IPO price per share (the price of the stock paid by the initial public investors to acquire their shares).

CHAPTER EIGHT
OUTSOURCING: TODAY'S BUSINESS-BUILDING NECESSITY

KEY POINTS

Use Outsourcing to Quickly Increase the Profitability of Your Business

The Five Main Reasons Companies Go Out of Business Today

The Definitions of Outsourcing

Why Outsourcing is So Important to Lowering Overhead and Increasing Productivity

Specific Areas Your Business Can Outsource

Tips on Finding the Outsourcing Company That is Right For You

CHAPTER EIGHT

OUTSOURCING: TODAY'S BUSINESS-BUILDING NECESSITY

As must be obvious, it is much easier to sell a thriving business than a failing business. And it is more profitable to sell a business that is making a lot of money than one which is making little or none. If your business' bottom line is not what you would like it to be, and your time frame does not dictate a hasty sale, you should give some thought to outsourcing.

There is no doubt about it: Outsourcing is today's business-building necessity—and today's top business-building consultants stand by that claim.

The theory behind this is simple: by outsourcing jobs in your company that do not have to do with your core business, you can quickly increase profits in a short period of time, while concentrating on building the business further. Outsourcing has helped numerous companies that were floundering become profitable again.

We'll begin this chapter on the value and importance of Outsourcing by first laying out the five main reasons companies are going out of business today:

1. Skyrocketing overhead costs.
2. Sales not increasing, and a loss of market share due to low margins and aggressive competition.

3. Management spending too much time putting out daily fires, leaving little time to work on their core business.
4. Difficulty in hiring competent employees, allowing companies to settle for inferior work from their in-house staff.
5. Owners burning out because of the increasing problems. Employees pick up on these feelings, causing even further business problems.

Well, strange but true, with proper outsourcing, all five problems above can be corrected in a very short period of time!

Outsourcing is the most powerful tool available for the speedy correction of business problems for small, medium and large companies. Here are important descriptions of what outsourcing does:

- Outsourcing brings in specialists who better understand the task at hand, and are more focused on that particular task than a full-time employee, one who may be earning many times more than the outsourced expert. These tasks include:
  - Sales
  - Bookkeeping
  - Copywriting
  - Graphic Design
  - Receptionists & Call Centers
  - Technical
  - Mechanical Service
  - Trucking & Transportation
  - Typing Services
  - Human Resources

  and the list goes on.
- Outsourcing allows a business to contract out non-core, non-revenue producing tasks, so that key employees can focus on core business activities. These include:
  - Increased Sales
  - New Business Acquisition
  - Customer satisfaction.

Through outsourcing, business owners and their top management no longer have to put out internal "fires," write out checks, listen to employee complaints. Outsourcing allows them to put 100% of their time into building the business while professionals outside the business expertly handle the non-core activities.

Today's best business consultants confirm that outsourcing is the fastest way to turn a company around.

Outsourcing can be used to perform any job in your company, except for the most intricate parts of your Core business. The only thing top management should be working on is their CORE BUSINESS.

Outsourcing allows, for example, a manufacturer to retain 10 key employees while still running and building upon a multi-million dollar company. In the old days, that manufacturer would have had to handle—and pay substantially for—design, distribution, warehousing, sales, service, freight, and so on. Now, a handful of top staff members can concentrate on core business functions, and outsource the rest of the tasks.

Outsourcing works during a business' good times as well as its bad times.

All companies, when they start growing, need bigger telephone systems, more computers, more sales force, more storage areas, more trucks, more drivers, more office space, and many more employees for different business areas needed to keep up with the growth. **If you use outsourcing properly, your business can increase in size, or downsize its payroll, without having a harmful effect on profits.**

Outsourcing is usually based on a flat fee per service, like storage and shipping. What actually happened to enable a company to drop from 4 million dollars in annual shipping costs to $500,000 a year? Before outsourcing, the company owned a large warehouse and trucks, and retained full-time employees to handle everything. By eliminating the need to pay rental fees and salaries during slower times, by reducing its huge payroll and benefits for employees that were often idle, by canceling unneeded insurance and by downsizing, costs went down 84%! And outsourcing ended the pressure management was feeling when faced with huge fixed costs, probably extending their individual life spans, as well.

Outsourcing benefits vary based on the type of business and how management pushes the envelope. **There are many reasons why outsourcing is becoming so important to lowering overhead and increasing productivity:**

- Increased focus and commitment to core business tasks. This is the most important item in the list. When management puts 95% of its time in its core business, instead of putting out all those fires and getting burnt out, they will increase sales while lowering overhead.
- Better budget control.
- Acquisition of fresh, innovative ideas.
- Higher quality service through the outsourced provider's dedication.
- Access to world-class capabilities.
- Sharing of risks.
- Freed resources for other purposes.
- Making more Capital Funds available.
- Reducing and controlling operating costs.
- Lowering costs due to economies of scale.
- Having greater flexibility and being able to define the required service more readily.
- Enabling improved security.
- Providing higher quality service due to improved focus of the supplier.
- Improving internal management disciplines.
- Lessening dependency upon internal resources.
- Speeding setup of the function or service.
- Lowering ongoing investment required in internal infrastructure.
- Improving ability to control delivery dates, avoiding penalties.
- Increasing flexibility to meet changing business conditions.

- Increasing commitment and energy in non-core areas.
- Improving credibility and image by associating, often, with superior providers, experts in their fields.
- Generating cash by transferring assets to the provider.
- Gaining market access and business opportunities through the supplier's network.

Outsourcing began in the data-processing industry and has since caught on to many other areas. **Here are some specific areas you can outsource:**

- Sales
- IT office and computer work
- Receptionists and fielding calls
- Call Centers
- Blackberry outsource systems that are revolutionizing corporate mentality
- Service at client's home location—machinery, computers, telephones, etc.
- Technical service—by telephone: computers, software, telephones, etc.
- Typing
- Back office outsourcing of papers and info
- Bookkeeping
- Office space and office space outsourced, even to other cities with lower overhead
- Warehouse and storage space
- Internet based software to run your companies on the Internet
- Trucking & Transportation & Storage
- Professional Services, where the skills of highly trained retirees such as lawyers, accountants, engineers, teachers, nurses, executives, etc. can be obtained directly from their homes to your offices

Outsourcing is a viable option for everything from payroll, accounting, manufacturing and delivery to customer service, employee training, property management and computer services.

The key advantage of outsourcing is that it enables you to invest your resources into more profitable activities. Companies, however, should be careful not to outsource functions that appear negligible, but that are actually essential, such as customer service operations in a small business that relies on building rapport with a loyal customer base.

It all boils down to this: Outsourcing is a strategic tool for making your business more productive and profitable—if you know when to take advantage of it. Here are some more criteria to follow when deciding whether to outsource:

- The activity isn't central to generating profits or competitive success.
- The job is a routine one that wastes valuable time and energy
- The task is a need that's only temporary or that recurs in cycles.
- It's less expensive to have someone else do it than to do it in-house.
- The activity can be done cheaper in-house, but drains resources that could be better used elsewhere.
- The skill required is so specialized that it's impractical to have a regular employee do it.
- The activity isn't one that people enjoy doing.

Once you've decided to outsource a particular area, follow these tips to find the company that's right for you:

- Do your homework. Ask companies in your area for recommendations on good outsourcing firms, and search the Internet for a more comprehensive list of services available. Ask the companies you research to give you client references, and interview these clients to find out how reliable and flexible their services are.
- Select a compatible company. Choose a company that understands your needs and can accommodate them. Devise a

contract that allows you to adjust the terms of the agreement to adapt to unforeseen changes. An arrangement that's satisfactory now may not work in the future if the company expands or competition increases.

- Establish the standards you expect. Outsourcing will mean the loss of direct control and supervision, so communicating the standards of performance you expect is a must. Outline these standards in the contract in detail, and check up on the company periodically to make sure that it's doing its job correctly.
- Arrange for constant communication. Schedule regular meetings with your outsourcing people to stay informed and discuss the day-to-day problems they've encountered. By staying aware of what's going on, you can prevent potential problems and improve how your business operates.
- Secure insurance for emergencies. Make sure you have a backup system in place in the event that the outsourcing company can't carry through. An accounting service, for example, should provide your company with a copy of backup records or store them in a separate location.

In a recent survey, nearly two-thirds of experienced outsourcers (those with 7 or more years of experience in outsourcing) reported that outsourcing improved their company's overall performance. The improved functions included better business processes and increased profits.

What it all comes down to is this:
Traditional thoughts on the need for full-time office employees are changing as technology, such as the Internet, e-mail, zip files and more, make it easier for specialists to offer their services to a company at costs much lower than employing someone full-time. Even better, these outsourced specialists can focus exclusively on the skill they do very well, and were specifically hired to accomplish. These outsourced services, in turn, help you to better build your company and quickly increase its profitability before selling.

CHAPTER NINE
MERGERS AND ACQUISITIONS

 **KEY POINTS**

Definitions

Acquisition—Purchase of One Entity by Another

Merger—Consolidation of Two or More Companies

Horizontal Merger—A Merger of Two Companies in the Same Field

Vertical Merger—A Merger of Supplier and Customer

Purpose of a Merger
     All Mergers and Acquisitions Have a Single Goal, Which is to Create Synergy Wherein the Value of the Combined Companies is Greater Than the Sum of Their Parts

The Importance of Recasting

Possible Pitfalls

Create a Win/Win Situation

CHAPTER NINE
MERGERS AND ACQUISITIONS

One consideration in planning an Exit Strategy involves the decision as to whether the time is ripe for a business owner to cash in his profits and positive cash flow and sell, or to use that surplus to locate a smaller company and merge to help his company expand and grow. Many industries are rapidly consolidating today. Over 75,000 mergers and acquisitions were recorded in 2008, the majority of them in the mid range (under $20 million). Big companies are looking for solid buys. Your business might be in either category—an acquirer or a seller, or perhaps it may be a candidate for a merger of equals.

It doesn't matter whether you are a giant corporation like Exxon or a small $300,000 net worth company. The theory and execution of a merger or an acquisition is identical. As a matter of fact, it has long bothered me that big corporations always seem to be the ones utilizing the tools involved in creating powerful mergers and acquisitions to build multi-million (and multi-billion) dollar companies, while America's small businesses have not taken advantage of these important tools to expand their own companies. One of our hopes for this book is to convey to the small businessman the wealth of knowledge and material available, and provide him with the tools needed, to consider and execute a successful Merger or Acquisition. You don't need to pay out huge sums to high-priced advisors to get your feet facing in the right direction. In *Exit Strategy,* we give you the benefit of our nearly 40 years of experience as Mergers and Acquisitions experts, so that when you DO find yourself in the offices of a professional, you are already armed with your own base of knowledge, as well as the security of knowing what you want.

It is apparent that there are several ways two or more companies can combine their efforts.
- They can partner on a project
- They can mutually agree to join forces and merge
- One company can outright acquire another company, taking over all its operations, including its holdings and debts, often replacing management with its own representatives.

Through a merger or an acquisition, a company can (at least in theory) develop a competitive advantage.

While the terms "Mergers" and "Acquisitions" are usually lumped together as if they were the same concept, each term actually refers to a different "exit strategy" for a particular business owner.

MOTIVES BEHIND M&A

These are some of the motives behind a merger or acquisition that are considered to add shareholder value:
- Economies of Scale: This refers to the fact that the combined company can often reduce duplicate departments or operations, lowering the costs of the company relative to, theoretically, the same revenue stream, thus increasing profit.
- Increased Revenue/Increased Market Share: This motive assumes that the company will be absorbing a major competitor and increasing its power (by capturing increased market share) to set prices.
- Vertical Selling Method: For example, a bank, buying a stock brokerage, could then sell its banking products to the stock broker's customers, while the broker can sign up the bank's customers for brokerage accounts. In the same vein, a manufacturer can acquire and sell complementary products.
- Synergy: Better use of complementary resources.
- Taxes: A profitable company can buy a loss maker to use the target's tax write-offs.
- Geographical or other diversification: This is designed to smooth the earnings results of a company, which over the long

term smooths the stock price of a company, giving conservative investors more confidence in investing in the company.

DEFINITIONS

MERGER: A general term used to refer to the consolidation of companies. A merger is a combination of two companies to form a new company. Examples would be Atlantic Corporation in its merger-of-equals with GTE Corporation to form Verizon Communications (which then bought MCI); McDonnell Douglas Corporation in its merger with The Boeing Company; and Mobil Corporation in its merger with Exxon Corporation, JP Morgan and Chase Manhattan Bank. (The new Company name—JP Morgan Chase.)

ACQUISITION: An acquisition involves the purchasing of one company by another with no new company being formed. Examples: Teva Pharmaceuticals bought Ivax. Ivax no longer trades. Hewlett Packard bought Compaq. Now it is just Hewlett Packard. Wachovia bought Prudential, with the company's name now being only Wachovia, and Bank of America purchased Fleet Bank, changing the name of all its branches to that of the parent company. This has been true of many bank purchases throughout the years. On the other hand, New York Community Bank bought Roslyn Savings Bank, but continues to run Roslyn banks in areas where there is brand recognition like Long Island, New York.

In fact, acquisitions occasionally, for continued brand recognition or consumer name loyalty, combine the acquired company's name with that of the buyer. Occasionally, the names are kept and hyphenated, even though the transaction was a purchase and not a merger. Example: Citigroup bought Smith-Barney, creating Citigroup-Smith Barney.

When the names are well known and stand alone, the acquiring company may benefit by letting the acquired company's name and logo continue to exist. Paramount Pictures, a division of Viacom, Inc., purchased DreamWorks SKG in 2006, but, as of this writing, intended to retain the well known DreamWorks SKG name. Time Warner bought AOL, but AOL is too well recognized by its millions of users to abandon the name. Pfizer bought Warner Lambert and

Pharmacia to create a pharmaceutical giant, but their individual names are retained, as the acquired companies are under new ownership, with changes on the executive level, yet both still exist as identifiable pharmaceutical companies.

Mergers and acquisitions, when plotted out, may look somewhat like a family tree, with parents, step-parents and grandparents. NBC Universal acquired iVillage because it envisions iVillage as the "centerpiece" of its digital strategy. However, General Electric owns 80 percent of NBC Universal (the other 20 percent of which is owned by Vivendi Universal), which makes it a part owner of iVillage. Obviously, acquisitions need not be total.

Please be aware that the "big" names used to describe mergers and acquisitions are familiar names used for example only. Small and mid-sized businesses merge and acquire each other all the time, profitably and successfully. And that is our aim: to empower the smaller business owner to know what the big boys know—and to win at merging and acquiring businesses like the pros.

EXPERIENCE COUNTS!

Many times in the past 40 years, I have merged two companies that were both losing money into a single entity that turned a huge profit almost immediately.

Just a year ago, we represented two companies that, between them, were losing $475,000 a year. After they merged, they showed a profit of over $2 million for the first 9 months of operation. How did this happen?

Among other innovative ways, we put both companies in one building instead of two, cutting rental and maintenance expenses in half, and eliminating other duplication of expenses, which, alone, increased the bottom line. Savings by merging bookkeeping, accounting/controller services, human relations, transportation and training amounted to 40% of their budgets. Upper management and executive expenses were nearly halved. A single computer system ran the merged company. The sales teams merged, selling two related products instead of just one. Advertising costs dropped 40%. On top of that, there was a tremendous increase in buying power, as the new, larger company was able to negotiate better deals. Savings in this alone amounted to 5% to 20% of a basic expense item. Furthermore, the owners managed to re-allocate personnel, creating more productivity in the work force. Employees, worried that the old companies might have gone out of business, became eager to make the merged enterprise succeed. A fear factor may have been involved here, since, when companies merge, some firings are inevitable. After a merge, workers tend to demonstrate their value to a new company by working more diligently, not only to help that company succeed, but to retain their jobs.

UNDERSTANDING ACQUISITIONS

Once again, an acquisition is a transaction in which one company acquires or takes over another—basically, a sale. Often, the selling business' identity ends and the acquiring business folds it into its business structure, although, occasionally, it may be deemed advantageous to have the acquired company retain its identity.

The advantages to the seller are obvious: he is paid for his business, sells off its assets, and can go on to other ventures or to retirement with the proceeds. Or, having been properly compensated, he may relinquish control but offer his expertise to the buyer, receiving a work contract wherein that experience factor may benefit the buyer.

And the buyer will now own a business which, after careful evaluation, he believes will add something of value to his bottom line. Perhaps there will be increased profits. Or the newly retained customer list may offer opportunity for expansion. Market share may also be increased.

Furthermore, the seller may have been a customer, but will now be using the buyer's products exclusively. This is what happens in a Vertical acquisition. For example, both Pepsi and Coke have purchased restaurants and fast food businesses that now carry only their individual beverages.

There may be new technology acquired that will be profitable down the line. Or perhaps the advantage will be in eliminating a competitor, as in a Horizontal acquisition. The cost of doing business will decrease.

Occasionally, an acquisition need not be complete. Porsche, which has a "family" relationship with Volkswagen, bought 20% of VW. The objective was to thwart a hostile takeover. A hostile takeover is always an acquisition. A friendly takeover may be disguised as a merger to make the acquisition more palatable to the owners, Board or stockholders of the company being acquired.

The most important points in considering a merger or acquisition as an Exit Strategy are:
1. If your business possesses strategic value to a particular acquirer, the acquisition will pay far more than if you sell to someone else.
2. If you get multiple acquirers involved in an auction or bidding war, the price you get for your business will be much higher.

Using the Vertical Horizontal Selling Method of selecting potential acquirers will improve the likelihood of success.

One plus one equals three!

Whatever the reason, the key principle in acquiring a company is to create value above and beyond the sum of the two companies involved. One plus one makes three! Two companies together are more valuable than two separate companies. This rationale is particularly alluring to companies when they feel endangered. A strong company buys a weaker one to create a more cost-efficient company. A target company may agree to be bought because, in a competitive environment, it knows it can not survive alone.

On the other hand, the weaker firm may have steady cash flow and predictable sales, but sluggish growth. The acquiring firm may be betting on a mix of asset sales, restructuring and other operational improvements to jump start growth or bolster profits. The companies will come together hoping to gain a greater market share or achieve greater efficiency. If the acquired company has unique technologies, a large company can keep or develop a competitive edge. And the acquisition can produce improved market reach and industry visibility.

The seller in an acquisition is in a favorable position to negotiate, not always with an individual buyer but with a buyer's representative. If the seller, using the tools described above, can persuade this individual that his employer will benefit far in excess of the negotiated price (best handled by the seller's representative, not the seller), a deal may be made based on the perceived value. One looks for a strategic fit, wherein the acquisition will create an entity, worth more than the parts thereof, upon which to capitalize.

MERGERS

A merger occurs when two companies decide to go forward as a single entity, rather than remain individually owned and operated. The owners decide the merge will be in both their best interests. In many cases, the merger will produce what is generally referred to as synergy. Note that when the merger is between companies that are decidedly not equal, it may be called a merger, but it would, to all intents and purposes, be an acquisition.

CREATING SYNERGY

Synergy occurs when a newly merged business entity achieves greater value because of increased cost efficiencies. There is enhancement of earnings, as well as reduction of costs.

When companies merge, the duplication of staff must be addressed. Salary expenses are reduced when the newly structured company realizes that two accounting, bookkeeping, human resources, marketing and other departmental staffs are no longer needed. And a merged company normally needs but one "boss" or CEO, enabling one of the two company heads to either reduce his contribution to the company's functioning (and his earnings), or to take a carefully worked out retirement package and go on to other enterprises.

Marketing and sales forces may be less affected, as the new company seeks to not only keep but to expand its customer base. Synergy also occurs when the new, larger business develops better buying power for equipment and supplies by virtue of its size. If the smaller company has a better pipeline for product development or new technology, that, too, will enhance the larger company's eventual bottom line.

HORIZONTAL AND VERTICAL MERGERS
HORIZONTAL MERGER
A horizontal merger occurs when two companies who are in direct competition with each other merge.

An example of this would be the merging of telephone companies like Nextel and Sprint, or AT&T and Cingular. Horizontally merged companies share the same or similar product lines and markets. Horizontal merging allows the resulting company to vastly increase its market share, providing, as a selling point, the fact that it may become a giant in the field with the potential to grow even larger. The often unpleasant feeling of selling out to a competitor is eliminated, as two owners realize the strength in unity. If personalities mesh, and old rivalries are buried, the entire situation works out very well.

When smaller businesses are contemplating a merger, it may be in preparation for the retirement or other necessary departure of one of the owners. In this event, a merger allows the merged company to benefit from the knowledge and experience of both principals, while acknowledging eventual transfer of authority to one.

In the pure sense of the term, a merger happens when two firms, often about the same size, agree to go forward as a new single company, rather than remain separately owned and operated. Both companies' stocks are surrendered, and stock in the new entity is issued. For example, both Daimler-Benz and Chrysler ceased to exist when the two firms merged, and a new company, Daimler-Chrysler was created.

In a horizontal merger, the benefits are obvious. Aside from the convenience of a merge into a single location, thus eliminating one rental expense, staffing is drastically reduced (you do not need two bookkeepers or extra receptionists), and utility costs for the second location are now zero. Advertising costs are likely to plummet. In effect, a situation is created in which the gross income from one of the merged businesses winds up being its net, as the bulk of expenses of that company are virtually eliminated. Assuming, for example, that two companies, each with a gross of $500,000 and a 50% overhead, merge. The net of the two individual companies, pre-merger, is $500,000. Now, the new company has a gross income of $1,000,000, but almost the entire $250,000 overhead of the second company may be eliminated. This makes the new company's net not $500,000, but $750,000, substantially increasing the bottom line.

VERTICAL MERGER

A vertical merger occurs when two companies that are related peripherally, perhaps as either suppliers or users, come together.

Hypothetically, let's consider a possible ice cream franchise—a Cold Stone Creamery or a Maggie Moo's, for example—that sells its ice cream, mixed, in-store, with other edibles like candy or cookies. Look at the economies which might be gained by merging with a bulk candy distributor, or with a manufacturer of other ingredients or waffle cones or paper products! The cost of doing business would be lowered. Merging with a supplier means that the now guaranteed constant supply is available at a cut-rate cost. And, as an added benefit, the merged companies would become, in effect, a conglomerate, expanding possibilities for further growth in other directions, and, if they have not already done so, the ability to (and advantages of) going public.

In our firm, we often find ourselves recasting financials (as explained further in the Recasting, and EBITDA chapters) for both companies to see how they mesh, whether in a vertical or horizontal merger.

By simply removing irrelevant data, and reflecting the true profits of these companies, we create an environment conducive to an effective merger. We demonstrate, in black and white, how duplication of essential in-house services may be eliminated. And we work out in detail how overhead is decreased, and the bottom line enhanced.

ALL MERGERS AND ACQUISITIONS HAVE A SINGLE GOAL: TO CREATE SYNERGY, WHEREIN THE VALUE OF THE COMBINED COMPANIES IS GREATER THAN THE SUM OF THE PARTS.

PITFALLS TO BE AWARE OF WHEN CREATING A MERGER

There are side effects, of course, to any merger.

Because of staff reductions, we know that mergers lead to job losses in accounting, marketing and other departments. Less affected might be the former CEO, who will, under most circumstances, leave with a compensation package. Business heads, seeking to create a merger, must always be aware of the consequences to employees, although all of this is more than balanced, at least in the eyes of the company, by planned economies of scale.

There may be cases in which a salesperson has achieved his dream of buying the company in which he has been employed, or perhaps that of a competitor. Despite his dreams and credentials, his managerial skills may be lacking. Unless he capitalizes on the knowledge and experience of the seller, even hiring the seller to come on board as a consultant or employee, his dream may very well become a nightmare.

Other potential problems: Mergers must be carefully planned out, as economies of scale are not automatically realized. Successful mergers are based on a fair selling price and a sensible plan for the future. But 1+1 may not ALWAYS equal 3.

- Economies of scale may not be as great as anticipated.
- Some key personnel may be too valuable to let go.
- Combining computer systems may not lead to greater efficiency if systems clash.
- Sheer size increase may not get suppliers to lower their costs.
- A large company may be too difficult for the owner to handle, and he may find himself spread too thin.
- Employees may find the new company different in its attitude toward management access or flexible work schedules and leave.

Occasionally, bidding wars or auctions break out, as in Johnson and Johnson's battle a few years back with Boston Scientific for Guidant. Having a bidding war is not necessarily a bad situation. It is one for which the orchestrators of a purchase or merger must be alert, and be ready to take advantage of when it occurs.

In the Time Warner/AOL deal alluded to earlier, there have been many problems. In fact, at the time of this writing, eight years after the acquisition, Time Warner was considering spinning off AOL.

What's more, the Justice Department has challenged many mergers in the consumer products industry, as in the recent challenge against the Maytag acquisition by Whirlpool. As noted, mergers and acquisitions may involve horizontal or vertical liaisons. Occasionally, a vertical acquisition in which a company purchases a customer or a supplier creates an alliance that effectively stymies competition. Unless we are dealing with a giant company in a small industry, it is unlikely that anti-trust issues will arise. Still, it is something to consider.

Any possible pitfalls must be anticipated and addressed by expert merger and acquisition consultants.

CREATE A WIN/WIN SITUATION

A merger may not immediately lead to the departure of key personnel. Planning ahead to create a positive outcome for all sides is necessary. One of our clients in the printing supplies business merged with an owner 25 years his junior, bringing experience and know-how, along with a solid customer base, to an energetic entrepreneurial go-getter. Our client knew he was ready to retire in a few years, so the buy-out was calculated to be fair to all parties. He wanted a win/win situation. The first year, he received, as a buy out, 18% of the previous years gross, then 20%, 22% and 24% in the following three years. That way, if the business, which he built up, continues to do well, he benefits. If business drops, however, his former partner is not saddled with insurmountable debt. Both participants in this merger remained friends, and the business continued to prosper.

A word of advice, when considering a merger or acquisition, is needed here. Cost cutting cannot be the only reason to merge. Businesses must be integrated in such a way that increased revenue results, as well. To make a merger work, careful planning and expert professional advice from experienced, competent accountants, attorneys, business brokers, mergers and acquisitions specialists, and other consultants familiar with both businesses must be sought and utilized.

CHAPTER TEN
PROJECTING AN IMAGE

KEY POINTS

The Importance of Corporate Image

Eye-Catching Graphic Design, Hard-Hitting Copy and Well-Planned Marketing Strategies are Vital to Your Company

Projecting That Image Facilitates a Profitable Sale or Merger

CHAPTER TEN
PROJECTING AN IMAGE

Appearances are important in life. Making a good first impression will help you sell yourself in social as well as in business situations. Don't underestimate the importance of corporate image as a means of building internal cohesion and external recognition. In a crowded marketplace, with dozens of companies selling the same service or product, the only method of differentiation and separation is through your branding and image. This is achieved with quality promotion and advertising. And what an asset you'll find these services have provided for you when it comes time to sell your business.

In selling a business, packaging is important. A well-prepared brochure with eye-catching graphics can put your company's best face forward, giving an impression of vision and success. Certainly, using a graphic designer early in your business formation may increase your success likelihood.

I am the owner of many successful companies, including:
- Pr.com
- BusinessBrokers.com
- MergerAcquisition.com
- BuyorSellaBusiness.com
- BusinessMultipleListingService.com
- FranchiseBusinessBroker.com
- AssociationofBusinessBrokers.com
- RealtyBrokers.com
- ManheimRealty.com

- ProfessionalPracticeBrokers.com
- MedicalDentalHealthCare.com

In building and running these companies, I have experienced this fact: harnessing the power of a talented promotional services agency can bring a wealth of new knocks on your business' door and make you a force to contend with against even your biggest competitors.

There are many companies whose experience and power you can use to project an image, whether building a business or preparing for a sale. It would be advantageous to use a solid advertising and graphic design company to create brochures and catalogs with copywriting of the highest caliber, along with uniquely designed flyers, result-grabbing public relations material, and hard-hitting website copy. Even simple business cards can be enhanced, for example:

The results:
- More clients
- More attention for my businesses
- My projected image is of success
- And there is more money in my business banking accounts

With a few of their targeted promotional campaigns under your company's belt, you just can't help but win, whether building a business in order to sell it, or as a new owner seeking to expand your new business' horizons.

My advice? Retain a good promotional services organization. They will perform many different services for your business, protecting and growing the value of your business and increasing your bottom line, so that when you're ready to sell, prospects are ready to buy.

If you are eager to raise the likelihood of a rapid and profitable sale, as an adjunct to preparing for a successful exit strategy, start upping cash flow today by contacting a strong promotional sales company. They will make the most of relationships you've created with existing customers. And they will help increase customer loyalty, even while generating new sales for your business.

It is the job of a good promotional services agency to understand, interpret, and graphically and verbally convey a company's personality in a way that is honest, unique, and memorable.

Doing this successfully requires close collaboration with principals of the client company. The promotional services team needs to know what you stand for, what unique products, services, and benefits you provide, and who your customers are. It is important to view advertising and promotional services as an investment, not an expense. A well-designed piece and a sharp presentation will make your company stand out, promoting a quick and profitable sale of your business when the time is right.

THE VALUE OF BRAND IMAGING

Branding combines unique strategies and insights, which are developed through of the business itself and its users (consumers, clients, customers, etc.). A good Graphic Arts company combines expertise in proprietary research, consumer insight, and strategic brand planning through identity design, advertising, web, direct, and non-traditional channels.

Whether building a business or packaging it for sale, a business owner should use his own insights and ideas, rather than a pre-defined media offering. Find a graphic artist who can listen to you and use his or her creative skills to enable you to put your best foot forward.

Following are some examples of brand imaging to give you some idea as to its value, whether promoting a brand or projecting an image of a successful business to a potential buyer.

CHAPTER ELEVEN
GENERAL ACCOUNTING ADVICE

 **KEY POINTS**

Anticipate Tax Consequences

Types of Deals Involved in the Sale of a Business
- Purchase of the Assets of the Business.
- Purchase of the Stock of the Company (Assuming it's a Corporation).

Anticipate Tax Consequences
- Structuring the Sale
- Fixed Assets vs. Goodwill

Individual Proprietorship

LLC

C Corporation

S Corporation

CHAPTER ELEVEN
GENERAL ACCOUNTING ADVICE

We are indebted to Jay H. Freeberg, CPA, CFP, CMFS, MBA of Janover-Rubenroit, *a major financial planning and accounting firm, for his valuable input for this section. Mr. Freeberg has helped many of our clients. He has been recognized as a* ReutersAdvicePoint 2008 Top Adviser *and was selected among the Top 150 best financial advisors for doctors in U.S. by* Medical Economics. *He is often quoted in the media, most recently in the premier issue of* Private Wealth's *magazine,* Advising the Exceptionally Affluent *and in the* Journal of Accountancy, CFA Magazine *and the* Washington Post.
Jay H. Freeberg is at 100 Quentin Roosevelt Blvd., Garden City, New York 11530. Telephone (516) 445-9898, e-mail free@jrllc.com. *His website is:* www.jrfadvisors.com. *He will be pleased to serve as a resource for readers of this book.*

ANTICIPATE TAX CONSEQUENCES

Buyers and Sellers, in most respects, are on opposite poles when it comes to evaluation and costs. The one item upon which they always agree is: "How can we minimize the amount we have to pay in taxes?" In evaluating the sale of a business for taxation purposes, the IRS is concerned only with who is going to pay, and how much they can get. This depends on how the business is structured. Here again, we recommend expert advice. Tax avoidance strategies may be quite efficient—or may lead to unanticipated disasters. The importance of expert advice can not be overstated.

For the seller, the objective must be to receive as much as possible, after taxes, for the company. In general, a business sale should be structured to show as much of the sale as recovery basis, then as a capital gain. Deferring income to a year or years down the line, when anticipated income is lower and tax bracket may be lower, sometimes works, and is often a good reason for the seller to self finance. And your advisory team (accountants and attorneys) must do all possible to avoid double taxation.

TYPES OF DEALS INVOLVED IN THE SALE OF A BUSINESS

There are basically two types of deals when purchasing a business:
- Purchase of the assets of the business.
- Purchase of the stock of the company (assuming it's a corporation).
- In addition, a merger is a special type of stock acquisition.

In general, sellers prefer to sell the stock of a business, while buyers prefer to purchase the assets. Most sellers of a company would prefer to sell stock in order to obtain tax favored capital gains treatment on the sale. On the other hand, the buyer of the assets does not generally inherit the liabilities of the business, while the stock purchaser does. This is a critical factor in deciding which type of deal is best for you as seller or buyer. There are some instances that can make the purchase of stock advantageous. Due diligence will determine if the business's contracts are assignable. If they are, the contracts will continue if you buy the stock of the company. If they are not assignable, and you wish to benefit from them, you must purchase the stock of the company. If the buyer is acquiring stock, that can be accomplished through direct stock purchases from all selling shareholders, or it may be done through a merger. As we have discussed above, a merger is a creature of state law (so you have to follow the legal rules in your state) that results in one entity being combined (or "merged") into another entity. After the merger, the merged out entity no longer exists, and the business of the combined entities continues in one company.

Mergers can have a number of advantages. A tax-free merger, where the selling shareholders receive stock in another company and don't have to pay immediate tax on the sale of their shares, may be possible. Mergers also have the advantage of not needing every shareholder to approve the deal. But mergers may be quite complicated, and, using some of the guidelines in Chapter One, you should enlist the guidance of an experienced corporate attorney.

ALWAYS CHECK THE TAX CONSEQUENCES OF A SALE WITH A TRUSTED ADVISOR

As a general rule, most businesses are individually owned, or are set up as S corporations, C corporations, or Limited Liability Corporations (LLCs). Taxes are assessed differently for each.

As a general rule, C Corporations generate capital gains, while the other corporations generate individual income taxes or taxes on dividends. C Corporations are governed by the most complicated tax rules, generating corporate revenue and incurring taxation at corporate rates. Owners and stockholders, of course, pay taxes on income, dividends and capital gains.

A corporation must meet certain conditions to be eligible for a subchapter S election. It must have no more than 75 shareholders. Only individuals, estates, certain trusts, certain partnerships, tax-exempt charitable organizations, and other Qualified Subchapter S trusts (QSSTs) may be shareholders. With an S corporation, income and losses are passed through to shareholders and included on their individual tax returns. As a result, there's just one level of federal tax to pay. There is no double taxation.

In addition, owners of S corporations who do not have inventory can use the cash method of accounting, which differs from the accrual method. Under this method, income is taxable when received and expenses are deductible when paid.

S corporations have some downsides. They are subject to many of the same requirements corporations must follow, which mean higher legal and tax service costs. They have to file articles of incorporation, hold directors and shareholders meetings, keep corporate minutes, and allow shareholders to vote on major corporate decisions. S corporations can only issue common stock, which can hamper capital-raising efforts.

If planning a sale shortly, and not yet an S corporation, you have a problem. A corporation must make the subchapter S election no later than two months and 15 days after the first day of the taxable year to elect. Subchapter S election requires the consent of all shareholders.

Since this book is meant for national use, we must point out that some states treat S corporations differently. Some disregard subchapter S status entirely, offering no tax break at all. Other states honor the federal election automatically. And some states require filing of a state-specific form to complete subchapter S election. Some local taxation authorities may not recognize S Corporation status. Consult an accountant and/or attorney in your state to determine the rules that apply to your business.

LLCs are more flexible. They, too, pass income through to owners or stockholders, who pay taxes at personal rates. This special tax status eliminates any possibility of double taxation, just as for S corporations. With LLCs, there is no limit on how many people, other businesses or trusts can own stock. They offer their owners limited liability protection as well. An LLC can have non-US Citizens as shareholders.

LLCs are more flexible in distributing profits than S corporations, wherein the corporation can only have one class of stock and your percentage of ownership determines the percentage of pass-through income. On the other hand, an LLC can have many different classes of interest, and the percentage of pass-through income is not tied to ownership percentage. The pass-through percentage can be set by agreement of the members in the LLCs operating agreement.

S corporations have several advantages over LLCs. One person can form an S corporation, while in a few states at least two people are required to form an LLC. Existence is perpetual for S corporations. Conversely, LLCs typically have limited life spans.

The stock of S corporations is freely transferable, subject to the contracts as written, while the interest (ownership) of LLCs is not. This free transferability of interest means the shareholders of S corporations are able to sell their interest without obtaining the approval of the other shareholders. In contrast, members of LLCs would need the approval of the other members in order to sell their interest. Lastly, S corporations may be advantageous in terms of self-employment taxes in comparison to LLCs.

Sole proprietorships' income naturally goes to the individual owner, who pays taxes at personal rates.

The Advantages of a Sole Proprietorship

- Owners can establish a sole proprietorship instantly, easily and inexpensively.
- Sole proprietorships carry few, if any, ongoing formalities.
- A sole proprietor need not pay unemployment tax on himself or herself (although he or she must pay unemployment tax on employees). Of course, he receives no benefits if unemployed.
- Owners may freely mix business or personal assets. (This requires major "Recasting" when preparing to sell.

Disadvantages of a Sole Proprietorship

- Owners are subject to unlimited personal liability for the debts, losses and liabilities of the business.
- Owners cannot raise capital by selling an interest in the business.
- Sole proprietorships rarely survive the death or incapacity of their owners and so do not retain value.

The sole proprietorship is the simplest business form under which one can operate a business. It is not a legal entity. The sole proprietorship is a popular business form due to its simplicity, ease of setup, and nominal cost. A distinct disadvantage, however, is that the owner of a sole proprietorship remains personally liable for all the business's debts. Sole proprietors can, and often do, co-mingle personal and business property and funds, with bank accounts in the name of the owner, something that partnerships, LLCs and corporations cannot do. Perhaps more than with any other form of ownership, sole proprietorships need serious recasting before they are ready to look for a buyer, since so many perks have been available to them and taken advantage of, that should not included as part of the bottom line.

CHAPTER TWELVE
INSURANCE NEEDS OF SELLERS AND BUYERS

KEY POINTS

The Purpose of Insurance

Insurance Needs of the Seller
- Health Insurance
- Disability Insurance
- Life Insurance
- Pension Plan
- Estate Planning

The Role of an Insurance Broker

Insurance Needs of the Buyer

Property and Casualty Insurance

Sole Proprietorships, Partnerships, Corporations

Other Insurance Needs

Buy/Sell Agreements

Ownership of Policies

Top Ten Do's and Don'ts

CHAPTER TWELVE

INSURANCE NEEDS OF SELLERS AND BUYERS

We are indebted to Charles Holzberg of The Charles Holzberg Agency, LLC, 275 Madison Avenue, New York, NY 10016 for his valuable insight and input in helping us prepare this chapter. He is available for consultation to all readers of this book, and we encourage you to use his wisdom. Phone (212) 279-7500 or e-mail <u>holzagency@elinkisp.com</u>.

The purpose of insurance is to transfer a risk that you can afford (payment of a premium with no guarantee of its return) to cover a risk you cannot afford.

You might ask what a book on planning an exit strategy has to do with insurance. The fact is that insurance is extremely important to the seller of a business, for reasons we shall elaborate. We have already mentioned that exit strategy should be considered, even when starting a business. For that reason, we will also deal with insurance needs of a buyer, as well.

When you are starting a business, you have a myriad of insurance needs you would not even begin to think about. Insurance is not only going to be important to you, but it will be important to your other business relationships. For example, if you choose to lease office space, the landlord will typically require that you furnish a certificate of insurance or be listed as an additional insured on your policy as assurance that your business will not disappear overnight in the event a loss occurs. The point is, you must protect yourself, and you must protect others from you.

INSURANCE NEEDS OF THE SELLER

We will assume that the successful business owner has protected himself and his family by following the advice of professionals, such as his accountant, financial planner, attorney and insurance broker. If so, there are many insurance policies that require attention as a business is sold or transferred.

HEALTH INSURANCE

An employee who is covered under a company health policy has the luxury of continuing coverage for 18 months under COBRA, a continuation of benefits provision. An owner has no such luxury. If not eligible for Medicare coverage, the seller must protect himself and his family through purchasing health insurance immediately. As is obvious, accidents, disability, illness and death never occur at convenient times. Proper planning for protection is essential, regardless of the current health of the seller.

DISABILITY INSURANCE

Disability policies may be continued if the seller immediately goes to work for another company, or goes into another business. If he is no longer working, he would be wise to reallocate the funds currently being used to pay disability insurance premiums into purchasing Long Term Care Insurance.

LIFE INSURANCE

If a cross purchase agreement funded by insurance is in existence, a well drawn agreement should include a provision for the buyer to allow the seller to take over these policies if deemed necessary or desirable.

PENSION PLAN

If there is a qualified pension or profit sharing plan, either being terminated or taken over by the buyer, a seller must sit down with his financial planner to determine what to do with the distribution. Should the funds be transferred into an IRA so they may continue to accumulate on a tax deferred basis? Should they be annuitized to provide monthly income? Or does the seller take a lump sum distribution, despite the huge tax liability this might create? Here, as throughout this book, we can not overemphasize the value of excellent legal and financial advice.

ESTATE PLANNING

Along with all of the above, the health and age of the principal, together with that of his spouse, should be taken into consideration so that Uncle Sam does not become a significant beneficiary. Wills and trusts should be revisited, especially considering the new circumstances related to the exit from a business. Now is the time to sit down with competent, trusted estate planning, tax, legal and accounting professionals. It is not the time to tell yourself that you want to save money on the fees involved. That could be a very costly error.

INSURANCE NEEDS WHEN STARTING A BUSINESS

A smart, well informed businessman plans ahead, anticipating potential problems so they may be avoided and protecting himself from the severe consequences of problems that can not be avoided. Hence, the need for insurance.

THE ROLE OF AN INSURANCE BROKER

Direct to consumer advertising permeates our environment, hawking everything from prescription drugs to plastic surgery. The insurance industry does its part to direct the consumer to major national insurance providers. Those who decide to "go direct" often do so at their own peril. While insurance needs may be fairly clearly defined, no two persons have exactly the same needs. Just as a buyer of do-it-yourself wills and boilerplate trusts does so at his own peril, an individual who haphazardly selects insurance from the smorgasbord in front of him may put himself at risk, often in the not too distant future.

Insurance is a commodity. However, it should be purchased, not as a commodity alone, but as part of a service provided. A broker provides value added services to enable the insured to maximize the use of the commodity. He can broker the type and amount of insurance that match the needs of an individual insured, and place that insurance with the best and most appropriate company. As in many aspects of life, the policy with the lowest cost is not necessarily the best. Nor is a national provider with huge assets (and advertising) always the best. Often, a local provider sensitive to and knowledgeable about local requirements may be a better fit. A good broker will know that.

An insurance broker represents the insured's interest. A broker who has expertise in the insured's field of endeavor is ideal. Not only will a property and casualty broker tailor a plan to meet individual needs, but the broker will be there to deal with the insurer should there be problems or claims in the future.

Now let's explore the basic insurance needs of someone who is buying or setting up a business.

PROPERTY AND CASUALTY INSURANCE
It is obvious that the owner of a business must be insured for known hazards—fire, theft and liability. There must be protection covering the cost of defense against litigation, whether from consumers, competitors or suppliers. Use and occupancy insurance must be in place.

There may also be insurance needs unique to a particular business, as, for example, a physician's need for medical malpractice insurance. An individual entrepreneur will certainly need business interruption insurance should he be unable to operate at his location due to events out of his control, such as fire or water damage. Unfortunately, in some locations, terrorism coverage may be necessary, as well.

Locally mandated insurance needs can only be determined and planned for by someone familiar with the territory. Different states have different laws regarding workman's compensation coverage for job or business related illness or injury. Unemployment insurance needs vary, as well, as does the requirement for posting these benefits prominently. Fines for failure to post them, in fact, can be costly. Disability insurance for non-employment related loss of ability to work must also be in place.

OTHER PROTECTION NEEDS
INDIVIDUAL PROPRIETORS
Rarely is a business purchased for a cost of zero dollars. Whether the purchase price comes from the individual buyer's personal assets, a

mortgage or a loan such as an SBA (Small Business Association) loan, you want to protect the capitalization of your investment. This is true, whether you are a sole proprietor, a closely held corporation or an LLC (Limited Liability Company).

An individual owner must be aware of what is required to go into a business, and what might happen to that business should he become disabled or die. Again, neither death nor disability happens at a convenient time. The need for life insurance is obvious. It is the least expensive way to replace the capital investment without jeopardizing the financial security of the owner's family. We will not go into the relative merits of various types of life insurance here, leaving that to a trusted insurance advisor.

Disability insurance is another requirement in order to protect assets, the type an amount to be determined after careful evaluation of the owner's circumstances. A balance must be determined between likely needs and costs involved. Since the proceeds of disability insurance are tax-free, the premiums are not tax deductible. On the other hand, overhead protection is tax deductible but one pays tax on the proceeds (offset by the overhead expenses actually incurred at the time).

There is, especially in these days of escalating costs, an absolute need to purchase health insurance. If the buyer has left a previous position in which health insurance was provided, he should be able to carry that insurance with him for eighteen months under the portability provisions of COBRA (Continuation of Benefits) law. This will allow the new owner time to build his organization and explore the new company's needs related to health insurance. A competent local insurance broker will be in a position to guide and advise him as to what may be needed with respect to group health and group life insurance that may be cost effective yet adequate enough to attract capable employees.

PARTNERSHIPS

When you have more than one person as an owner of a business, whether it be a partnership, a closely held corporation or an LLC (Limited Liability Company), things get more complicated when it comes to insurance needs. Certainly, you get involved with personalities.

One partner may be conservative, the other adventuresome. One may have a young family, while the other may be a bachelor or be paying alimony. And they may have different fields of expertise. One may be a super salesman, while his partner is purely an administrator with zero ability to sell. In such a case, the loss of services of either for any significant length of time would throw a considerable monkey wrench into the company's operations, and adversely affect the bottom line. A good partnership agreement is at least as important as having a properly prepared and frequently updated will.

A good partnership agreement protects against the dreaded three "D's"—Death, Disability and Divorce. It establishes a fair market price for the business for today, and a means of reevaluating its value annually in the future. It creates a partnership or corporate buy-out agreement, whether it involve cross purchase, stock redemption or a combination of both.

The agreement also must provide a restriction as to whom the partnership or corporation might be willing to accept as a co-owner. Obviously, no organization wants an unwanted partner, whether it be a surviving spouse or surrogate, looking over its shoulder. A buy-out, as part of a partnership agreement, prevents such a calamity. You need key man insurance to fund a buyout.

In the event of a major disability of one of the owners, the question arises as to how long, and how much, to pay the disabled party, especially while also paying someone to replace him. It may seem a luxury, but you need a disability buy-out policy to fund such an eventuality, supplementing the partner's own disability insurance. A good insurance broker can juggle these needs and arrange a cost effective method of protecting you and your company.

PROTECTION RELATED TO DEATH OR DEPARTURE OF AN OWNER

In a two person partnership, as part of a well drawn agreement, upon death or departure of one partner from the firm, the partnership is over. Upon death of a partner, there must be a buy-sell agreement. Even in a corporation, the agreement must state that the entity or co-stock holders must buy the deceased partner's interest, and, importantly, the

INSURANCE NEEDS OF SELLERS AND BUYERS

estate must sell its interest. A simple cross purchase agreement clearly states that partner A shall buy from partner B, and partner B's estate must sell to partner A. This eventuality must be funded by life insurance. Generally speaking, and this is not commonly appreciated, it is much more advantageous for individuals to buy the insurance policies out of their own pockets rather than have the entity pay the premiums. As the owner of the policy, you receive the benefits free of taxation and give it to the estate of the deceased, upon which you now own 100% of the company. You have a stepped up cost basis, and, when you sell, the capital gain will be substantially less. In addition, the proceeds of the policy would not be available to creditors, creating another level of protection. I know this does not sound easy, and, in fact, it's not all that easy as it does sound. You need a competent insurance broker, working in concert with your accountant and attorney, to sort this out. By the way, it is important to note that, as your business grows, insurance covering a buy/sell agreement can and should be increased.

In contrast, assume a redemption agreement wherein the corporation redeems the stock of the deceased and redeems it. Creditors can attack this dollar amount. Generally speaking, it is usually preferable to have a cross purchase agreement rather than a stock redemption plan. In general, one does not have a corporation, therefore, as a beneficiary, unless the partnership is so large that any other arrangement is impossible. While having a trustee as beneficiary might be an option, the most important point I will make, again and again, is that an insurance broker, acting in concert with professional advisors, is an urgent and necessary part of your team.

OTHER POLICIES

D and O—Directors' and Officers' liability polices—and Product Liability policies—might merit your attention. Ask an advisor about these.

Employment Practices Liability Coverage is now carried by many companies. While employment practice liabilities are rarely encountered in a small operation, the threat of wrongful termination or sexual harassment lawsuits, which are excluded under most business policies, become more prevalent as the size of your organization grows.

All risk policies might include computer hardware and software, plus your valuable records. A properly written policy will include loss of income that might result from breakdowns, as well as loss of income from other hazards that would temporarily close down your business.

Some policies will exclude Products and Completed Operations and/or Personal Injury and Advertising Coverage depending on the services your business provides. In these instances, a Professional Liability, Malpractice, or Errors and Omissions Policy might be available for your type of operation that will cover the errors and omissions that might result in suits against your company. This is particularly true of professions that are held to a higher degree of care or standard, for example, attorneys, engineering consultants, insurance agents, realtors, doctors and dentists.

We have not even touched upon excess personal liability or umbrella policies, which cover extraordinary damages, and should be explored.

WHO SHOULD OWN THE POLICIES?

In general, personal insurance should be carried personally. It is NOT cheaper to let the business pay for it. If they do, the proceeds are taxable personally, and this can be a huge number. Property and Casualty Insurance premiums are tax deductible as a normal business expense. Life insurance premiums are almost never deductible, no matter who pays, because the proceeds are tax free. The exceptions are group coverage—ask your broker—and insurance provided in a qualified insurance plan. As mentioned, you should never deduct disability insurance premiums since, to do so, causes the proceeds to be taxable as ordinary income.

SUMMARY

In starting your own business, there are many insurance aspects that require research. You will have liability concerns. If you have employees, you will have their concerns. Before starting, you must speak to an insurance professional who represents several types of companies and can offer a wide range of products.

INSURANCE NEEDS OF SELLERS AND BUYERS

You must tell your insurance professional what you're doing and let him research exactly what type of insurance you need. Personal liability concerns are to protect others from you. Professional liability concerns are to protect others from your making a wrong recommendation to them. Employment practices liability coverage protects you from litigious employees.

Your business may have inventory, computers, or supplies that you must have coverage for in the event of physical loss, a fire, or a theft. Employees will open up another avenue. There are laws governing workers compensation insurance needs. You may need your own health insurance. You may need your own disability insurance. And you will need group health and life coverage if you wish to attract capable employees.

TOP TEN DO'S AND DON'TS

- Do bring an insurance broker into your start-up process.
- Do include excess liability "Commercial Umbrella" coverage for your business.
- Do consider health insurance coverage to recruit and keep good employees.
- Do consider employment practices liability coverage.
- Do increase insurance coverage appropriately as your business grows.
- Do maintain a buy-sell agreement with your partners, funded by life insurance where possible.
- Do not self-insure any part of your worker's compensation risk.
- Do not feel that you can't afford insurance. You can't afford not to have it.
- Do not allow insurance policies to lapse.
- Do not go uninsured in any category of insurable and significant risk.

CHAPTER THIRTEEN
LEGAL ASPECTS OF BUSINESS SALES

 **KEY POINTS**

Form of a Sale

Letter of Intent

Due Diligence
- Financial
- Non-Financial
- Legal

Purchase Agreement

Protecting Buyer and Seller

Full Disclosure

CHAPTER THIRTEEN
LEGAL ASPECTS OF BUSINESS SALES

We are indebted to Herbert W. Solomon, Esq., for his assistance in preparing this section. Attorney Solomon has assisted our clients with closing many deals, both as buyer's and seller's legal counsel, and has done so quickly and efficiently. In addition, he has served as Counsel to the National Association of Publishers' Representatives, Inc. (NAPR) since 1981, and authored a series of articles for their Journal concerning legal aspects of selling a representative's business. The NAPR consists of firms that sell advertising for magazines and internet sites. These firms gross as little as $100,000 annually, and some up to $10,000,000 or more. Thus, we are dealing with the sale of a business entity whose principal asset concerns its rights to sell advertising for a publisher, rather than a product. Legal aspects, however, are quite universal in business sales. (Portions of Mr. Solomon's series have been extrapolated, with his permission, for this chapter.)

It must be stressed that this chapter is intended to provide guidance, not legal advice, and the contents of this Chapter should not be utilized without consultation with a competent legal counsel and a tax advisor.

SALE OF REPRESENTATIVE'S BUSINESS

By Herbert W. Solomon, Esq.[1]

(Abridged by the Author)

---

1   Herbert W. Solomon, Esq., P.C., of the New York bar, is Counsel to the law firm of Meltzer, Lippe, Goldstein & Breitstone, LLP, 190 Willis Avenue, Mineola, New York 11501 (516) 747-0300 ext. 152, e-mail: hsolomon@meltzerlippe.com.

EXIT STRATEGY

The key question is, "What does a Representative have to sell?" That question is easy. All the Representative has to sell are his agreements and his relations with his publishers. Accordingly, NO SALE CAN PRACTICALLY BE ACCOMPLISHED WITHOUT THE CONSENT OF THE PUBLISHER. *(Author's note: This concept applies in the sale of a service oriented business, such as a professional practice, nail salon or hairdresser, etc. If the clients of the business, or patients, refuse to use the buyer's services, the buyer receives nothing for his investment. Conditional sales such as that discussed below may be required. However, professional practice sales must beware of any arrangement that violates fee-splitting restrictions.)*

We must therefore assume that the PUBLISHER has consented or will consent to the sale. Initially there should be a negotiation of the price. In my experience the price is usually based upon a multiple or the revenues expected. Years ago, NAPR requested the opinion of its members as to what they would sell their businesses for and received 14 responses ranging from 1 times gross revenues to 3 times with an average of 1.7. *(Author's note: This is what the sellers **want**. It is not necessarily what they get. Each industry has different guidelines as to what multiple of gross or net constitutes a reasonable asking price for a business.)*

Of course, each situation will depend upon its specific facts. Price is a function of term or length of time to complete a purchase. How long does the buyer have to pay off the price? Most purchasers of a Representative's business will want to negotiate a term of payment that can range for as long as four or five years or more. Furthermore, a purchaser may want a provision that if it is unable to retain the business of the publications purchased, the purchase price will be reduced. A buyer will want to pay as soon as possible. We will discuss this subsequently.

The sale of the Representative's business can take various forms:
- Sale of stock.
- Sale of assets.
- Issuance of shares to a non-stockholder, and, following this a redemption of the existing shareholders' ownership interest.

Each form of the transaction is likely to have different tax consequences. Accordingly, the seller must work closely with his certified public accountant or other tax advisor. This article will not discuss the tax consequences involved. Suffice it is to say that they must be carefully considered for each proposed transaction.

There are various components to the transaction consisting of the specific sale of the stock of the corporation to be sold or assets to be sold:

- price
- payment terms
- allocations of price
- closing conditions
- schedules of assets, liabilities, agreements, etc.
- security for the sale
- guarantees
- representations and warranties
- consulting agreements
- restrictive covenants
- dispute mechanisms

This list is not complete, but it does contain the major items to be considered.

First to be considered is the form of the transaction. Will it be a sale of stock or a sale of assets? If a sale of stock, the purchaser will be acquiring all the assets of the business being sold. But the purchaser will also be acquiring all of its liabilities as well. Expect, in either situation, that the purchaser will also be performing substantial due diligence.

This leads to the need for a Confidentiality Agreement before the buyer is permitted to review any of the seller's records and papers. The proposed purchaser must not be able to utilize any confidential information ascertained in doing his Due Diligence, and should not be allowed to solicit any publications of the proposed seller if no deal is consummated. The State law must be considered, as laws may vary from state to state.

Accordingly, after the Confidentiality Agreement is signed, it is advisable to prepare a letter of intent, or at least a proposed term sheet, so that the key points of the transaction are understood up front. If there is no initial agreement on the key points, the parties should not proceed further.

It should be noted at this point that a Representative's business can be sold to a third party who is a stranger, or to someone already involved in the business being sold. This can be an important consideration, in that the purchaser will want to know that he is acceptable to the publisher. However, if the publisher knows the seller is looking to sell his business, it may start looking for a new Representative. The issue of publisher consent is also a very tricky point, since the seller may be very much concerned about informing the publishers of a proposed sale. This is, then, a consideration to be discussed. It concerns the timing. Should the publisher be asked for approval before, or after, an agreement between the seller and the buyer is reached? This will depend upon the situation. Note, also, that should the purchaser be someone already affiliated with the seller, and the publisher knows of this person because he worked on the account, it may be easier to get the publisher's consent. *(Author's note: This, in general, does not apply in usual business or professional practice sales. As readers will recall, one of the reasons for using a business broker involves the extremely important concept of confidentiality. Release of information that a business is being sold can have devastating effects, as we have noted. Sellers may not extend credit, customers and/or employees may leave, and competitors may aggressively solicit customer base.)*

In a sale of assets, or even of stock, there are issues pertaining to what specific assets of a seller's business are being sold. Besides the representative's agreements, there are accounts receivable, cash in the business, fixed assets, and all other assets of the business. The opposite of this is the liabilities the business may have. The purchaser will not want to assume any liabilities. Expect a thorough search by the purchaser. Further, is there any litigation that the seller is party to? Are all of its taxes paid? What employees of the old business are going with the new business? Does the business being sold have a lease? Is the lease being assigned? What binding agreements is the business subject to? The foregoing and numerous other questions concerning the assets of the business and its liabilities will need to be discussed and resolved. (*Author's note: See "due diligence" below.*)

Up front, we discussed the issue of a reduction in price if the key accounts acquired are lost. This needs to be resolved. I believe that only if the account is lost during the first year or two after sale should the price be adjusted. Provision can be made for a decreasing reduction in the purchase price with respect to a loss of the publication subsequent to closing, with a decreased percentage of reduction for that year after closing.

The sale of the Representative's business will include various other aspects. First to be discussed concerns the seller receiving security in the event the unpaid portion of the purchase price is not paid. Primary consideration should be whether or not the purchaser, if it consists of a corporation or an LLC, will have the unpaid portion of the purchase price personally guaranteed by its shareholders or members of the LLC. If so, a personal guaranty should be carefully discussed which will provide that the persons guaranteeing payment agree, unconditionally, to pay the unpaid portion of the price in the event of a default.

Further, the seller should negotiate a security agreement, pursuant to which the Seller will be secured by the accounts receivable, unpaid commissions, fixed assets and all other assets of the purchaser. The security agreement and necessary state filings should all be prepared and filed in accordance with the appropriate provisions of the Uniform Commercial Code.

With respect to the payments to be made by the Purchaser, they should be paid, over a term agreed upon, in equal installments, and with interest on the unpaid balance. A grace period such as 10 or 15 days may be permitted. In the event of any default, the entire unpaid balance should become immediately due and payable. Attorneys' fees may be provided upon default. At that time, the seller would be entitled to pursue all of his remedies, including claims on any personal guarantees and the foreclosure of any secured interests. Critical is that the seller demand prompt and immediate payment in accordance with the terms of the purchase agreement.

Also to be negotiated with reference to the sale is a consulting arrangement between the seller and the purchaser that may be utilized following the closing. The purchaser may want the seller to devote time to the business purchased after closing. The questions are for how long, and for how many hours, the seller is to devote to the purchased business. Time negotiated may be for as little as a month and for as much as a year or two. Critical is a description of what the seller must do, and what his compensation will be for his efforts. Is the seller required to spend any time at the place of business, or can he devote his time by being available by telephone or modem?

Another factor to be considered is the question of whether or not the money to be paid to the seller for consulting is to be considered part of the purchase price, or is the amount to be paid additional consideration. Allocations of the purchase price relate to tax considerations and are to be negotiated separately. Some items may be considered ordinary income and other capital gains. Issues of allocation also relate to depreciation and how quickly the purchaser may write off, and what he can write off, from the consideration paid. It is significant to note that the issues of allocation must be carefully considered and the income tax consequences carefully reviewed.

The last point I want to mention is the issue of restrictive covenants. The purchaser will want to make sure that, so long as he complies with the terms of sale, the seller will not represent directly or indirectly the publications that have been sold. This is significant, and a portion of the purchase price will be applicable to the restrictive covenant. *(Authors' note: Legal and ethical guidelines in the professions require that a restrictive covenant, contained in the confidentiality agreement be fair to both the proposed buyer and the seller, and must be limited in duration and scope.)*

In conclusion, there are many aspects involved in the sale of a business and they must be carefully negotiated with all issues resolved before a contract is signed and a closing takes place.

DUE DILIGENCE

Purchase of a business can be a dream come true. Full disclosure can never be taken for granted. Due diligence, properly performed with competent advice and counsel, is needed to keep the dream from becoming a nightmare.

It is absolutely necessary to review certain documents when performing due diligence in getting ready to buy a business. The checklist below is not necessarily complete. The specifics of each deal must be considered. This list, we must stress, is in no way to take the place of adequate qualified and experienced legal counsel.

ACCOUNTING AND FINANCIAL INFORMATION

From a financial standpoint, due diligence requires an examination in detail of:
- financial statements
- terms of loans and leases
- asset valuation
- cost allocation
- company stability
- pension (and health) benefits

Documents required usually include:
- the previous three years' tax returns, possibly personal as well as corporate
- the previous three years' bank statements
- financial statements including assets, liabilities, accounts receivable and payable, inventory and cash position and requirements
- prospective financial information including:
    - Earnings projection
    - Projection of cash requirements
    - Projected financial statements
    - Capital and operating budgets
    - Long-term plans

LEGAL INFORMATION
From a legal standpoint, due diligence requires an examination in detail of Corporate Documents of the Company and Subsidiaries including the following materials or information relating to the target company and any subsidiaries (together, the "Company"):

- Articles of Incorporation and all amendments thereto.
- Bylaws and all amendments thereto.
- Minutes of all Board of Directors, committee and shareholders meetings.
- Stockholders' information.
- A list of states and jurisdictions in which qualified to do business and in which the Company has offices, holds property or conducts business.
- All contracts, arrangements, or public or private documents or commitments relating to the Company.
- All significant and relevant contracts and agreements.
- Leases, deeds and mortgages.
- Legal proceedings, current, pending and anticipated.
- Lien and litigation searches.
- Potential or actual liabilities.
- Determine position on key points such as:
    - Representations and warranties.
    - Liabilities to be retained/assumed by buyer.
    - Conditions to closing.
    - Damages clause in the event of failure of buyer or seller to close.
- Prepare agreements involving:
    - Confidentiality
    - Asset or Stock Sale
    - Assignment & Assumption
    - Real Estate Purchase
    - Environmental factors
    - Bills of Sale (and other instruments of transfer)

Legal due diligence also requires obtaining:
- Copies of any leases, mortgages, appraisals of property or other relevant documents.
- Copies of covenants for key employees or Executive Personnel.
- Contracts and agreements.
- Title reports (if real estate is involved).

There should be an arbitration clause, and a non-compete provision. As you can see, your legal advisor earns his fee, as this is only a partial list.

GENERAL DUE DILIGENCE

From a business standpoint, due diligence requires that you evaluate:
- the company's background
- the company's product lines
- the company's market
- customer relationships
- management and employees
- competition
- marketing
- internal reports
- environmental problems and liabilities
- information regarding employees, patents and trademarks

You must also establish conditions with respect to:
- Treatment of employees & benefit plans.
- Pre-closing restrictive covenants of seller and buyer (such as access to records).

It is also necessary to establish a prorating and allocation of closing costs:
- transfer taxes
- escrow fees
    - title insurance premiums
    - recording fees

Asset Schedules:
- Establish whether there will be a detailed listing or a descriptive approach?
- Are there any assets subject to liens?
- Are any assets leased or licensed?

POST-CLOSING TRANSITION

Is this an As-is sale with all faults?

Are there Disclaimers of representations or warranties?

Will there be an assumption by the buyer of designated existing contracts and of deferred obligations?

Personal contact with suppliers and customers can be helpful and revealing, either reassuring or alarming, but worthwhile pursuing.

CHAPTER FOURTEEN
FRANCHISES

 **KEY POINTS**

What is a Franchise?

Franchise Systems

Costs, Fees, and Other Financial Requirements

Controls

The Franchise Disclosure Document

The Franchise Agreement

Exiting the System

The Amicable Separation

The Adversarial Separation

Restrictive Covenants

CHAPTER FOURTEEN
FRANCHISES

We are indebted to Justin M. Klein and David S. Paris for their valuable input for this chapter. Their company, Marks & Klein, LLP, is a boutique law firm representing franchisees and emerging franchisors across the country. They have helped so many of our clients throughout the years when we have dealt with franchises. Justin Klein and David Paris have both been recognized as a "2008 Legal Eagle" by the Franchise Times, *a designation reserved for the top franchise attorneys in the country. They will be pleased to offer their services to our readers with queries regarding franchise acquisitions or sales. Contact Marks & Klein, LLP, 63 Riverside Avenue, Red Bank, NJ 07701, by e-mail, David@Marksklein.com, or phone (732) 747-7100.*

CONSIDERATIONS IN BUYING (OR SELLING) A FRANCHISE

While the intent while writing *Exit Strategy* was to assist those who are preparing to sell or transfer a business, we would be remiss were we not to include advice to those who are exploring the various categories of business ownership. As we have stated in the first few chapters, planning an Exit Strategy should begin when starting a business, For those who are selling a franchise business, they must be aware of various methods of separation and how separation can be accomplished as smoothly and hassle-free as possible. This chapter, therefore, is aimed at both buyers and sellers.

Many persons will explore purchase of a franchise, the rationale for doing so being rooted in the public's perception of franchising as a safe and proven path to achieving the "American Dream" of business ownership. Unfortunately, many prospective buyers fail to perform the comprehensive investigation required to allow them to make a truly informed decision about investing in a franchise. More importantly, and consistent with our basic premise, they fail to even consider how and when they plan to exit the investment. Often, they sign their franchise agreements without giving serious thought to the many issues that may arise during the purchase of a franchise, the operation of a franchise, or during their transition out of a franchise system. In the end, these individuals may find themselves in uncharted waters, with no exit strategy in place.

I. WHAT IS A FRANCHISE?

While the allure of franchising is rooted in the prospect of business ownership and success, potential investors often do not actually know what a franchise is. The textbook definition of a franchise is a streamlined mechanism of product or service distribution. There are generally two types of franchises—Product Distribution franchises and Business Format Franchises.

Product Distribution franchises typically sell the franchisor's products through a supplier-dealer relationship. In this format, the franchisor licenses its trademarks to the franchisee, but does provide a supporting relationship or system for running the business. While the franchisee essentially operates the business independently, he or she does benefit from the marketing and advertising efforts of the franchise system. Common examples of such franchises include auto dealerships, gas stations, and soft-drink bottling companies.

The Business Format Franchise is the type of system that gleans the most interest in today's market. These franchises are characterized by an ongoing business relationship between franchisor and franchisee. The franchisee benefits, not only from the franchise trademarks, but also from a comprehensive operational and marketing system. Business format franchises are recognizable throughout the world, and include as participants, famous concepts such as Century 21, Medicine Shoppes, Dunkin' Donuts and McDonald's.

II. BEFORE SELECTING A FRANCHISE SYSTEM

Determining the ideal franchise system to enter is an extremely individualized process which requires a considerable amount of research and due diligence. Once a decision is reached as to which franchise systems best conform to personal criteria, complete information should be obtained with respect to: costs (getting into the system), controls (operating within the system), and termination and renewal (exiting the system).

A. Self-analysis

The first step taken by a potential franchisee should be a self-analysis, to assess among other things, personal finances, interests and abilities. This initial assessment is integral in determining which of the thousands of available franchise systems presents the right "fit" for the individual.

Personal finances should be evaluated as the first level of the filtration process in selecting a franchise. As the costs and risks associated with franchises vary widely from system to system, the amount of money available for investment and the investor's ability to sustain a loss should be the two paramount financial factors in the decision making process. Other critical financial information to be considered are whether the investment will be made independently or through a partnership, the credit worthiness of the investor(s), and the necessity for and availability of financing.

Once the field of available franchise concepts has been narrowed by financial criteria, the abilities and goals of the prospective franchisee should be appraised. More specifically, the franchisee should consider each potential opportunity against the backdrop of his or her own practical experience, relevant education, and technical skills. Additional consideration should be afforded to personal goals such as interest in a particular industry, the amount of time that must be committed to operating the franchise, the ability to own multiple units within the chosen system, and the attainable level of income.

B. Costs, Fees, and Other Financial Requirements

With thousands of franchisors existing on almost every economic level, the costs, fees and financial requirements in connection with owning and operating a franchise can vary significantly. Generally, these expenditures are borne by franchisees in exchange for the right to use and benefit from the franchise trademarks, marketing system, ongoing support and business format.

The sales prices of franchises offered to new franchisees should ideally be standardized, irrespective of the franchisee's state of residence or the state in which the franchise is located. More to the point, the sales price should be consistent, regardless of who the prospective franchisee is, how the cost of the franchise is being financed, and whether or not it was purchased through a franchise consultant. To ensure that new franchisees all pay the same fee based prices, franchisors are required to make full disclosure of those prices in their Uniform Franchise Offering Circulars, which are commonly referred to as UFOCs[2]. UFOCs, which are discussed later in this chapter in greater detail, are franchise documents, mandated by the Federal Trade Commission, which include a required set of disclosures each franchisor must complete and have available for anyone interested in purchasing a franchise.

Initially, as a means to screen out unqualified applicants, some franchise systems impose preliminary criteria, such as minimum capital requirements. To that end, candidates interested in investing in these franchises are required to establish that the value of their net worth (total assets less total liabilities) exceeds the franchisor's pre-determined minimum dollar requirement. Franchisors may also require other types of pre-sale qualifications, such as a minimum level of experience in the industry or licensure in a given field.

Typically, in exchange for starting up a new franchisee, franchisors charge an initial franchise fee. More specifically, the initial fee is levied to pay for the new franchisee acquisition, training, site selection and other franchisor costs. This fee, which may be non-refundable, ranges between thousands and hundreds of thousands of dollars. When researching the viability of specific franchise systems, it is critical to rule out those that derive most of their revenue by initiating new franchisees and collecting franchise fees, in favor of

---

2   As of July 2008, due to changes in the law, these documents will be referred to as Franchise Disclosure Documents, or FDDs.

those concepts which prosper by virtue of the sale and distribution of their products through the franchise network. Those systems which rely on franchise fees to pay their bills almost always become unstable and problematic.

Once the franchise fee has been paid and operations have commenced, most, if not all franchisors require their franchisees to pay continuing royalties. Royalties are generally paid for the right to use the franchise name, and are often based on a percentage of the franchisee's weekly or monthly gross sales (generally 5%-10%). Some franchisors may employ alternative methods to collect their royalty fees. Such means may include: charging their royalty as a flat fee, to be paid weekly or monthly, or adjustable fees based on certain milestones in sales. Royalty payments are characteristically required throughout the duration of the franchise agreement.

While performing their diligence, prospective franchisees should be cognizant of each franchisor's royalty requirements as certain franchisors require the payment of royalties, even during time periods when the franchisee has not generated significant revenues. Furthermore, some franchisors mandate that royalties be paid even if they fail to provide the support and services bargained for in the franchise agreement.

Yet another fee frequently borne by the franchisee comes in the form of an advertising fee. As with royalty payments, advertising fees are most frequently calculated as a percentage of the franchisee's weekly or monthly gross sales (generally 1%-5%). These fees are generally paid into an advertising fund, and expended for the purpose of national, regional, or local advertising, to attract new franchise owners, and to increase customer acquisitions. However, in some of the more favorable franchise relationships, the franchisors make reciprocal contributions to the advertising fund—some even matching those made by franchisees.

In addition to the foregoing, there are numerous other costs required to get the business fully operational. The amounts of such costs depend on the type of franchise and the scope of its operations. One such cost that is generally inescapable is rent. Unless the franchise is home based, or the franchisee owns the land (another substantial cost), monthly rent must generally be paid to either a landlord, or in some instances, to the franchisor, where the franchisor holds the lease and enters a sublease with the franchisee. The amount in rent hinges on a number of factors, including the nature of the space (commercial, as if located in a strip mall, or non-commercial, as if located in a church or a school), the size of the space, and the geographic and demographic location of the space.

Another potentially significant expense can be the build-out of the franchise store. For those franchisees that purchase undeveloped or "new" locations, it will generally be incumbent upon them to bear the cost for the design and construction of their franchise store. This process, which can range from hundreds of thousands of dollars to more than a million dollars, usually requires the hiring of an architect and various contractors to complete the job. As a word of caution, some franchisors actually mandate which architects and contractors a franchisee can employ, irrespective of the fact that other, equally qualified professionals on the open market can do the same job at a lower price. There may also be a requirement that future changes in décor may be needed, at franchisee's expense, to maintain uniformity throughout the country.

In the case of a product-based franchise concept, franchisees may be required to purchase an initial inventory from the franchisor directly, or from a franchisor approved vendor. In even more restrictive concepts, the franchisees obligations go beyond initial inventory, as they are required to continually purchase and carry a minimum product inventory from the franchisor or an approved vendor. Again, just as with build-out costs, these requirements can be enforced regardless of the fact that similar products of equal or greater quality can be purchased on the open market for less money.

There are a host of other miscellaneous start-up costs which the franchisee may be forced to cover, depending upon management capabilities and requirements. These costs include operating licenses, insurance, or "grand opening" costs required in connection with the promotion of a new franchise. It should be noted, however, that in most instances, a franchisee will not need to have 100% of the initial costs to start up a franchise. In fact, many franchisees borrow funds or have partners, while others use their retirement accounts as collateral or leverage the SBA for loan guarantees.

As a word of caution, debt service is another significant cost to consider when investing in a franchise. After all, one major misconception of franchise investment is that the business will start making money on day one. That result is highly unlikely. Franchises are no different than independently owned businesses in this sense, and as in any business, cash flow will dictate the early success. As such, a prospective franchisee should strongly consider the impact such a loan can have on their bottom line.

C. Controls

As a means to ensure uniformity throughout the franchise system, franchisors often exercise a substantial degree of control over how their franchisees conduct business. These controls are frequently restrictive, and as such, may impinge on the franchisee's ability to exercise his or her personal business judgment.

One of the more prevalent issues over which franchisors commonly exercise control is franchise site selection. The rationale behind this control is that the franchisor has, at least in theory, conducted extensive geographic research and demographic market studies to determine which locations in a given area would create the most productive franchise stores. When researching a potential franchise opportunity, one issue to identify is whether the franchisor provides site selection assistance, and if so, to what extent.

A related control which is often exercised pertains to restrictions of sales area. Franchisors may limit your business to a specific territory. A territory is typically defined in terms of population or geography, and can include a town, county, state or region. Such restrictions will determine whether or not the franchisee has any "exclusivity" over his or her territory. Some franchisors offer exclusive territories, which will limit same-system encroachment of sales. Other systems provide no territorial protection, and thereby force franchisees to fend for themselves and compete for sales within a smaller geographical region.

In most systems, the franchisor maintains control over the design and appearance standards with respect to the franchise store. The franchisor's involvement in the aesthetics of its franchise is ostensibly to ensure customers experience uniformity in the quality of goods and services at each unit. Some franchisors even include provisions in their franchise agreements mandating that the franchisee refurbish and/or remodel their stores periodically throughout the duration of their agreement. It is important for prospective franchisees to determine whether such requirements exist within systems they are considering, since a refurbish or remodel can cost hundreds of thousands of dollars.

Another constraint often implemented by the franchisors comes in the form of restrictions on the goods or services offered for sale by the franchisee. For instance, with respect to the sale of products, certain franchisors mandate that the franchisees stock and sell only those items manufactured by the franchisor (or an affiliate of the franchisor), while others require that the products sold in the franchise store only be purchased from a list of approved third-party vendors. As with other franchisor restrictions, the requirements exist irrespective of the fact that other product, of equal or better quality, may be obtained from the open market for a lower price.

As with the controls exercised on design and appearance, the main thrust behind the restrictions on goods and services provided is to promote uniformity throughout the system. However, in many cases, there is also financial motivation for the franchisor that underlies these restrictions. More specifically, many franchisors receive rebates in connection with the goods sold to franchisees by the vendors included on their "approved" lists. Such rebates are required to be disclosed in the UFOC. It is intended that these rebates will be used by the franchisor to help grow the franchise business. Franchisors that do not properly disclose any rebates, or usurp that rebate capital and do not re-invest it in the franchise company may be problematic and should be avoided.

Some franchisors also place restrictions on the franchisee's methods of operation. In those systems, the controls exercised over franchisees include parameters regarding hours of operation, approval requirements for signage and displays, employee uniforms, and advertisements. Under these restraints, some franchisors also mandate that the franchisee abide by certain accounting or bookkeeping procedures—sometimes dictating which accounting and payroll professionals may be retained to facilitate those services.

Simply stated, as demonstrated by the level of control that can be exercised by the franchisor, no franchisee is truly an independent business person.

D. The Franchise Disclosure Document and the Franchise Agreement

1. The Franchise Disclosure Document

For the last three decades, federal law has required franchisors in the United States to deliver a UFOC to all prospective franchisees. In July 2008, for the first time in almost as many years, the disclosure document will undergo a facelift. One of the most significant changes is that the UFOC will now be recognized as the "Franchise Disclosure Document" or "FDD." For consistency in this article, from this point forward we will refer to this document as the "FDD."

Despite the change in the face of the FDD and a number of its internal provisions, the FDD remains the crucial document in any franchise operation. The legal due diligence process begins with a careful inspection of the FDDs used by the franchisor in each state where it has done business over the last four years. Loosely related to a stock prospectus, the FDD details the financial and legal elements of the franchisor-franchisee relationship and includes information about the financial investment and other commitments required of franchisees, the services to be offered by the franchisor—for example, training services and marketing help—and the business and professional background of the franchisor and its senior executive team, including any bankruptcies and securities violations, among other items.

The FDD additionally contains a list of current and former franchisees and provides contact information for each of those individuals. This list is a key resource which should be utilized by a prospective franchisee in the due diligence phase of his or her decision making process. The prospective franchisee should contact many, if not all, of the individuals on this list to learn first-hand of the experiences, both positive and negative, they have had with the system. These individuals can also advise the prospective franchisee about the accuracy (or inaccuracy) of the other information contained within the FDD, including that which pertains to the franchisor's treatment of its franchisees.

The FDD also includes relevant financial data for the franchise company, which should allow the prospective franchisee to obtain a clear picture of the franchisor's financial disposition. Additionally, the FDD will include various agreements that the franchisor may require a franchisee to sign, including the franchise agreement.

2. The Franchise Agreement

The entire franchise investment begins and ends with the franchise agreement. The Franchise Agreement is the legal document that governs the franchisee/franchisor relationship. There is no standard format for a Franchise Agreement because the terms and conditions and operations vary from franchise to franchise and industry to industry. Although widely preached but less frequently practiced, a prospective franchisee should have the agreement reviewed by an attorney that is well versed in franchise law, especially since most agreements are extremely one-sided in favor of the franchisor.

The core purpose of a franchise agreement is to ensure that the franchise will be operated in a manner that is identical to the way in which all other franchises are being run within the system. The agreement also addresses potential issues which may arise in the future of the relationship, such as defining how a default will be remedied.

The important terms of the franchise agreement will define the franchise relationship during the operation of the franchise and equally as importantly, upon termination or expiration of the franchise agreement. Some of the more critical provisions in the franchise agreement, which are focused include: training fees and requirements, royalty and advertising fees, definition of the territory to be serviced, the term of the agreement, and the legal parameters in defining the use of the franchisor's trade name and marks. The franchise agreement will also define the obligations and rights of the franchisor, which may include, for example, the right to open other franchises outside of the franchisee's territory or the right to sell the franchisor's products over the internet, or via other non-traditional channels. Additionally, the franchise agreement can identify the types of conduct that is prohibited by the franchisor, including the sale of unapproved products or services. Participation in such conduct can result in termination of the agreement, which is discussed later in this chapter.

The franchise agreement also contains provisions which establish the post term rights and responsibilities of the parties. These provisions often include restrictive covenants, which are discussed in the next section of this chapter. Additionally, the franchise agreement will most likely contain a dispute resolution provision that will dictate how disputes between the franchisee and franchisor will be handled (whether during the operation or post term). This provision may significantly alter the rights a franchisee might otherwise have. More specifically, the provision may mandate that any disputes arising between franchisee and franchisor must be arbitrated, or dictate the venue and controlling law in the context of litigation. Furthermore, the provision may call for limitations on damages and waiver of a trial by jury.

E. Exiting the System

When researching a particular franchise, most potential investors do not exercise the foresight required to appreciate the potential issues which may arise in the context of exiting the system. For franchisees, however, planning an exit strategy is something to consider long before investing in that first unit or concept.

1. The Amicable Separation

The conclusion of the franchise relationship can either take the form of an amicable parting of the ways or an adversarial and frequently litigious divorce-type situation. The former, which is clearly the preferable means of exiting a franchise system, typically comes as a mid-term sale of the franchise or at the expiration of the franchise agreement. Under either set of circumstances, both parties are assumed to have fulfilled their contractual obligations, and the franchisee has decided to move on in pursuit of other endeavors, or perhaps even retirement.

In the context of a mid-term sale, where the franchisee is able to exit the system on his or her own terms, timing is everything. The optimal time to sell is at a point when performance is meeting projections, and the franchisee has been in the system long enough to obtain the return on investment they had planned for.

When attempting to sell a franchise, confidentiality can only be maintained by using the services of an intermediary, such as a business broker. We have repeatedly stated the many reasons for maintaining confidentiality throughout this book, and it would be wise for the reader to review them. Either the business broker, or, if the franchisee insists on finding a buyer himself, the franchisee will first look to another franchisee in the system who is seeking to expand. They should begin in the local or regional market. If those efforts prove fruitless, the scope of the search for a qualified purchaser should be expanded outward on a national scale within the franchisee's system. If successful, a buyer from within the system can plug the franchisee's units into their infrastructure, adding value for themselves and dollars to the franchisee's selling price.

If a sale to a franchisee within the system doesn't work out, the next place to look is to the franchisor itself. Logically, there is no one with a greater understanding of the business and its value than the franchisor, and if it is motivated to buy back franchised units, it has the infrastructure to handle it.

A franchisor's determination to buy back franchised stores hinges on a number of factors. For instance, the decision may depend on the franchisor's need to protect its good will by keeping the franchise unit operational. Typically, franchisors will not pay top dollar to buy back franchised units, although that is not a hard and fast rule. If the franchisor operates its own units, and the units for sale are in a contiguous territory, chances of receiving a more favorable price improve. Correspondingly, if the franchised units are distant or in a secondary market, the franchisor will probably offer less.

In the event the franchise cannot be sold within the system, there are often willing and qualified buyers outside the system. Under these circumstances, however, the franchisor frequently retains the right to approve or disapprove any purchaser (typically, any sale or transfer of an interest in a franchise can be subject to franchisor approval). Ordinarily, that decision will include an element of reasonableness on the part of the franchisor; however, certain circumstances may give rise to the rejection of potential buyer. For instance, franchisors usually favor a buyer who enters the system with capital and can grow the brand further, especially if they are experienced operators in the same industry. On the other hand, if the purchase is highly leveraged and the buyer has little industry experience, that represents a greater financial risk the franchisor will more likely reject.

Finally, there is always the possibility that the franchise relationship will run its course and the agreement will arrive at its natural expiration date. Franchise agreements typically run for 10 to 20 years. Upon their expiration, the franchisee is often faced with the decision whether or not to renew the agreement. That determination is contingent on a number of factors. First and foremost, the franchisee may be required to pay a fee for the ability to renew. Often this payment may be substantial and renewal may not provide the terms and conditions contained in the original agreement. In fact, the new set of terms may be significantly less favorable. For instance, the franchisor may raise the royalty payments, or impose new design standards and sales restrictions. Additionally, the original territory may be reduced, possibly resulting in more competition from company-owned outlets or other franchisees.

2. *The Adversarial Separation*

Despite franchising's general acclaim, the franchise relationship can become adversarial. As a result, disputes between franchisee and franchisor arise, which sometimes result in the termination of the franchisee. Such situations generally take the form of "self-termination," wherein the franchisee unilaterally elects to discontinue operating his or her franchise, or outright termination, where the franchisor forces the franchisee to cease operations, usually based on allegations of failure to fulfill obligations under the franchise agreement.

Premature self-termination of a franchise can occur for a wide variety of reasons. Grounds for self-termination have ranged from changes in personal circumstances to the need to cut losses and exit a failing franchise business. While at times it is seemingly an economically efficient strategy, self-termination can also result in substantial additional damages to the franchisee.

As a means to thwart self-termination, some franchise agreements include provisions for liquidated damages, which are pre-determined damages, included as a term of the franchise agreement to deter the franchisee from prematurely terminating the contract. Other franchise agreements include a penalty for self-termination which takes the form of future royalty payments. Indeed, such provisions will require that the self-terminating franchisee pay all future royalties that will go unpaid as a result of the pre-mature termination of the agreement.

In stark contrast with self-termination, the outright termination of a franchisee by the franchisor is often based on allegations of misconduct or contractual violations on the part of the franchisee. For example, a franchisor can seek to end the franchise relationship when the franchisee fails to pay royalties or abide by performance standards and sales restrictions. Should a professional franchisee, such as an optometrist or pharmacist, run into licensing difficulties, severance of the relationship should be automatic, though not penalty-free.

Most franchise agreements and certain state laws limit the ability of a franchisor to terminate (or not renew) a franchisee, requiring that any such outright termination (or non-renewal) be predicated on good cause. To that end, in most situations, a franchisee must be given the opportunity to remedy any cited defaults or deficiencies prior to facing the finality of termination.

3. Restrictive Covenants

Most franchise agreements will contain restrictive covenants, which are designed to limit any negative impact that a terminated franchisee can have on the franchise company. More specifically, these provisions seek to preclude the former franchisee from convincing existing franchise clients to sever their relationship with the franchise and be serviced by the former franchisee's new employer or company. Restrictive covenants also seek to prohibit the former franchisee from soliciting or encouraging other key employees to leave the franchise company.

In addition to the foregoing, the vast majority of franchise agreements will include a covenant not to compete. These provisions will limit the former franchisee's ability to compete against his or her former franchise after the franchisee's employment with the company is terminated (typically franchise agreements also include these types of restrictions to prevent competition during the operation of the franchise as well). Covenants not to compete are typically defined by geographic proximity and duration of time. For example, a terminated franchisee may be prohibited from working for any competitor within two miles of his former franchise for two years. Restrictive covenants must be reasonable in order to be enforced.

Finally, a well drafted franchise agreement will also include a confidentiality provision. These types of restrictive covenants require the former franchisee to keep the business practices and operations of the franchise confidential both during and after the term of his or her employment. These provisions may also require that the franchisee return and not remove from the franchise any proprietary information, records, or reports.

4. Real Estate Leases

Many franchisees that enter franchise agreements are required to concurrently enter lease agreements for the locations at which they will operate their businesses. As discussed earlier in this chapter, these agreements can exist as leases between the franchisee and an independent landlord, or as subleases from the franchisor, where the franchisor holds the master lease with the landlord.

When entering into a new lease and starting a relationship with the landlord, it is important that a franchisee think about what would happen if he or she wants to get out of that relationship. Unfortunately, situations do arise where it is necessary for a franchisee to terminate a lease earlier than planned, as in a condemnation situation, or if a fire occurs in the building and the landlord is not able to restore the facility within a particular period of time. A forward thinking franchisee may want to negotiate for the inclusion of a termination clause.

Moreover, franchisees entering into a long term lease may want the right to terminate that lease if sales fall short of expectations, or if terminated by the franchisor. For instance, if a tenant signs a 10-year lease, he or she should seek the inclusion of a "safety-hatch" provision in the form of an option to terminate the lease at the five-year mark if sales are so low that it becomes economically impracticable to continue operating the business.

Finally, those franchisees that are located in shopping centers or strip malls also should include termination rights that protect the business if a major anchor tenant leaves, or if other small shop space falls below a certain occupancy level.

F. Conclusion

Contrary to popular belief, investing in a franchise is far from a sure bet. While buying a franchise may reduce your investment risk by enabling you to associate with an established company, it can be costly. You also may be required to relinquish significant control over your business, while taking on contractual obligations with the franchisor.

Undoubtedly, the amount of time and effort dedicated to conducting proper due diligence prior to investing in a franchise is key to making that franchise a success. Correspondingly, before making the leap, a prospective franchisee should learn as much as possible about the market he or she is entering. Once the franchisee has selected a concept based on his or her own financial position and interests, an investigation should be launched into the demand for the particular product or service in the chosen area. Things to consider when performing this evaluation are the level of competition in the target market and whether a concept has only seasonal marketability.

It is also imperative for the potential franchisee to study the FDD and find out what training and support the franchisor provides. More importantly, the prospective franchisee should use franchisees that are presently in the target system as resources for accurate information and insight into the system. Finally, it is imperative to plan an exit strategy and consider the factors that impact that plan. That means determining how to position the business so it is tax-favorable for a sale, maximizing sales price by retaining the real estate if possible, and avoiding the over-complication of the business so that people can understand it when they're looking to purchase it.

Most franchisees don't think in detail about their exit strategy when they enter the system—but they should because one day, sooner or later, they'll want to be out of it. When buying a franchise, buy toward the thought of sale. Today's market is too volatile and unpredictable to believe a business interest will be held forever.

Again, we are indebted to Justin M. Klein and David S. Paris. Mr. Klein and Mr. Paris would be pleased to offer our readers the benefit of their extensive experience in representing franchisees and emerging franchisors across the country. In considering a franchise purchase, or the purchase or sale of any business, there is no substitute for expert professional guidance. We urge our readers to use such services.

CHAPTER FIFTEEN
FINANCING THE DEAL

 **KEY POINTS**

Equity Financing or Debt Financing
- Cash From the Buyer
- Seller Financing
- Lender Financing
- Combination of Lender Debt and Seller Debt

What Lenders Look At
- Historical Financial Performance of the Business
- Transaction Structure
- What the Borrower Brings to the Table

SBA Financing

Alternative Methods of Financing

CHAPTER FIFTEEN
FINANCING THE DEAL

We are indebted to Bradley Colehour of Popular Small Business Capital, a Division of Banco Popular North America, for his assistance in preparing this section of the chapter. He has handled many of our deals, both locally and nationally, and is an excellent source of information and assistance in financing business sales. Mr. Colehour can be reached at (847) 671-5666 or by e-mail at bbcolehour@bpop.com. A knowledgeable business broker can be an excellent source of referrals to finance sources, especially in times when such sources may not be readily available.

We have a motivated seller and an eager buyer. The question now is how the deal is to be financed. The seller knows what he wants to get for the business, and has worked with his advisors to determine how much he is willing to finance himself via a promissory note in order to facilitate the deal. The buyer, being proactive, has worked with a lender early on, and has either lined up financing or obtained good advice as to how to make it happen. That is the ideal situation, with both buyer and seller pre-qualified for financing. Unfortunately, such is not always the case. To help consider these facets in advance, or to assist in achieving financing, we have written this chapter, calling upon two experts in the field. We are grateful to them for their assistance, and urge readers to contact them to assist in their financing needs.

FINANCING ALTERNATIVES

Now that a borrower has found a business on which he/she wants to make an offer, it is time to start thinking about how the to finance the deal. There are two main ways to finance a business equity financing and debt financing. Equity financing is pretty straightforward, involving cash from the buyer or investor for the business being purchased. Debt financing involves money from a lender, or, often, from the seller. In most instances seller financing will be subordinated to lender financing. We are left with alternatives, individually or combined, with each having strengths and weaknesses.

CASH FROM BUYER

The first alternative is all cash from the buyer. This is a very quick and easy way to finance a deal. If the buyer has $200,000 in the bank, he can buy a business for that amount in a relatively short amount of time. This is done most often with cash businesses, especially when tax returns may not support the true cash flow for lender financing, and when the seller is unwilling to take a note back for part of the purchase price. (See the Chapter on *Recasting* for methods of handling discrepancies between tax returns and the true value of a business.) Cash from a buyer would also be needed if, for some reason, (bad credit, judgments or tax liens) a lender is unwilling to fund a business they otherwise would for a better qualified borrower.

If using all cash, the buyer can typically negotiate a lower selling price, since there is no further repayment exposure for the seller. One of the downsides to using cash is that the return on equity for the borrower drops significantly. Some buyers might be of the mindset that they do not like debt. It must be stressed that paying cash when one does not have to do so severely lowers one's return on investment. In addition, it pays for buyers to hold on to their cash because buying a business presents all sorts of opportunities, as well as unexpected pitfalls. Using debt helps keep this money available should either situation arise.

SELLER FINANCING

The next alternative is seller financing. This can be a quick and easy way to finance a deal, as well, but there are often some negotiations that go on that can slow up the process. One of the main benefits of seller financing is that is will delay any tax liability on the sale, and help spread it over a period of years. In this situation, the seller basically becomes the bank and assumes all risk of repayment. The main question arises as to what will happen, should there be a default on the note. This is a situation in which having qualified attorneys, whose primary field involves business acquisitions, pays off. You will want to align yourself with advisors that will help, not hinder the process of buying a business. Another risk in seller financing, from the buyers perspective, is that there may not be a third party assessment of the deal quality, which is what you get from a lender review.

Seller financing is also an alternative to be considered when the underlying tax returns do not support bank financing for the purchase. Many times, for these types of purchases, a combination of seller financing and owner equity will be enough to get the deal closed. Seller financing indicates confidence on the part of the seller that the business will generate enough cash flow for repayment of the loan.

LENDER FINANCING

Now we come to Lender financing. Lender financing refers to both bank and non-bank lenders who provide financing for business acquisitions. It is important to be wary of some loan brokers, who can be helpful, but also have been known to take advantage of small business owners who find themselves in need of fast cash. There are many to be found on the Internet who require significant fees in advance to obtain a business loan for a vulnerable buyer. Careful investigation of these companies or their principals, via Google.com or BBB.com, will often find that the parties behind these companies may have been involved in fraudulent schemes under various company names in the past.

Obviously, lender financing takes more time to fund due to underwriting concerns and closing issues that may arise. This is because there is significant risk on the lender's part. A bank has no upside in a loan, but has 100% downside of losing all its principal and interest. A bank needs to be right 99% of the time to have a profitable loan portfolio. The mortgage market can, and has, collapsed in the past, especially in the sub-prime housing market. While lending institutions may be more cautious (and better regulated) at this time, there is still a great deal of capital that lending institutions are willing to loan out to **qualified** borrowers. The sellers, of course, are out of the deal as they cash out at closing. All of the risk has shifted to the bank, and, of course, the borrower. Some borrowers may prefer this, as they want to sever any connection to the seller at closing. The lenders, however, would prefer some seller note, as it will keep the sellers involved in making sure the transition is smooth.

Combination lender and seller debt
This brings us to the last scenario; a combination of lender debt and seller debt. It has the same timing issues, but should offer all parties involved a stake in making sure the transaction is successful in the coming years. Again, the seller debt is subordinated to the lender, and all parties must agree as to the terms of the financing.

LENDER FINANCING—WHAT THEY LOOK FOR
There are three areas lenders explore when deciding whether or not to lend funds for business acquisitions. They are:
- The historical financial performance of the business
- The transaction structure
- What the borrower brings to the table

Historical Financial Performance
In evaluating the financial performance of the business a lender will first look at the stability of revenue and cash flows. A lender will look for revenue that is flat to rising over the prior three years. Declining revenue is a red flag for underwriters who do not want to finance a sinking ship. If there are legitimate reasons for any decline in the bottom line, they must be clearly explainable.

If a company has been in business for a significant number of years, that also helps a lender be more comfortable. On the other hand, if a seller is departing after two years, it may give the impression that the seller is trying to get out of a bad situation. A company that has been around for a while, and has built up a clientele, is more likely to receive a favorable decision.

Industry ratios will also be compared to the relative size of the company, making sure gross and net margins are in line with like companies.

The last issue which is probably the most important to any lending decision is the quality of cash flow. "Cash is King," as they say in the banking business. It is no different when looking at a business' financial

FINANCING A DEAL

status. The amount of cash a business throws off is used in deciding how much a lender is willing to put at risk. The lenders usually are most conservative when determining a cash flow figure. They will use the most recent three year tax returns for the basis of their decision. If the seller has hidden income or has taken excess deductions, this will affect the chances of a lender issuing a loan. Typically lenders will take net income, add back depreciation, interest and owner salary, and get to a base number. From this they will deduct a salary the new owner will need to cover living expenses. This leaves a net cash flow figure. Most lenders will want a cushion built into the loan as well, which is called a debt service coverage ratio. This can range from 1.2x to 1.5x, depending on the lender and the amount of collateral supporting the loan. Basically, if you have annual debt payment of $100,000 you will need at least $120,000 in net cash flow.

There are other adjustments that can be made to cash flow; rent can be added back if property is being acquired, and pension liabilities as well, since these are not a necessary business expense. Another component in figuring the cash flow figure is outside income. This can come from an other business, which will need to be disclosed, spousal income or rental income. Income from these sources can typically be used to lower the cash needed from the business for living expenses, thus increasing cash flow used for debt. Remember, cash flow from tax returns is the number one tool in deciding business valuation, and in analyzing capacity for repayment of acquisition debt.

TRANSACTION STRUCTURE

The transaction structure includes the purchase price, the down payment of buyer, the structure and term of bank financing, the structure and term of seller financing, and working capital needs.

Purchase Price

The purchase price is one element for lender financing, especially for SBA financing. SBA financing states that the company must be properly valued in order to obtain the government guarantee. Most buyers of main street businesses are looking for a 20-35% return on their equity, which means they will pay 3-5 times owner cash flow (after consideration for fair market owner compensation). Businesses for sale falling within this range will be strongly considered for lender financing with an adequate down payment and qualified buyer. There are many variables that can take place after a purchase wherein a buyer paying too much will get buried if there are any hiccups.

Equity Injection
Buyer down payment is an area that needs proper documentation, and should be provided for upfront. The industry standard for Small Business Association (SBA) financing is around 20% down payment, but as little as 10% and as much as 30% is not uncommon. More recently, professional (partner buyout) and medical practices (dental, medical and veterinary) have been able to obtain 100% financing of acquisitions due to the extremely low rate of loss on these types of deals. The down payment is based upon the total financing package, which can include purchase price of business, working capital, new equipment, soft costs such as attorney and accounting fees, and SBA guarantee fees. The lender will correlate borrower funds with the personal financial statement.

Some areas that have been used to finance a purchase are cash or savings:
- Cash gifts from relatives may be used, but must be verified, along with a gift letter stating that the money is freely given and that no repayment is expected.
- A home equity loan which, of course, requires repayment, can be used, but the source will be taken into consideration when calculating the borrowers living expenses.
- Seller financing is an excellent option if the seller is willing. In many cases, if the buyer is short on funds, a seller note in a stand-by basis (meaning it can accrue interest but not be repaid for a period of time) may be useful. Arrangements like this must be clearly presented to all parties early to avoid surprises at closing. Often, if seller financing is utilized, only 50% of the needed equity injection can come from a seller note.
- The last method that has been gaining some traction recently has been to use IRA/401(k) funds to capitalize a business. The beauty of this program is that it keeps intact the tax deferral and

avoids triggering the tax penalty. These transactions are clearly within the letter of the law as spelled out in the Employee Retirement Income Security Act of 1974 (ERISA). Typically, a service provider prepares documentation and administers the program for a nominal fee. The advantages and disadvantages of using this method are detailed in an addendum to this Chapter.

Debt Structure

Structure of the debt, as it relates to lenders, is based upon term and interest rate of the note. Most business acquisition terms through the SBA are for 10 years. The interest rate can be fixed or variable, but most lenders who use the SBA prefer variable rate financing. The rate is tied to the prime rate and cannot exceed 2.75% over the prime rate. When real estate is involved the borrower can get a longer term, up to 25 years, and often a better interest rate. In addition, a lower down payment will also be discussed, depending upon the percentage of the total package being real estate. Needless to say, but important to note, Adjustable Rate Mortgages (ARMs) may lead to unanticipated and unwanted circumstances, as painfully demonstrated in the housing market crunch that dominated the news in 2007.

Seller financing terms will depend upon whether the money is used as part of the down payment, or if it is in addition to the buyer's fully funded down payment. If it is used for equity in the eyes of the lender, the note will be considered on a stand by basis. This means that no principal or interest payments can be made for a defined period of time, dependent upon the lenders underwriting guidelines. Interest may accrue, and the borrower can request refinancing of this note after several years, if the financial statements support such action. If a seller note is used in addition to the buyer's down payment, the term is negotiable, as long as cash flow covers this debt service. Lenders need to agree to the terms, and the note will be subordinated to the lending institution.

One of the biggest mistake buyers make is underestimating how much working capital they will need after they close the deal. Finding a lender who understands this will keep more buyers in business, as they will be able to absorb unforeseen issues. What happens when vendors will not' give terms, when a key customer goes elsewhere, when customers take longer to pay then they had previously, or when a buyer wants to take advantage of new opportunities that arise?. Initial working capital can cover a lot of these issues. As it is said, banks will lend umbrellas when it is sunny, but demand them back when it rains.

A typical transaction structure, then, may look like this:

Purchase price	$ 800,000
Working capital (for fees and liquidity)	$ 60,000
Total project cost	$ 860,000
Buyer down payment (20%)	$ 172,000
Seller financing (10%)	$ 86,000
Bank loan (70%)	$ 602,000
Total cash at closing	$ 860,000

BUYER QUALIFICATIONS

Once the lender becomes comfortable with the financial performance of the company, it will want to be certain the buyer is qualified. This is the single biggest risk to the lender, since there are so many uncertainties. To become comfortable with the buyer's qualifications, the lender will look at a management resume, personal credit history and personal financial statement.

Work History

The work histories of buyers shed light on the skill sets they will bring, in running prospective businesses. Most lenders will want at least a year of direct industry experience or three years of relevant industry experience. If a buyer has been running a manufacturing facility and now wants to run a restaurant, it will be difficult for a lender to see the correlation. There are ways to help mitigate a buyer's lack of experience. One might be for the buyer to write a small business plan, highlighting how his work experience and developed skills will be used in the new venture. This would show that the buyer has a good understanding of the industry. Another could be to give a small ownership position to someone who does have direct industry experience, whether it is a general manager currently employed at the company or an outside person that is brought in. Franchise purchases may make lenders a bit more comfortable, since there is usually Franchiser training involved, and Franchisers tend to look for strong net worth ownership.

Credit History

It is always a good idea for buyers to check their credit history before pursuing the purchase of a business. Bad personal credit can kill a deal quickly, especially if a bankruptcy has taken place in the past eight years. Buyers can check their credit history by going to www.annualcreditreport.com. This is a service that allows people, once a year, to check their credit history free of charge. It does not give credit scores, but there are sites that will for a small fee. A buyer should read the report carefully, and be prepared to document the reason for any late payments, liens or judgments thoroughly. The credit score most lenders look for is a minimum of 640. If the buyer's score is below 640, he should attempt to repair it before applying for a loan. If this is not feasible, it is possible that bringing in a stronger borrower for part ownership will help mitigate this risk. Lenders are well aware that how you repay your bills personally is a direct reflection of how your business will pay its bills.

Personal Financial Statement

One of the documents lenders will look at is the personal financial statement or the buyer. This is, pretty much, a balance sheet for individuals. The lender will look to see that there is enough liquidity, and that borrower is not going to be hamstrung by the first little problem encountered in the business. When it comes to SBA loans, lenders will look to see if there is additional collateral available, since there often will be a shortfall on the new business assets. The most common collateral requested is a second lien on a person's home or other real estate. The SBA also has rules regarding liquid net worth. If a borrower has $1,000,000 in cash and stocks, they ask why he needs to finance a $300,000 business. The SBA is set up for people who can not get reasonable terms conventionally.

The concept of using OPM (Other People's Money) is not one the SBA appreciates. According to the SBA website, www.sba.org, "The U.S. Small Business Association was created in 1953 as an independent agency of the Federal government to aid, counsel, assist and protect the interests of small business concerns, to preserve free competitive enterprise, and to maintain and strengthen the overall economy of the Nation." In practical terms, the SBA program is used by people who are unable to handle terms like short amortization, high interest rates, or balloon payments, or who have a collateral shortfall.

Buyers must know that they will have to personally guarantee the loan. These are required on all SBA deals for borrowers who have 20% or more ownership, and for most conventional deals as well.

All of the previous factors (and more!) are considered when lenders make a loan decision. Believe it or not, however, there can be is flexibility with regard to bank financing. A strong buyer or strong transaction structure can offset weak financials. Strong financials and a strong buyer can offset a weak transaction structure (from the bank's perspective). Assessing strengths and mitigating weaknesses is what bankers get paid to do—managing risk!

SBA FINANCING

Why SBA financing?

Most transactions are highly levered. Banks traditionally have a hard time financing small deals where risk is higher, and leverage is above 2:1. The SBA program offers longer terms, up to 10 years on business only acquisitions. Most banks want any non-collateralized debt paid back within 1-2 years, thus severely crimping cash flow for a new owner. The biggest issues is that there is usually significant goodwill on business purchases, especially for professional practices. What a borrower is really buying is more than the cash flow stream of the company, although the SBA does not believe that. The transaction might be called an asset sale, but if those assets are not generating cash, it should probably be referred to as a liquidation sale. In some instances, especially with respect to service businesses, 100% financing for goodwill is available, though the borrower may need to pledge personal assets, if available. Cash flow had best be strong as well, for the buyer's benefit, in these transactions. SBA financing helps a lender be comfortable with the above risks, because a portion of any loan loss is guaranteed by the government.

Programs of the SBA

The SBA has two main programs, the 7(a) and the 504 programs.

- The 7(a) loan program is the most common general purpose SBA loan program. Loan proceeds may be used for the purchase of machinery and equipment, inventory, furniture and fixtures, land for construction, building construction, leasehold improvements, real property, working capital, and goodwill. This program can be used for most acquisitions under $3,000,000 by utilizing SBA debt, seller debt, and owner equity.
- The 504 program is a special purpose SBA loan program that provides long term, below market rate, subordinated financing for businesses to expand their operations, help the local economy and create jobs. Eligible project costs include land acquisitions, building acquisitions, building construction, renovations, expansions, or financing of machinery and equipment with a useful life of 10 years or more. The majority of loans will include owner occupied commercial real estate mortgages. As with the 7(a), under the 504 program businesses can purchase property for as little as 10% down. The basic structure with the 504 program is 50% traditional bank financing, 40% SBA loan through a certified development company and 10% equity injection.

Since the SBA program is intended for small businesses there are some eligibility issues to be aware of. For the 7(a) program, depending upon the type of business, according to SIC codes, the eligibility rules are either based upon revenue (for retail, service and construction businesses) or number of employees (for wholesaling and manufacturing businesses). The eligibility standards are often updated, so it is best to check with the lender to be safe.

It is important that professional advisors get serious buyers in front of lenders early in the game. This way they can help qualify the buyers, and give them direction when filling out applications. When applying for and SBA loan, in order to minimize delay in processing, it is important to have all documents readily available. These include:

For the seller:
- Most recent three years business tax returns
- Recent interim financial statements
- IRS form 4506 signed by seller—used to verify tax returns
- Schedule of outstanding debt
- A/R and A/P ageing tied to balance sheet. (stock purchase only)

For the buyer:
- Most recent three year personal tax returns
- Personal Financial Statement
- Statement of Personal History (SBA form 912)
- Management resume

Other documents will be needed along the way, and vary from lender to lender, but these mentioned are pretty standard across the industry.

ALTERNATIVE METHODS OF FINANCING

Business Funding with Retirement Savings

Special thanks to Guidant Financial Group™ for providing the information for this section. When selecting a company to utilize this funding strategy, we highly recommend using Guidant, based on their industry reputation, meticulous attention to detail and their capacity to meet the needs of entrepreneurs. More about this funding option or about Guidant can be learned by visiting www.guidantfinancial.com or calling Guidant directly at (888) 472-4455. The comments below are those of Guidant, and are not those of the author. While this may be eminently suitable for some entrepreneurs, careful consideration must be given as to safety of the business purchased, as well as the potential for loss of retirement savings, before embarking on this funding option.

Determining how to fund a business venture is one of the most important aspects of business ownership. Selecting the most appropriate funding option could ultimately result in the success or failure of the business. With a multitude of funding options available, it is good to research all options to determine which works best for your business purchase.

FINANCING A DEAL

An often overlooked funding option is utilizing one's retirement funds as an investment into the new business. This can be accomplished prior to retirement age, and without taking a distribution or paying penalties. Don't feel badly if this is a new concept for you, since it is for most.

Through an account structure similar to self-directed IRAs and Employee Stock Ownership Plans (ESOP), the purchase of a business or franchise can be made with IRA or 401(k) monies as an *investment* on behalf of that retirement account. It's similar to the concept of investing in stocks and bonds, but, in this case, you're investing in your own business. Please see the next Chapter on ESOPs to explore this option further.

But Wait, There's More!

The more you explore this funding option, the better it looks. Obviously, using one's own hard-earned money is better than using leverage to finance a business. The flexibility of this account structure also allows for multi-party purchases (ideal for husband and wife teams) or for combining with loan money. Providing a chunk of change as a down payment on a loan can make the difference between closing a deal or scrapping the dream. Tapping IRA or 401(k) monies allows individuals not only to secure their business but to launch it with significantly less overhead—translating into greater profits.

Let's take, for example, a typical person looking to purchase a small business for $200,000. Most likely, he will turn to the SBA for help. A 10-year 10.75% SBA loan for that amount, however, could stunt the business's growth for the first 10 years, with the monthly debt payment of roughly $2,700. By using his own retirement funds instead of the SBA loan, his loan payments could be reinvested, instead, into the business. Who wouldn't rather use that money for advertising, signage or salaries?

While growing their business, individuals who use this funding option are also growing their retirement nest egg. Business owners can add up to $45,000 per year, based on 2007 data, to their retirement account through deferrals and contributions (and up to $50,000 if the client is over 50 years of age).

Too Good to Be True?

Nope. This funding option has been available since 1974, when Congress enacted the Employee Retirement Income Security Act (ERISA). At that time, what we've come to know as the IRA and 401(k) came into being, and the responsibility for retirement plan investing shifted from the employer to the employee. For the past few decades, and with only a few exceptions, individuals could choose how and where to invest their retirement money. Because the government wanted to encourage employees to save for their retirement, those investments, however, were to be used for the exclusive purpose of growing their retirement account and not for personal spending sprees.

There are a few reasons why this investment strategy is starting to gain momentum. Every day, thousands of Baby Boomers are crossing the retirement threshold, and they're discovering that their IRAs and 401(k)s just aren't big enough to support a comfortable lifestyle. So they're exploring their retirement account options in ways they never did before. Also, those who are still a few years from retirement age and have accumulated a nice chunk of change in their IRAs are seeking to start making those funds work for them *now*.

Secondly, when ERISA was passed, the banks and brokerage houses took the concept of retirement-account investing to the mass market. As a result, many IRA/401(k) holders presumed that all they could do was purchase stocks, bonds and mutual funds inside their account. But, in reality, there are a near-endless number of investment options available to individuals—including one's own business.

There are a few guidelines that business owners should be aware of and that should be discussed with the financial entity structuring the account. While the Internal Revenue Code sets guidelines that state an IRA may not purchase a business dealing with life insurance or collectibles, specific service providers have some additional guidelines. Guidant Financial Group, one of the largest providers of these structures, sets forth these following guidelines. A business owner must:

- Own a minimum of 5% of the new business personally (based on the amount of retirement money being invested).
- Work for the business a minimum of 1000 hours per year.
- Pay himself a reasonable salary.
- Defer 1% of his salary to the company's 401(k) as soon as he is eligible.
- And offer employees participation in the company's 401(k).

Additional guidelines should be discussed with the financial entity creating this structure, as each situation is unique.

Don't Try This At Home, Kids!

If you're getting the impression that purchasing a business with retirement money may require expert assistance, you'd be absolutely right. The set up involves structuring new customized and conforming retirement accounts, rollovers, the creation of a unique C corporation and careful documentation.

MAKING A GRACEFUL EXIT

At some point, after a long, successful run, and when retirement age has been reached, business owners will eventually want to exit this structure and start taking a distribution. So how does one exit out of this special retirement account strategy? The exit strategy is actually quite simple. Taking distributions will require liquidity. The stock held by the customized 401(k) can be liquidated by either of two routes: sell the company or sell the stock of the company; or go through a corporate stock buy-back.

If there are enough cash reserves available, and the owner decides to invest that money back into his business by buying the stock back from the retirement fund, there are a few steps that need to be taken:

- The price of the stock must be set at Fair Market Value (FMV) by having the value of the company determined through a third-party appraisal.
- The 401(k) must be eliminated as a shareholder in the corporation by having the C corporation use its cash reserves to re-purchase the stock from the 401(k) at the FMV price.

- An S election can then be made, changing the C Corporation to an S Corporation.

There is a calendar issue to be aware of—business owners will want to make the S election before March 15 of any calendar year. An S election made before March 15 is retroactive back to January 1 of that year, freezing the built-in gain. An S election made after March 15 is not effective until the following January, subjecting all company profits to double taxation inherent in a C corporation. So clients will minimize the amount of profit in the company subject to double tax if they make the S election before March 15.

The built-in gain exemption comes into play when the company is sold in the future. Double tax will only apply to the profit attributed to operating their business as a C corporation, before the S election is made. If the business is operated as an S corporation for at least 10 years, there is no double tax on the built-in gain.

What's Not to Love?

A financing strategy that saves money, lowers business overhead, increases success rates, eliminates personal liability, creates tax-deferred savings, builds retirement savings, and allows entrepreneurs to invest in his- or herself... Think you or someone you know could benefit? You may be surprised what a big difference this little bit of knowledge could make when it comes to financing failure or funding success!

Urgent Author's note:
Again, caution is urged when using this funding option. Buyers must thoroughly explore this with their personal expert advisors, and only then contact a reputable, experienced firm like Guidant to explore the possibilities.

CHAPTER SIXTEEN
EMPLOYEE STOCK OWNERSHIP PLANS (ESOP)

KEY POINTS

Unlock the Hidden Value of Your Business

Imagine Selling Your Business For Cash
- Deferring the Capital Gains Tax Indefinitely
- Having the Transaction Financed by a Financial Institution
- Having the Company that You Have Sold Pay Back the Loan With Tax-free Dollars
- Selling a Majority Interest in Your Company and Still Maintaining Control
- Using Loan Proceeds to Expand Acquiring Another Company With Tax-free Dollars
- Creating an "Ownership Culture" in Your Company

Employee Stock Ownership Plans (ESOPs) Are an Often Misunderstood Employee Benefit Plan

Explaining an ESOP

What Makes a Good ESOP Candidate?

Business Owners Face Tremendous Potential Tax "Leakage"

CHAPTER SIXTEEN
EMPLOYEE STOCK OWNERSHIP PLANS (ESOP)

We are indebted to Jerry Shapiro, Managing Partner of RJ Group, for his contribution of the information regarding this little known method of selling a business. He can be reached at RJGroupbbn@aol.com or directly at (732) 462-1859.

UNLOCK THE HIDDEN VALUE OF YOUR BUSINESS
Imagine for a moment:

- **Selling your business for cash** (no stock or seller financing) to a ready, willing and able buyer right in your community, in a private transaction, **at fair market value** (no endless haggling over the price and terms).
- **Deferring the capital gains tax indefinitely** on the sale of part or all of your company.
- Having the transaction financed by a financial institution, and **the company that you have sold, all or part of, paying back the loan with tax-free dollars** (an ESOP is a tax free entity).
- **Selling** a majority interest in your company (as much as 99%) **and still maintaining complete control of your business.**
- Using the loan proceeds to **Expand by acquiring another company with tax-free dollars.**
- **Creating an "ownership culture" in your company** that improves the morale, loyalty and productivity of your employees.

An ESOP can bring this image to reality.

WHAT'S THE MAGIC ABOUT AN ESOP?

Employee Stock Ownership Plans (ESOPs) **are not magic but they are probably one of the most misunderstood employee benefit plans in existence today. It is true they are a tax-qualified retirement plan like a profit-sharing or 401-k plan with two important distinctions:**

1. Employees are required to make **NO** investment. Other plans require employees investments to be diversified.
2. It is the only employee benefit plan that may use corporate credit to finance the buy back purchase of company stock from shareholders. For other plans, this would be a prohibited transaction.

ESOPs are much more than a retirement plan. The owner of a privately held business can sell some or all of his or her business at fair market value to a ready able and willing buyer (the ESOP) and with the proper corporate structure elect to pay no tax on the sale. Or, they can sell a significant portion of their business to diversify their personal net worth and still maintain control of their company. An ESOP can borrow money to finance the transaction and pay down the debt with tax deductible contributions to the ESOP creating a deduction for both the principal payment and the interest. This unique leveraging ability allows business owners to use their ESOP to grow their business by making tax advantaged acquisitions.

Why does the government allow these potent tax advantages to ESOP sponsors? Because ESOPs are a marvelous tool to help companies become more profitable and enable employees to "share in the wealth." And wealth distribution is a major contributing factor to the long-term health of a free and democratic society.

Academic and commercial research studies show that ESOPs motivate employees to higher levels of productivity and profitability.

With all of these advantages, **what's the catch?** The formation and implementation of an ESOP is complex requiring multiple levels of tax, legal, actuarial, financial and administrative expertise. That's where we come in. Our experienced experts meet all of your ESOPs needs.

R&J Group's ESOP Specialists

The R&J Group's independent specialists include a wholly owned subsidiary of one of the largest independent valuation firms in the U.S. with 10 offices across the country and over 70 years of experience. The R&J Group's affiliate specialists create and manage strategic alliances with professional ESOP service providers to deliver comprehensive, "one stop" ESOP services to its clients. The R&J Group's affiliates are comprised of highly skilled and experienced insurance and investment advisors who aid their clients in maximizing their profits during the formation and in working with the established ESOP. Specialized services provided include: feasibility studies, ESOP design and formation, valuation and financial consulting, ESOP financing, life insurance funding strategies, repurchase liability studies, preparation of legal and regulatory documents, IRS filings and plan administration services. You can use one or all of our services depending on your needs and we commonly work in tandem with your existing advisors. The R&J approach allows you to delegate the responsibility of coordinating and directing the day to day activities of five or six ESOP specialists and focus on what you do best—running your business.

The R&J Group and our Affiliates "quarterback" the process on your behalf. The process ensures that you do not make the decision to implement an ESOP in isolation. Working with you, full consideration is given to your personal financial needs, other employee benefit plans, the needs of your shareholders and key people as well.

Why should you consider the services of the R&J Group's and its affiliates?

- The employee benefit and ESOP legal and regulatory world is complex requiring specialized expertise.
- The R&J Group's professional service providers are nationally recognized experts in their respective fields.
- Our experts remove the burden from your shoulders, of managing the feasibility and implementation process required to establish an ESOP.
- The R&J Group's affiliate project management experts help keep your plan implementation process on time and within budget.

- Our experts remove the burden from you and your staff of keeping up with and interpreting all the "gray areas" and inevitable regulatory revisions that exist in the ESOP and employee benefit world today.
- Since plan administration is of major importance and is a core service of one of our affiliates, your plan administrator will be in constant contact with you after your plan is installed.
- Our unique, holistic approach will consider your personal needs and those of your shareholders and employees in any potential transaction.
- The R&J Group can introduce you to other business transition professionals such as merger and acquisition or investment banking specialists if it's determined that an ESOP is not the right solution for you.

WHAT MAKES A GOOD ESOP CANDIDATE?

A business owner with any of the following goals should consider the advantages of an ESOP:

- Improve worker performance through equity incentives.
- Enable you, as the owner, or all current shareholders to sell your/their stock, to the ESOP, on a tax free basis. (Postpone Capital Gains Tax indefinitely.)
- Enable you and other shareholders to diversify your/their holdings in the company on a tax free basis and still maintain control of the company.
- Buy-out inactive minority shareholders on a tax-deductible basis for the corporation and a tax-free basis for the selling shareholders.
- Grow the company through acquisition on a tax free basis.
- Share equity in the company with employees to attract, retain and reward a productive workforce while retaining complete control.

In addition, the best ESOP candidates have:
- Eligible payroll of approximately $800,000 or more.
- At least a three year business history.

- A business with a current minimum market value of at least $3 million.
- C or S corporation tax status.
- Capable successor managers.
- Good revenue and earnings history creating the ability to secure financing.

What's the first step to determine if an ESOP is right for you and your Company?

The first step in determining if an ESOP is right for you and your company is to complete a feasibility process with the assistance of the The R&J Group's team. The feasibility process starts with a thorough review of your goals and objectives. After establishing your goals and objectives and reviewing your Company's financial statements, we offer two levels of feasibility analysis:

1. Preliminary Analysis which includes:
- A current estimated market value of your company.
- Modeling and structuring a basic transaction based on your goals and objectives.
- Evaluating the impact of the ESOP transaction on the company's current financial statements and cash flow.
- Assessing your financing options.

2. Feasibility Study

Our Feasibility Study is a more rigorous and expanded version of our Preliminary Analysis. The Feasibility Study will consider:
- Projections of the net income and cash flow of your company into the future both with and without an ESOP.
- Projections of covered payroll of participating employees.
- Thorough analysis of both the pre-transaction and post-transaction value of your business.
- Forecast employee accumulations in the ESOP and in your other benefit plans.
- Forecast the net wealth effect of the transaction on you and all other shareholders.

- Analyze the effect of the transaction on corporate governance issues.
- Prepare an employee communications plan.
- Forecast the repurchase obligation created by the installation of the plan.

If the analysis concludes that an ESOP is feasible for your Company, The R&J Group's team will prepare a project management plan to establish a timeline and budget that meets your requirements.

3. Strategy Development

- Goal & Objective Setting—determine if an ESOP can help you achieve your business and personal goals.
- Feasibility Analysis—conduct rigorous quantitative analysis to determine if an ESOP is financially feasible and advisable for your company.
- Alternatives to Consider—compare an ESOP with other potential solutions.
- Cost/Benefit Analysis– determine if the benefits of implementing an ESOP for your company exceed the benefits achieved with other options.

4. Strategy Implementation

- Plan Design and ESOP Formation—drafting the necessary legal, corporate, shareholder and employee documents and agreements to tax qualify the plan with the IRS and make it effective in the eyes of the regulatory authorities.
- Plan Trustee—the ESOP trustee ensures that the creation and maintenance of the plan adheres to fiduciary standards.
- Business Valuation—must be conducted by an independent, third party qualified appraiser to establish a fair market value of the business according to Revenue Ruling 59-60.
- Financing Alternatives—compare internal versus external funding for the plan. Secure financing for the ESOP if required.
- 1042 Investment Planning—adherence to the IRS requirements

enabling a selling shareholder to indefinitely defer the capital gain on the sale of their shares to the ESOP.
- Repurchase Obligations—forecasting your obligation to repurchase the shares of departing ESOP participants and evaluating pre-funding strategies.
- Employee Communications—communication strategies to maximize the desired employee productivity results.
- Administration & Compliance—the administrator must collect and maintain all required participant data, prepare the management and participant reports, and ensure that the plan complies with government reporting and disclosure requirements.

THE CHALLENGE

Business Owners Face Tremendous Potential Tax "Leakage" in the Life Cycle of Owning their Business:

Life Stage	Challenge	Leakage	
Building and managing the business for growth	Income taxes	Pre-tax income:	$16.67 million
		Income taxes (40%):	$6.67 million
		Net income:	$10 million
Transitioning the business during the owner's lifetime	Capital gains taxes	Net proceeds upon sale:	
		Selling price:	$10 million
		Transaction fees (7%):	$700,000
		Cost basis:	$0
		Gain:	$9.3 million
		Taxes (20%):	$1.86 million
		Net proceeds:	$7.44 million
Passing the owner's estate to the next generation	Death taxes	Net proceeds at death:	$7.44 million
		Taxes (55%):	$4.09 million
		Transfer to heirs:	$3.35 million
		Total tax leakage:	$11.98 million

The Big Picture
$16.67M in hard earned income, after years of work, building a business worth $10M after tax netted the owner $7.44 million. Upon the Seller's death, after taxes and fees, the remainder passed onto his/her heirs would be approximately $3.35 million. Total tax leakage: nearly $11.98 million.

Required Planning
While this example is purposely over simplified, it illustrates the tremendous tax loss that can occur during your lifetime if you don't engage in planning at three levels:

1. The optimal business strategies to minimize current income taxes and maximize employee motivation to grow the value of the business.
2. Strategies to enable you to exit your company with minimal disruptions to the business and maximum net sales proceeds in your pocket.
3. Strategies that maximize the net proceeds you can pass on to your heirs.

This can be accomplished with an ESOP.

(Author's Note: Since this is a highly specialized field, we have reproduced the chapter exactly as R&J Group submitted it. If you have questions concerning the feasibility of using ESOP, or simply for more information, call The R&J Group at (732) 462-1859. They are eager to help readers of **Exit Strategy.***)*

CHAPTER SEVENTEEN
THE ART OF CLOSING A DEAL

KEY POINTS

CPR—Control, Power, Rescue
- Know Basic Selling Techniques
- The Importance of Speed in Closing a Deal

A Deal Will Close More Quickly When:
- Everyone is Prepared
- Everyone Wants to Make the Deal

Problems and Solutions

CHAPTER SEVENTEEN
THE ART OF CLOSING A DEAL

For a deal to close quickly, it must be a first-rate deal for both the buyer and the seller. Deals go to contract and close faster when both the buyer and the seller are very motivated.

However, very often, we find that either the buyer or the seller holds the perception that he is not getting a fair shake. Assuming the broker knows that the deal to which both have agreed is the very best deal for all parties involved, it is the broker's obligation to make the deal happen, and to close it successfully.

There are most certainly many time-tested techniques used to close a deal, whether it be selling television sets ("Would you like the 42-inch or the 45-inch size? "), or buying a new car "Do you want the bronze or the silver model?), or getting someone to sign any contract ("Would you like to use my pen or yours?"). The "art" comes in when you are considering when and how to apply these techniques.

Not asking the right question, preferably at the right time, is the most common situation leading to a sale not closing. Every step you need in order to get you closer to a profitable sale, such as setting up a meeting or properly qualifying a buyer, will come only if the right questions are asked.

Often, it's not only the questions that matter, but how they are presented.

The best salespeople are merchandise or product advisors. They help potential buyers make decisions that are good for them. When selling a business, keeping the focus on the benefits that will accrue to the buyer will make the sale. The ability to do that makes the difference between an average salesperson and a great one.

As an owner and seller, your job is to have your company presented in such a way that the buyer will be able to see the benefit of owning your company. It is usually best that you not, however, be the one presenting this information to the buyer. Just watch how a good business broker can do this! Should a deal start coming apart at the end, and many tend to do so, an experienced broker will put it back together using skills learned over many years and through many deals.

A deal will close more quickly if:
- Everyone wants to make the deal.
- Everyone is prepared in advance.

THE IMPORTANCE OF SPEED IN CLOSING A DEAL
Time kills deals!

Speed in closing a sale is vitally important. The longer it takes to close a deal, the greater the likelihood things can go wrong. Examples abound: the economy goes suddenly sour, or interest rates may go up. Let us look at an actual case in which a hardware and home furnishings store was well on its way to being sold to a motivated buyer at our Manheim Business Brokers office. It was suddenly rumored that a Home Depot would be opening in the town next to the business our buyer had his eye on. Whether the rumor was true or not, the deal was gone. The same could be true for a Mom and Pop card store getting ready to go to closing on a sale, when a 50% off card store or a major franchise opens down the block.

I remember a French restaurant we had on the verge of being sold until anti-French sentiment came to the fore during the early days of the first Iraq conflict. A local boycott caused the owner's business to fall 50% in a few months, and the deal was off. A steak restaurant had its sale fall through when Mad Cow Disease was being talked about in the news. Sudden sickness or death of a buyer or seller can also happen during the course of the deal, as can a sudden divorce or breakup of partners.

So much can go wrong when there are delays in the sale process. There may also be seller's remorse—"Maybe I should hold on to the business a while." There may be buyer's remorse—"What am I getting into?" or "What if I can't improve sales?"

Whatever the case may be, when a deal seems to be dying, it is the broker's job to resuscitate it. A good broker has learned the **CPR** (**C**ontrol, **P**ersuasion, **R**escue) needed to do so. He is prepared for it.

When given the responsibility of selling a business, brokers realize their obligation to the seller. They use all the tools at their disposal to control the event, and bring an effective, timely and profitable sale to conclusion. Most brokers adhere to McLuhan's affirmation regarding the "folklore of an industrial society"—Promotion/Marketing/Persuasion. It takes all three to be an effective business broker or merger and acquisition specialist. We can promote a purchase or merger, and market it aggressively. We must be able to gently persuade both parties, when we know it to be true, that the deal is a win/win situation for both.

So how can you help speed matters up in order to see the sale of the business through? Preparation is extremely important. Line up your advisors. And be absolutely certain that all relevant documents are available the minute the seller decides to proceed. These documents include, but are not necessarily limited to:

- Three years' tax returns
- Bank statements for the current year
- Invoices for major expenditures
- Equipment purchase dates and costs
- Depreciation schedules
- Spreadsheets with income, expenses, profit analysis
- Copies of leases
- A lawyer who specializes in the selling of businesses

NEGOTIATIONS

Many people are uncomfortable with negotiation. We do not go shopping in supermarkets and offer 75% of the marked price, and we are too quick to pay full price quoted in other retail shops when a bit of bargaining is expected (bargaining is much more common in Europe and Mexico, for example).

Studies show the number one thing people dislike about buying a car is the negotiation process. No matter what the result, the buyer feels he did not bargain well enough, and the seller is upset by not making his anticipated profit on a sale. There is resentment on both sides.

That's why a business broker or merger and acquisition specialist is essential to the lucrative sale of your business. Business brokerage is all about negotiation. A good business brokerage aims to create an environment where negotiation is comfortable.

A broker orchestrates the sale from beginning to end. To begin with, the broker must ask the seller, using the seller's data as presented, how much a buyer can make per year. Most often, someone working a business grossing under $2,000,000 makes 10% to 20% on gross sales per year, as a guideline. The broker then relays this information to the buyer. It is likely that the seller is telling the truth, because mortgage money will not be available to buyers if the seller is dishonest. Very often, a problem arises when the non-recast financials are presented to the buyer's accountant. An accountant, unaware of recasting and EBITDA methods, will most often advise the buyer not to buy based on the financials. A broker, knowing this and educating the buyer (and accountant) beforehand, can rescue a deal before it melts away.

In larger businesses, the sale price is determined based on 2 to 10 times yearly earnings. In small businesses, this formula does not work because they are often "cash" businesses. (Cash may not have been taken into account in the financials. Financials are intentionally prepared to show no profit or a loss for the sole purpose of paying no taxes). Again, a buyer must know all this before non-knowledgeable advisors scare him off. If the broker can honestly see the benefits to the buyer of purchasing a business, it is the broker's obligation to point this out. The broker's job is to stress the benefits to the buyer, without ever misleading for his own profit.

Bargaining should never be done between a buyer and seller directly. There **must** be an intermediary. A broker can go back and forth as many times as needed to craft, in good faith, a fair and mutually beneficial sale. Buyers and sellers cannot do so without weakening the position of both. If a business broker is not involved, then the respective attorneys should do the negotiations and report back to their clients. But be very careful here! I have personally seen attorneys making business decisions and renegotiating business prices where the deals quickly fell apart.

LETTER OF INTENT

As negotiations proceed, a proper Letter of Intent or binder is mandatory as an aid to preventing snags.

A binder is a small good faith deposit. A Letter of Intent to Purchase a Business is the prelude to a definitive agreement. It must be preceded by a signed Confidentiality Agreement between the parties. The Letter of Intent confirms the Buyer's and Seller's mutual intentions with respect to the potential deal, and describes the business being acquired. In legal parlance, the "Buyer is agreeing to acquire substantially all of the assets, tangible and intangible, owned by Seller that are used in, or necessary for the conduct of, its business, including, without limitation, intellectual property, fixed assets, customer lists, as well as goodwill, all free and clear of any security interests, mortgages, liens or other encumbrances." It specifies the Consideration (purchase price), and is contingent upon the Buyer's Due Diligence Review (see Appendix).

EXAMINATION OF DOCUMENTS

Promptly following the execution of the letter of intent, the Seller agrees to allow complete examination of financial, accounting and business records, contracts and other legal documents. Now is the time to bring out the RECAST earnings statements, using EBITDA and all other methods of showing the business in the best light.

We have seen deals collapse when a Seller decides to hold back on one or more requested documents, whether through ignorance as to the necessity of cooperation or sheer obstinacy. Both parties must agree to cooperate to complete due diligence expeditiously. There is usually a standard clause which indicates that the purchase is subject to the

Seller having continued to conduct business "in the ordinary course" during the period between the date of the Letter of Intent and the date of closing, and there having been "no material adverse change in the Seller's business, financial condition or prospects." As mentioned in previous chapters, it is the duty of the Seller to continue to run the business being sold as if he were planning on staying forever.

The next step in reaching a closing is a Definitive Purchase Agreement. All terms and conditions of the proposed deal are stated, to be negotiated, agreed and executed by the Buyer and the Seller.

FINANCING

While this will be dealt with in greater depth in a future chapter, it should be obvious at this point that nothing will stifle a deal faster than the Buyer not being able to come up with the money needed to make the purchase. A good business broker will have pre-qualified the Buyer. Credit scores, D&B ratings, financial statements and personal interviews will have led to presentation of a suitable candidate. But that person must also be aware that, since financials as filed with the IRS may not simply poorly portray the true value of the business, they may lead to a bank's refusal to lend money on that basis.

In view of the above, the Broker must educate the Buyer to understand that banks will not lend money (SBA loan) on the purchase of some businesses because there is no collateral, unless the Buyer puts up a house or other collateral. This, of course, can be dangerous for a Buyer. Businesses must have debt repayment ability to get a loan, the reason being that a Bank does not have the skill to come in and run the business should they take it as collateral. With owner financing, the owner has the skill (if not the desire) to take the business as collateral, then take it back and run it should the Buyer default on its notes. It is often a better idea for a seller to loan the money (Purchase Money Mortgage) to the buyer. The Seller will lend the Buyer money only if he knows the business will be good enough for the Buyer to be able to pay the notes. Another option might be, with proper planning of an Exit Strategy, an Employee Stock Ownership Program as explored elsewhere in this volume.

CLOSING THE DEAL

We have located acquisition candidates, evaluated investment opportunities, structured the deal, raised financing and done our due diligence. Now it is up to the lawyers. What you, as Buyer or Seller, must do, is to make sure the lawyer has prepared all necessary documents beforehand, such as employment contracts or restrictive covenants. You should review these documents, and, if there is language you do not understand, ask questions to clarify that. At the closing, it would be wise to review all the documents before you sign them. Once you have all this done, the only thing left to do is sign the check, shake hands all around, and get busy: as the buyer, start implementing all the great ideas you have on how to improve the business; as the seller, start instituting your next move—business or pleasure, another project or some well deserved leisure. Congratulations. If you are going on to another business venture, we hope you have learned that now is the time to plan your Exit Strategy for a year or ten or twenty years from now.

PHILOSOPHICAL ADVICE

Think win/win

Put first things first

Begin with the end in mind

Be proactive

Seek first to understand, then be understood

Sharpen the saw (improve mentally and physically)

Synergize (the whole is greater than the parts)

In 1990, a leadership guru named Stephen R. Covey wrote a book entitled *The 7 Habits of Highly Effective People*. He put forth basic rules for achieving success in one's personal and professional life. These rules apply in selling and buying a business, and in facilitating such deals. First and foremost, he stressed thinking "win/win." Any deal moves more quickly when both participants are happy. Putting first things first always helps. Taking care of the important things early in negotiations makes the small things more manageable as they arise. At least they will not be deal breakers. Another way of stating that is,

"Don't sweat the small stuff," the corollary of which is, "It's all small stuff."

Beginning with the end in mind keeps you goal oriented. Know what you want to accomplish and work toward that goal. Don't get detoured and lost along the way. Being proactive will grease the way toward closing a deal. Anticipate what has to be done, and have the means or plans to accomplish that at your fingertips.

If you seek to understand, then to be understood, you are in the driver's seat. I have always said that nobody learns anything while he or she is talking—only when listening. If you do not understand the needs of your buyer or seller, you can never act to meet those needs or desires.

Mental awareness and sharpness will enable a seller, ready to leave a business, to plan an exit strategy, and a buyer to be sharp enough to take advantage of, and not miss, an opportunity. And synergy, making a whole greater than its parts, is the basic tenet of any merger or acquisition.

In 2006, Covey wrote *The 8th Habit: From Effectiveness to Greatness* (Free Press) in which he advises, "Find your voice and inspire others to find theirs." Leadership, he says, is not telling others what to do, but communicating to them their potential, so they may willingly contribute to a company's success. Whether starting a business or winding down, empower those with whom you work to be an asset, and all will benefit from that input. In fact, the employee you empower may wind up being your buyer, and perhaps even your employer, should you stay on.

BEWARE OF HOURLY FEES IF POSSIBLE

No matter how well prepared you may be, snags do occur at the very end of the purchase process. In fact, most brokers agree that more time is spent on a deal at the conclusion than at the beginning. Egos get involved, personalities clash. It sometimes takes superhuman efforts to calm both parties down to conclude a sale, even if the buyer and seller want to do so. The business broker becomes confidante, psychologist, and even baby sitter. The value (and mettle) of a broker is often most tested at such times.

THE ART OF CLOSING A DEAL

Assuming all parties to the transaction agree—the Seller wants to sell and the Buyer wants to buy—why isn't closing the deal always a piece of cake? Certainly, problems may surface at the last minute, but they can be overcome. Occasionally, the legal consultants on either side may feel the need to delay a closing. A minor snag, one which may easily be handled after closing between two parties of good will, becomes an insurmountable obstacle. Perhaps the attorneys are intent on totally protecting their clients. Perhaps they want to make their overall efforts more appreciated by clients. Or perhaps, in rare instances, a large hourly fee may come in the way of a rapid closing of a deal.

As noted above, "A deal will close more quickly if everyone wants to make the deal." As much as we respect the legal profession, it is not unusual for attorneys, often believing they are acting in the best interests of their respective clients, to raise questions which might seem inconsequential (and often are) to the involved parties, at or prior to closing. This is why we strongly recommend that both buyers and sellers hire attorneys who are willing to take the case on a fixed fee basis. In fact, some attorneys will take a case based upon a commission structure that requires a deal to be **concluded** in order to earn **any** fee.

The way this works would be to set a percentage of the sale price, usually 1% to 1.5% of the total, as the attorney's fee **IF** the deal closes. If the deal falls apart, the lawyer gets **no** fee. This usually ends up benefiting the buyer and the seller, since all parties are eager to conclude the deal rather than dicker over unimportant points.

We are not suggesting attorneys on either side neglect their clients' interests, but rather that, if all parties are eager to close, and there are no **major** impediments that can not be worked out at a later date, having all parties motivated leads to smoother closings. We **are** suggesting that an hourly rate is not a good thing in hiring a legal expert, especially for a business sale, and a fixed fee (plus disbursements) or a negotiated contingency fee, if ethical in your state, might be worth pursuing, if the deal is a simple sale.

HOWEVER, IF YOU NEED THE BEST, YOU WILL NOT GET HIM OR HER UNLESS YOU PAY THE PRICE!

In a transaction in which there are many potential legal issues, **do not look for a bargain.** It is unlikely you will get the best in the field under conditions that you, yourself, lay down. There are many circumstances in which getting a bargain when choosing a consultant may be a very costly decision. Use good judgment.

PROBLEMS AND SOLUTIONS

Nobody ever said buying or selling a business would be problem-free. This book is aimed at helping you avoid problems as much as possible, but problems do arise.

PROBLEM: The buyer runs in to a temporary problem with financing.

SOLUTION: Even if you prefer not to do so, in order to expedite a sale, the seller may have to take paper. Taking paper indicates to the buyer that you have confidence in his ability to run the business. It also means a continual income flow, so don't dismiss the possibility and ruin the sale at the last minute. A bird in the hand is worth several in the bush, and a different qualified buyer may not come around that quickly.

PROBLEM: The seller wants to sell it himself without a broker, in order to save a commission.

SOLUTION: While it is possible to sell a business without a broker, it is rare that the seller will (a) get the best price, or (b) have the largest pool of prospective buyers. A good broker might create an auction, or bidding war, that will effectively make up for any commission charged. In addition, time is a factor. A broker will certainly be able to sell a business more quickly, and time is money.

Alternatively, the seller can try to negotiate a cap on the commission if possible. Or he might arrange for a bottom line price with any overage being split with the broker. Another possibility might be to have a broker find a buyer who is willing to pay the commission, although this is rare.

PROBLEM: The buyer discovers at the last minute that there are problems with liens against the seller, or lease issues.

SOLUTION: Business sales often go awry when a buyer finds that important information affecting the business has been withheld—an act that may constitute fraud. The seller's attorney and all other interested parties, including the business broker, must be told everything that may affect the sale. They can prevent such a happening. That said, there is really no substitute for effective due diligence on the part of the buyer and his legal and financial advisors. If a last minute snafu occurs, short of walking away from the deal, a buyer might, with legal advice, be able to close, leaving a reasonable amount in escrow until such issues can be resolved.

PROBLEM: The lease on the property or equipment is expiring.

SOLUTION: There is no substitute for anticipating this in advance. Real estate leases should be evaluated as soon as a decision to sell is contemplated, especially if a business is tied to its location. We have had many instances in which the landlord had to be compensated financially for allowing a buyer to take over or extend a lease, often with increases added on. A buyer with a strong credit history must be presented in such a manner that the landlord will see the benefit to having such a tenant, especially as compared to having an empty property.

PROBLEM: Key employees hear about the impending sale and decide to leave.

SOLUTION: Departure of key employees during a sale will very often kill a deal. It is important that such employees not hear about the pending sale from a third party. It is critical to determine which employees will be crucial to the new owner's success, and make their remaining during and following the transaction rewarding to them.

PROBLEM: From K.B.:
"I was a business broker for three years. In each deal there was a "moment of truth" in the final stage, where it was either going to fall apart of go to closing. That moment usually involved either financing or inventory discrepancies, with the latter being more prevalent. When I sold a lumber yard, the inventory was off by $200,000, though the owner had sworn his "perpetual inventory system" was highly accurate.

Apparently, he forgot to do annual inventories to reconcile his routine counts."

SOLUTION: Do inventory checks when relevant before the closing date, and make certain the selling price reflects that.

PROBLEM: The buyer has no assets and a less than perfect credit score.

SOLUTION: At the height of the credit crunch in 2008, we had a dental office grossing $1,500,000 sold for the bargain rate of $675,000. In better times, the buyer's DDS degree alone, combined with the obvious value inherent in a busy high gross practice, would have gotten her a loan. We found a mortgage broker locally who dealt with Asian banks. Though he charged the buyer a 5% fee, he was able to get her an $800,000 loan at very favorable rates. A good business broker will have such sources of financing available. Buyers should not hesitate to use the broker's knowledge and experience. Other brokers reading this book are welcome to call the author, Sheldon Manheim, at (516) 520-2000, for referrals to our finance sources as needed. For future editions, we welcome reader responses describing problems and solutions. Should you run into a problem, we will be happy to have one of our experienced brokers assist you if you call.

CHAPTER EIGHTEEN
WHAT THE BUYER WANTS TO KNOW

 **KEY POINTS**

The Buyer of Your Business Will be Asking Himself:
- Do I Really Want to Own a Business?
- What Sort of Business Do I Want to Own?
- Have I Considered Buying a Franchise?

Questions to Consider
- How Long Has the Operation Been in Business?
- Why is the Owner Selling?
- Is the Purchase Price Negotiable?
- Can the Buyer Afford the Purchase?
- Show Recast Earnings

Is All Income Being Reported?

Other Factors to Consider
- Inventory
- Appraisal
- Location
- Maintenance
- Put Up Your Antennae

- Determine Future Profitability
- Analyze Accounts Receivable and Payable
- Check For Liens
- Thoroughly Review Lease
- Inspect All Inventory and Equipment
- Conduct an Independent Business Appraisal

CHAPTER EIGHTEEN
WHAT THE BUYER WANTS TO KNOW

Business ownership is the American Dream. Our goal as business brokers has been to help as many people as we can realize that dream, and, at the same time, prevent them from walking into a nightmare. While this chapter is aimed at helping the prospective seller to be forewarned and forearmed to deal with relevant inquiries, a prospective buyer of a business should read this and learn what would be important in his or her considerations, as well. As we have repeatedly said, a deal is good if it is a win/win situation.

DOES THE BUYER REALLY WANT TO OWN A BUSINESS?

Many people say they want to own a business, but not all are aware of the positive and negative aspects of business ownership. It's great to be your own boss. But some people would rather work 9-5, and go home without worrying about earnings or orders that did not come in that day, or what bills to pay, or products to develop or market. An owner reaps rewards, but makes sacrifices as well. As science fiction writer Robert Heinlein wrote, "TANSTAAFL—There Ain't No Such Thing As A Free Lunch!"

WHAT SORT OF BUSINESS DOES HE WANT TO OWN?

What are the buyer's interests and abilities? What experience does he have? What amount does he feel comfortable in investing in a business? (The buyer must be pre-qualified. Is he really ready to be an owner?) How large a company does he want to run? What financing will he need? What income does he need to generate? Does he want a cash cow or is he willing to buy a turnaround business? What are his greatest strengths? What are his weaknesses? Does he want to manage the business, or just be an investor? Where does he want to live? Is he willing to commute?

How will he search for the right kind of business? Word of mouth? Newspaper listings? Referrals? Industry magazines? The internet? All these are doable, but the search can be shortened by using a competent, knowledgeable business broker familiar with the area, both geographical and type of business, a buyer is exploring.

Nationally, according to the Association of Business Brokers, 90% of those coming to a broker to buy a particular business will decide upon a different type of business, when presented with appropriate opportunities to do so. (That does not include specialized fields, of course, like plumbers, chefs, professionals and others.) A good businessman can do well in any environment, as long as it is not narrowly specialized. The moral is, "Keep your options open."

IS THE BUYER READY TO BUY A BUSINESS?
The business broker will have already asked these questions. If you are on your own, you should ask: Have you selected and spoken to a good accountant, attorney or lender? Is financing in place, i.e., are you pre-approved for an amount sufficient to buy the business and still have working capital? Will you want me, as the seller to take paper? (According to a national survey, 70-75% of sellers do.) If I do take paper, what down payment are you ready to make? (Down payments, if you do take paper, ordinarily are not more than one year's recast profits.)

A broker will have already pointed out that buying an established business may be more expensive than starting a business from scratch, but it is usually much less risky to do so. In taking over an existing customer base and location, a buyer has a major head start in earning a good income. In addition, purchase of new fixtures and equipment is much more costly than buying serviceable fixed assets from the seller.

No federal tax is due when you buy a business, but buyers should beware that they are not assuming outstanding tax liabilities, or facing potential tax audits or bills for years before taking over the business. Due diligence is extremely important here on the part of the buyer, and total honesty is mandatory on the part of the seller. In a recent potential sale, the buyer reneged the day before scheduled closing because his new attorney finally was able to discover undisclosed debts, overstated earnings, overvalued inventory and pending lawsuits. Even the accounts receivable that looked solid proved to have been uncollectible, and some of the inventory was defective or dated. His previous attorney was not business savvy. Having him for a bargain price almost became a costly disaster.

BUYING A BUSINESS OR A FRANCHISE?

(Sellers will use these features to encourage the sale of a business. Buyers must evaluate the relevance of these features to their individual needs.)

Advantages of Buying an Existing Business:
1. Actual results rather than pro-forma.
2. Immediate cash flow: you can use cash flow to pay the notes and have some income for yourself right away.
3. Trained employees in place.
4. Equipment at far less cost than if purchased new.
5. Established suppliers and credit.
6. Established customers and referral business.
7. Existing licenses and permits.
8. Training by the Seller: Seller will teach Buyer everything the Buyer needs to know.
9. The availability of owner financing.
10. You can take everything they are doing and improve on it.

Advantages of buying a Franchise:
1. Known name means instant recognition.
2. Proven product or service.

3. Ongoing support means you are in business for yourself but not by yourself.
4. More than 90% of new franchises are successful. (But re-sales are, in general, a much better deal.)
5. Operating system in place—all the mistakes have already been made and rectified.
6. Opportunity to add additional units within the franchise system.
7. Training by the seller and the franchise company.
8. The availability of owner financing.
9. Often, when insurance providers are involved, as in eye stores, a franchise guarantees a directed and motivated clientele.

QUESTIONS SELLERS WILL BE ASKED

Buyers must ask these questions.
Sellers must be prepared to answer them.

How long has the operation been in business?

A business with a long track record will be well known in the area. People are used to visiting the business, adding to the value of Goodwill. If the business has been owned by the same person or persons all that time, so much the better.

Why is the owner selling?

One important question to be asked is the reason for the owner's selling. Often, it is self-evident. An owner is ill or retiring, or perhaps moving to a distant location. However, if the buyer perceives that he is moving because he can't make a living in the business any more, the buyer must be sure he can turn things around quickly, **and** get the business at a price that takes into account declining sales or increased overhead. The more valid the reason for the sale, the more realistic the seller will be in considering a buyer's offer. However, a buyer must keep in mind that after five or six years or more, people do get restless, or "burn-out" sets in, or people look for new challenges. Why the seller is selling is an important question—have the answer ready.

Is the purchase price negotiable?

You, as a seller, have a particular number in mind, and are entitled to ask for that amount. However, if the numbers provided do not support that figure, negotiations are certainly in order. A careful buyer checks out fair market value, replacement value and book cost. The buyer may wish to use a method of appraisal that differs from the one or two used by the seller. We address the alternate methods of appraisal elsewhere in this volume.

If a seller has many other interested buyers, negotiation efforts may be limited. If an owner is desperate, and must sell, the buyer is in a very strong position. The expression, **BATNA**, **B**est **A**lternative **T**o a **N**egotiated **A**greement, comes into play. It works both ways. If the buyer has many choices, and you want to be the one he chooses, your negotiation advantage as a seller is reduced.

In general, a deal that is fair to all parties is the ideal arrangement. A cordial relationship pre-closing will be advantageous for all parties, if it can be maintained. If tempers cannot be controlled, let the advisors do the negotiating.

Can the buyer afford the purchase?

Does the buyer have enough capital for the purchase and for working capital, as well as an amount set aside for contingencies?

Initial cash flow is often a problem, which must be addressed when considering financing requirements. It is always best for him to be pre-approved for an amount greater than the amount he expects to pay for the business itself. Some owners include accounts receivable in the purchase price, allowing a cushion for the new owner during the first few months.

It would be important to provide audited financial statements for the previous three years, and copies of the seller's tax returns for that period, as well. A sales tax report to substantiate sales volume claims, if available, should be offered on request. Current records should clearly and completely show what the business is doing. The financial records of the practice are a good indication of how well the practice has been doing over the years. Keep in mind that tax records are not designed to show the business in the best light; no one likes to pay more taxes than they have to, and the owners of businesses are no different. See the chapter on Recasting, and point this all out to the prospective buyer.

A business forecast will show the buyer what he can expect. Current and projected cash flow, sales and profits can be used to determine future profitability. A budget and analysis of accounts receivable and payable must be provided.

OTHER IMPORTANT CONSIDERATIONS
Keep negotiations cordial and honest
If a deal just doesn't feel right to a buyer, there is usually a reason. Due diligence then becomes even more important to him. It is an aphorism that time kills deals, and, when a buyer is given the impression that all is not right, there will not be a rush in to do a deal. If everything is presented in a way that will keep the antennae from being raised, the deal will go smoothly. If a buyer feels pushed to act impulsively, he may fear less than perfect results, and delay the sale or walk away.

Look at recast earnings
Tax returns are rarely helpful. You must provide RECAST earnings (see previous chapter on Recasting) to discover how much in expenses are really perks. Look at non-cash items, such as depreciation, (see EBITDA chapter above), as well as business use of home and vehicles, "business trips" that are really vacations, etc. A professional business broker, happy to assist in a sale, can point these items out to a buyer. Buyers must know that recast earnings will be much more likely to indicate the true earnings of a business, especially that of a professional or of a sole proprietor.

Financial records are only history. There are no guarantees that they will or can be duplicated or repeated. All of your profits are future. In the final analysis, the financial records of the practice are an indicator of what the business has done. What a buyer does with its future is up to him!

Is all the income being reported?
Can anyone determine if you, as a seller, are reporting all income? The simple answer is NO! A seller will often tell a buyer, off the

record, just how much cash is not being reported. This can be in the thousands of dollars, especially in primarily cash type businesses. This "underground economy" has been well-documented and is in the billions of dollars nationally. The problem in using these underground dollars in evaluating how much you are asking as a sales price is that you can not document it. Sellers have no way of proving these amounts. Unreported income can not be substantiated, no matter what the seller whispers in the buyer's ear. If you factor that income into your asking price, and it turns out not to be true, to whom can a buyer turn? Certainly not the courts. In determining whether a business is the right one for him, and how much to pay for it, a prudent buyer will primarily base the decision on the real figures, able to be documented, which are supplied by the seller.

We had a dental practice in which the sellers were asking an extraordinary sum, in excess of twice a year's reported gross. The going rate for a good practice such as theirs was, at the time, no more than 85% of a year's gross. They explained that a large amount of income was unreported, and the perks extracted were extraordinary as well. Needless to say, we were unable to get anyone to look past the asking price, to no one's surprise but theirs. The rule for a buyer is that income that can not be proven must not be the basis for the final selling price.

Leases and liens

An important factor that often is overlooked until the last minute involves leases and liens. A copy of the lease must be provided, along with any agreements as to sublease allowance, transferability and lease extension. Any liens against the property or the business are easy to discover if not disclosed. Don't hold anything back! Non-disclosure will give a buyer pause as to why a seller is not being forthcoming about this, and cause concern as to what else might be non-disclosed.

Inventory

Inventory will be checked. If the business involves sales, a prudent buyer will attempt to determine if the inventory is saleable. How much is slow-moving or obsolete, and should not be priced at full value in the sale? A stipulation that the inventory at closing should not be in dollar value less than at the time of contract is standard. If inventory is depleted by a sudden upturn in sales, but not replenished, a suitable adjustment in selling price is in order.

Look at your fixtures and equipment. How old are they? Have they been maintained? A buyer will ask for service records. What must be replaced or upgraded to make it serviceable? Sellers always, in our experience, tend to over-value fixed assets.

Appraisal

The value of an independent appraisal has been discussed above. If there is real estate involved, it is important to get an individual appraisal of the real property. If there has been an earlier appraisal, it is often less expensive to contact that appraiser and ask for an update, rather than start anew.

Location

Obviously, location is a most important factor in buying a retail business. Is the neighborhood safe? Is it growing or deteriorating? Will the clientele continue to support what you are selling? Does the location generate walk in traffic? Is it handicapped accessible? Is parking available? Are there plans for a mega-store to come into the area diverting customers from your business? Full disclosure is, again, mandatory, to prevent allegations of fraud later on.

Maintenance

Is the business property clean and well maintained? Will a buyer need to invest a disproportionate amount to freshen it up, and make it safe and appealing (if retail), or safe and efficient (if a warehouse or factory)? For a retail establishment, a good test would be to ask your family members if they have enjoyed shopping in the store. They will be honest and tell you what needs to be done before you can entice a buyer.

There are many more caveats, but the above should give the prospective seller some ideas as to what to do to make sure a buyer sees a business that is ready for him to buy, and to give a prospective buyer an idea of what to look for.

WHAT THE BUYER WILL NEED TO SEE

After confidentiality agreements are signed, and a contract is either being prepared or has been signed, the buyer will have to do due diligence, The seller will have to provide prior 3 years audited financial statements, prior 3 years seller's tax returns, and sales tax reports if they are relevant. The buyer should obtain financing pre-approval for more than the purchase price. He should see the current and projected cash flow, as well as the current and projected sales and profits to determine future profitability. His advisors should analyze accounts receivable and payable, review the lease and check for liens. He should inspect the inventory and equipment, and should have the business appraised.

Full disclosure is not just important—again, it is mandatory! Full disclosure will lead to a decision. It may not be the decision either of you want. Your buyer may decide that the business he really was counting on owning is not destined to be his because of things discovered during full disclosure. But without provision of all data, and complete honesty, any deal, whether closed or not, will lead to problems.

TO PROSPECTIVE BUYERS: DO YOU SINCERELY WANT TO OWN A BUSINESS?

(Information a motivated seller will be happy to share in order to ensure proper transition)

A seller should tell his prospective buyer: "Being in business for yourself can be scary. There are no guarantees. Most buyers need to earn a living off their purchase right away, and have reasonable expectations of growth. If it looks good, feels good, and you can afford to make this investment in your future, you can go forward."

At some point, after your investigation is completed, you have to make that "leap of faith" that is necessary to proceed with the purchase. You will have to work hard, perhaps even cut back on personal expenses for a while, and perform many different jobs to be successful in your own business. But, when you are running your own show and making your own decisions, and you do not have to worry about job security, you will enjoy owning your own business. Nearly all business owners will tell you that they would never go back to being an employee.

A prospective buyer should always enter the process as well prepared and fully informed as possible. Often this means enlisting the guidance of a professional broker. Prospective buyers often need assistance in locating businesses and companies for sale, gathering and evaluating information on these opportunities, structuring an attractive purchase offer, and obtaining the financing necessary to buy the business. An experienced, competent business broker can be a major asset. Most business brokers charge commission only to the seller, not to the buyer. In general, that works out better for the buyer.

Now, all that's left is to unite the seller and the buyer of a business, negotiate a price and terms, and close the deal!

Good luck to both!

CHAPTER NINETEEN
PROFESSIONAL PRACTICE SALES

KEY POINTS

    A Profession is a Business

19A   **Selling a Professional Practice**

    Are You Ready to Sell?

    Special Circumstances Affecting Professional Practice Valuation
- The Value of Goodwill
- Recast Earnings

    This is No Job For an Amateur!

    What is a Practice Worth?

    The Vertical Horizontal Selling Method for Professional Practices

    Is There Life After Practice?

19B   **Buying a Professional Practice**

19C   **Professional Mergers**

CHAPTER NINETEEN
PROFESSIONAL PRACTICE SALES

FOREWORD

Whether they admit or not, regardless of how idealistic and self-sacrificing they may be, professionals are businessmen. (By their own admission, many are poor businessmen, at that.) And even those in the healing arts need to make a living so they can stay in business. We have come a long way from the $5 house calls and $2 fillings of 50 years ago, but, as fees have increased, so have expenses. Furthermore, with the encroachment by managed care (or, as doctors like to say, "managed costs and mangled care"), many professionals, who would have practiced until they died, are deciding to retire or move on. Without an exit strategy, these professionals will be likely to lock the door and walk away, or just sell their charts for a paltry sum. This would not be a fitting end to an often illustrious career.

Ideally, several years before retirement, a smart professional will take in an associate. Regardless of how close the relationship is between doctor and associate, it is mandatory to have a non-compete agreement. Be forewarned—an agreement such as this that is too restrictive, either in distance or duration, and that has no teeth in it to ensure compliance, will be unenforceable. You need a competent and knowledgeable attorney to frame this document. This is no place for a do-it-yourselfer.

When the associate demonstrates competence and compatibility, an agreement should be drawn up—again, by a professional. It should include not only whether there will be a buy-in or a working towards partnership arrangement, but, also, an outline of timing until equal partnership. Agreements that wind up 51%/49% usually do not satisfy the younger partners, and lead to dissatisfaction and eventual dissolution, thoroughly fouling up the owner's carefully planned exit strategy.

Just as the buy-in must be spelled out, so must a phase-out or buy-out be structured. Contingencies, such as bringing in a replacement partner who would do the buying out, must be considered. It is rare that a doctor who takes in an associate who buys in will find that associate also willing to buy him or her out. Here again, it's best in the long run to be fair. It does not take the wisdom of a Solomon to arrange this. To use an appropriate analogy, consider the wisdom of a mother who tells her children to share a pie, having the first child cut the pie in half, and the second child selecting which piece he wants. How close to equal will those pieces be? Very equal!

Sometimes, it is not possible to plan that far in advance. A solo practitioner (dentist, doctor, chiropractor, optometrist—it matters not) may become ill, or decide on the spur of the moment that he or she wants out. What are the choices?

If there is time, the solo practitioner should work hard at building up the practice during the six months to a year before the sale. A growing practice commands a higher selling price than one which is stagnant, or one which may be falling in patient volume or income. The year before you sell is **not** the time to take extra vacations, or to lay off part time professional help. It **is** the time to advertise for new patients, go into the community to give free lectures, and entice new blood into the practice. Continue to cultivate your referring doctors or dentists and encourage them to continue to refer patients to you. As mentioned in the previous chapters, confidentiality is most important. Once your staff or your patients learn you will be leaving, a significant number will leave a sinking ship and find work or care elsewhere. Ditto for referring professionals, as well.

Start getting your financials in order. Any documentation from the past three to five years that you do not have should be obtained from your accountant, or, if necessary, from the Internal Revenue Service. You will need that to back up your stated income and expenses, and the buyer may need that documentation for financing.

Once you have all the information, you should start RECASTING these data (see above). You are not creating another set of books to fool anyone. You are putting into proper perspective the true income and expenses taken by a solo practitioner. Income should be truly stated, and honest deductions that might be marginal, or might be "perks" that will not be relevant to the buyer, should be added in. You will find it amazing to see how much in the way of expense will not be carried over to the new owner, including your car, family on payroll, home office deductions, relatives' cell phones, trips to Costco and all the other items noted in that chapter.

Consider outsourcing (see the chapter on this subject above). Once thought of as appropriate just for large corporations, outsourcing is now within reach for any professional. Even for small offices, the time spent calculating tax deductions and making bank deposits is best designated to others. Many companies are available to do this and more. You can find one on the Internet or get a recommendation from a colleague. Warning: Personally sign payroll checks, and always give the checks a once over for anything that doesn't seem right. There are unsavory people in every field, and you must protect yourself. We highly recommend a billing or bookkeeping service. A physician who had to suddenly sell his practice took his accounts receivable to a billing service. He found that his long time receptionist who cost him a great deal of money in billable hours doing his billing had been either grossly negligent or dishonest (he never found out which). She cost him hundreds of thousands of dollars in billings she failed to pursue. There were payment denials that should have been resubmitted. She wrote them off. Other claim forms were buried and never filed. A small expense hiring a professional biller would have saved him a fortune. Many billing services are available. The cost of having someone do your billing outside your office is almost always offset by better collection efforts. Get timely profit and loss statements to allow you to better understand the business of your practice. As a side benefit, if this is all done outside your office, you save on in-office payroll. In our experience this is one service that quickly pays for itself with the benefits of increased and timely cash flow and better reporting, increasing your bottom line and the value of your practice.

Valuation of a professional practice will certainly depend on the financial statements, the cash flow, the recasted earnings sheets, EBITDA (see above) and other hard data, but there are other intangibles that must be considered. Good will, the relationship of a professional to his or her clientele, has a dollar value. Whether key employees will remain and for how long will be an issue. Location is always important. Is the practice in a safe area? If it depends on walk-in or transient business, is it visible from the street? Is parking available? Is the office handicapped accessible? We have devised a questionnaire (see Appendix) for medical and dental practices that may help a competent professional practice broker evaluate your practice's worth, and help you sell it.

In appraising a medical or dental, or any other professional practice, the rules are the same as with any business. You need a qualified, experienced appraiser. Look for independent valuation and financial advisory services specifically tailored to the healthcare industry. Financial advisory services are used for transaction due diligence and valuation, corporate compliance, and financial reporting.

Our organization has found that more dentists than ever are selling their practices and moving on to an active retirement or a new vocation. The retirees who postponed their retirement due to the stock market decline post 9/11, the baby boomers who are beginning to retire, and the dentists who are moving to new areas have created an increase in practice sales.

In the past several years, events national and global have caused many professionals to consider retirement or moving on to other endeavors. Many were hurt in the stock market decline post 9/11. They deferred their retirement and then were hurt by the market decline associated with the sub-prime debacle. The truth is that you can't time the market, and you can't time your retirement. All you can do is plan for it, then, when the time is right, as Nike says, "Just do it." But to do it, you need to have had an Exit Strategy.

The fact is that there are always more buyers than sellers. Especially now, when baby boomers are approaching that age, and dentists starting out or moving to new areas have created an enormous demand. I have ten buyers for every quality practice in my firm. Good practices, priced appropriately, move quickly.

As more boomers sell, this buyer-seller ratio will undoubtedly be altered, making it harder to sell a practice. Medical schools will soon be faced with a declining number of qualified applicants as college admissions fall. Many of the best and brightest may decide on other careers as managed care and Federal mandates increase, making the individuality prized as an attribute by admissions committees harder to find. Although some new dental schools are planned, the number of new dental graduates has not increased. Attrition due to death, disability, illness or retirement has exceeded the number of new graduates in recent years. This may, indeed, make practices harder to sell in years to come.

On the other hand, the demand has increased for medical and dental services, especially in the metropolitan areas, due to population increase and the need/desire for cosmetic procedures, particularly in dentistry. Because of this demand, and the shortage for the time being of practices for sale, many doctors are going into group practices, rather than seeking to strike out on their own, and new dentists are starting practices from scratch, spending $350,000 to $450,000 to do so. This investment is in addition to their student debt, which can range from $100,000 to $200,000. The likelihood of success, more rapidly, would appear to be a lower cash investment by purchasing an existing practice. Why are doctors and dentists selling?

The old standard reasons still apply:
- Disability
- Retirement
- Burnout
- Death

Add to that the newer reasons imposed by managed costs and mangled care:
- Paperwork

- Medical Liability
- Dealing with insurance companies
- Loss of autonomy
- Subjugation of medical judgment to financial restrictions

The decision to retire is never easy, and the time is not always perfect. But, again, when the time comes, that decision will be easier, and more positive financially, when Exit Strategy has been planned. After the post 9/11 stock market decline, many professionals were forced to delay their retirement five to seven years due to the stock market decline following 9/11. Then oil prices and sub-prime housing hit in 2007/2008, making more professionals feel they have to continue working. Following the plans outlined in this book will prepare those who want to sell be able to do so at the right time for them.

Even in a tight money market, 100 percent financing may still be available to buyers with a professional degree, enabling them to buy a practice. Lenders have tightened their requirements. Interest rates/terms are still reasonable for buyers. As of now, lenders rarely require the buyer to have a down payment, have a spousal signature or have their residence as collateral in order to buy a practice. There is no guarantee that this will be the case in the future. Lenders now may also extend loans beyond the traditional five to seven years, and drop prepayment penalties. Conditions are buyer-friendly now, but may change as lenders tighten their requirements.

At the time of this writing it is possible that tax laws may change with a new administration. The capital gains tax for sellers at 15 percent is very favorable. Buyers may depreciate and/or amortize the entire amount of the practice purchase price. These tax laws are also subject to change.

What does all this mean?

If you have any thought of leaving practice within the near future:
- Have your practice evaluated
- Plan ahead
- Have a written, proactive financial plan that is reviewed and updated annually

If you have any thought of buying a practice:
- Start looking now
- When you find the right one for you, two things will happen:
    - You will know it
    - You will be prepared to buy it

That is the purpose of these chapters.

19A SELLING A PROFESSIONAL PRACTICE

ARE YOU READY TO SELL?

This is a time to call in your professional advisors and get the basics laid out. Can you afford to sell? Your financial advisor must assist you, using knowledge of your life style as well as the assets you possess. I have had professionals, ready to sell, who, after such meetings, tell me they can retire in style, as long as they don't live too long, and don't buy anything while they do. That is not the way to approach retirement!

Are you still practicing capably? That is hard for any professional to judge for himself. But, if there is any thought that the quality of care you are providing is not as it has been, you are most assuredly ready to retire.

Do you have any interests outside your professional life? You need a plan. We all know people who, once they stopped working, started dying. You must have a plan for life after practice.

It is important to know that the sale does not have to be immediate and complete. There can be a transition time built in to a sale. The longer the transition, the easier the sale, as the retiring professional introduces the new doctor to the patients, putting his stamp of approval on the newcomer. By inertia alone, most patients will stay with the buyer, but a period of introduction makes patient retention much more likely.

SPECIAL CIRCUMSTANCES AFFECTING MEDICAL PRACTICE VALUATION

In putting a dollar value on a professional practice, many of the concepts listed in the previous chapters apply. After all, a professional practice is a business. However, increasingly onerous regulations, irrational governmental fines, insurer demands for refunds of moneys received for previously approved claims, and unit fees that grow less than the rate of inflation (or even shrink) are all factors making evaluation of a medical practice's worth difficult.

Therefore, market data approaches alone do not work well in valuing a medical practice. An appraiser must use an income approach. Cash flow is the key, but it must be capitalized, and then discounted. There are risks associated with buying medical practices today that did not exist a few short years ago.

The market risk is related first and foremost to the source of income. What portion of income is derived from Medicare and Medicaid, from HMOs and PPOs, from capitation plans, and from all their respective fee limitations? Key regulatory factors must be known to the CPA, certified appraiser, professional practice broker and to the prospective buyer. Stark and Stark II laws, anti-kickback statutes and other regulations restrict physicians' ability to profit from ownership in related businesses. These regulations reduce income potential as they do for no entrepreneurs in any other field. Such oversight has reduced abuse of the system, but those physicians who have worked honestly within the system have been impacted as well.

After realizing and factoring in these restrictions upon future income, a value must be placed upon the cost of a physician's services, were the buyer to hire a non-owner replacement physician of equal experience to run the practice. Then, a selling price must be further adjusted, based on the relative risk of various medical specialties and a realistic growth rate.

THIS IS NO JOB FOR AN AMATEUR!

It takes years to plan the proper Exit Strategy, especially if you want to get the maximum value from your practice. No matter whether you are selling (or giving) your practice to a colleague, selling it to another professional, or (hopefully not) just walking away, you must take the time to do it right. There are State mandated regulations involving patient notification and chart retention, along with a personal need to notify insurers, hospitals, and medical boards. Disposition of accounts receivable must be arranged, and continued liability coverage arranged. If you are a solo practitioner exiting the practice, you need to find a buyer, hire an associate who will eventually take over, affiliate with another practice, or, as mentioned, just close the doors. This is no job for an amateur. If you do walk away and just close the doors, assets like medical records become liabilities. You must keep records for a specified period of time, so that they can be available in case of litigation. You then must pay for storage, and be able to retrieve records when needed.

THINKING "OUTSIDE THE BOX"
JOINT VENTURES
With the encroachment of financial and political constraints on the professional today, there is often a need for thinking "out of the box," expanding the possibilities of both providing health care **and** earning a significant income. One such possibility is entering into a joint venture. Equity joint ventures between hospitals and physicians exist today which seek the alignment of their interests without unacceptable regulatory risk. Increasing competition between hospitals and physicians requires the consideration of non-equity models such as service line leases, "under arrangement" deals, clinical co-management agreements, and pay-for-performance arrangements. Joint ventures may include not only hospitals. There might be real estate, equipment, and management company joint ventures as well. Anything you can do to maximize profits without sacrificing patient care would be a win/win situation, one worth exploring.

There are many types of medical and dental groups being developed across the country, some of which are being reconfigured or restructured in view of the current economic and legislative environment. If you are getting involved with such an enterprise, you will need advisors familiar with current issues that face groups handled by practice management companies.

PROFESSIONAL PRACTICE SALES

REAL ESTATE INVESTMENT

In buying a practice, consider, if possible, capturing the upside of any real estate "boom" by purchasing the building which houses the practice. Physicians' and dentists' appetites for investment opportunities in medical office buildings have grown as compensation pressures increase. In fact, professionals have become increasingly interested in real estate investment in general—an asset class that has over time, despite intermittent "crashes" in 1969, 1978, 1989-1992, and 2008, experienced substantial value appreciation. Aside from the investment potential, being your own landlord and not having to deal with rent increases or lease renewals can be a blessing. Rental income from other tenants sweetens the deal, as well. There are key negotiating points and pitfalls, and best structures for any given situation, that require expert advice.

Other aspects of professional practice purchasing and selling, too specialized to go into in this book, include the formation of Multi-specialty Clinics and Ambulatory Surgery Centers. If considering deals such as these, there is no substitute for truly expert advice.

CAN YOU SELL YOUR OWN PRACTICE?

Sure you can! After all, you have successfully owned and operated a practice for years, and know all there is to know about it, right? But selling your own practice is never easy. There are countless complex issues involved. How will you market your practice, and maintain confidentiality? What is your practice worth? How do you structure the sale? Will you have to provide owner financing, and how does that work? How long will it take you to properly transition out of the practice? And how will you handle important tax and legal issues, like minimizing taxes?

Selling a practice is a complex and emotional process. Even large business owners, who have operated multi-million dollar, global companies, choose to utilize the services of a professional business broker or merger & acquisition advisor, not because larger companies are more complex, but, having an objective, third-party advisor direct the process is the right thing to do. In fact, using an intermediary can not only increase the likelihood of a successful transaction, but also can increase the price paid for your practice. As mentioned earlier in this volume, it should be noted that even in real estate sales, sale prices are 16% higher when a broker is involved in a sale than if a homeowner goes it alone. Similar figures apply to professional practice sales, as well, saving in time and adding in value a dollar amount far in excess of any commissions paid.

When coming up with an asking price, a seller must be practical. If income will not cover debt service, a smart buyer will be reticent to even look at the practice. And in most instances, a buyer of a professional practice cannot pass along the acquisition price or increased future costs to the patients. A restaurant might raise prices, but a doctor, in this highly regulated era, can not. The doctor cannot even reduce portion sizes (although, today, he might find himself forced to spend less time with each patient). A seller must use pragmatism, not greed, in setting a price.

An experienced professional practice broker, perhaps a retired professional utilizing his or her experience to help other professionals with their Exit Strategy, will understand your ultimate goals and objectives, and have the ability to accurately value your business. By only bringing you pre-qualified buyers, a broker saves you valuable time. By knowing the "market place," a broker may get you a higher sale price. Brokers will complete all negotiations, can assist buyers in obtaining financing, and, their document and negotiation skills can insure successful closing and transition.

WHAT IS A PRACTICE WORTH?

There have been rules of thumb, through the years, involving the value of a professional practice. In the 1960's, a practice would sell for two years' gross earnings! With the advent of managed care, and the disproportionate increase in overhead (medical liability insurance, salaries, supplies, etc.), the 1980's brought valuations of one year's gross, on average. With the onset of the 21st century, it is rare for a medical or dental practice to be sold for anywhere near that amount, barring exceptional circumstances. In fact, the latest figures for dental and medical sales indicate that most will sell for 45% to (rarely) 85% of a year's gross. Buyers and sellers obviously will have different concepts as to what a practice is worth. A seller wants to be compensated for the considerable effort put in over the years building a successful practice. A buyer wants to be certain he can handle his overhead and debt service, and earn a reasonable income, during the first few years, while further building the practice. Negotiation is necessary.

Variables determining the sale price include the practice's financial health and recent growth or stagnation, location, type and value of equipment, clinical nature of the practice, staff continuity, etc. A professional appraisal is the only way to determine actual value. In fact, I would suggest that a professional appraisal is required for any successful practice transition. Many lenders require a professional appraisal before providing funding.

Cash flow is really the lifeblood of any business. Most solo professional practices, however, are "owner-operated." The doctor or dentist, for example, is being paid for his or her efforts. Take-home earnings represent the profit of the business. (This is true primarily for practices with revenues under $1 million per year.) If you are planning to purchase a practice and manage it, one important factor you must discover is whether there will be enough profit or free cash flow for an absentee owner to pay a salary to a doctor and a manager. (Businesses with little or no profits would be valued differently.) By the same token, that bottom line is rarely a true figure representing actual cash flow. As mentioned above in the section on Recasting, a potential buyer must add back the "perks" and non-recurring expenses anticipated for an absentee (or new) owner into the bottom line.

How does one calculate free cash flow into a possible selling price? Available cash flow is separated into two categories: salary and debt service. The cash remaining after subtracting a reasonable amount for your salary provides the maximum cash available to service the debt. When applying for a business loan, most banks will allow a sufficient cushion when providing a loan so as not to overextend the professional buyer. It is in their best interests that he succeed.

If we have a situation in which the buyer definitely wants to buy a practice, and the seller is eager to sell, skillful negotiations, perhaps through an experienced professional practice broker, can make or break a deal. Let's assume a situation in which there is a reasonable gap—let's say $30,000—between the amount the buyer wants to pay and the bottom line below which the seller refuses to go. Should the buyer walk away or should he compromise? It would almost always be in the best interest of the buyer to recalculate the offering price based upon the value of the money involved. Emotionally, the buyer may believe the price is too high. However, the consequences of not purchasing the practice include (a) loss of equity (since continuing as an employee will not create equity in a business) or (b) a possible loss of higher income as an individual practitioner. These factors may make taking the risk a better option. The real question must be whether the existing cash flow of the business can support an increased payment of a few hundred dollars a month, the cost of a ten year bank loan. If the buyer can anticipate increased revenues of $350 per month, or $90/week, then the extra $30,000 seems less abhorrent. An extra $350 a month is not going to make any difference to the buyer in the long run. By the same token, a seller must realize he or she has an eager buyer, ready and willing to take over a practice so the seller can go on to whatever exit strategy is planned. Should a few thousand dollars stand in the way of a rapid sale to a pre-qualified buyer?

In other words, if negotiations have gone as far as they can go, and the deal is in danger of being lost, a buyer must step back and determine that the goodwill created with the seller will most likely create an even better transition if he or she agrees to a slightly higher price. It's not always how much you pay, but how much you benefit from the opportunity. A seller must remain flexible when a ready and willing buyer might not be easy to find again. There are always risks in every opportunity. However, most people never recognize the loss from a missed opportunity, which can be much more substantial than a few extra dollars per month. It is often said, in selling a home, that the first offer is your best offer, though it might not seem so at the time. While that is not always the case with a professional practice sale, it is worth thinking about here, as well.

THE VERTICAL HORIZONTAL SELLING METHOD FOR PROFESSIONAL PRACTICES

A review of the chapter above, entitled Vertical Horizontal Selling Method, a method we have devised to help sell businesses of any size and nature, will elaborate on the ideal way to find the right buyer for your practice. A professional practice broker, ideally a retired professional who knows what you are going through and has the knowledge and contacts to expedite finding the right buyer in a timely fashion, will do all this for you. The broker will seek a buyer without divulging your identity, since knowledge of impending sale of a practice has, as noted, sometimes led to a "rats deserting a sinking ship" mentality among both staff and patients. You do not want patients to know you are thinking of retiring, and seeking a replacement for your services before you go. As mentioned, you should do all you can to maintain or build up your bottom line, not let it decrease. Confidentiality can only be maintained if you have a third party doing the search. What you also do not want, from a morale standpoint, is to have potential buyers, especially non-prequalified buyers, parading through your office in front of patients and staff.

What a broker will do, other than advertise, is make contacts with colleagues in your field. The broker will speak to cronies in training programs or alumni organizations to see who is looking for a position. The broker, if a retired professional, will often be friendly with staff in hospitals or state and local dental and medical societies, and get information in that way. In addition, brokers get inquiries constantly from professionals who have a strong business sense and are buying up practices, and managing and staffing them, without working there. These groups also have the deep pockets to purchase high-grossing practices without worrying about financing.

Horizontally, a broker can do what you would have difficulty doing. While protecting your confidentiality (and avoiding a colleague angling to take your patients the minute you move on, or even before then), a broker can make discrete inquiries as to whether another practitioner in your area would like to merge or buy you out. The broker, especially if a professional, can attend conferences and let the word out that a practice may be available. Your privacy is intact, and qualified buyers who have signed confidentiality agreements (see Appendix for an example) will be brought to you at your convenience.

NOTIFYING YOUR PATIENTS

There are rules concerning patient abandonment. The retiring doctor certainly does not want to have an Office of Professional Medical Conduct calling him on the carpet for failure to give patients the opportunity and time to find a new medical home. A minimum of three months is recommended. All active patients should receive a letter indicating exit date, name of doctor taking over (if that is what is happening), and/or names of doctors willing to take on new patients in the area. (See Appendix for a sample letter.) The exiting doctor must also tell patients where records will be stored if the practice is not sold. Some states also require an ad to be placed in a local newspaper.

IS THERE LIFE AFTER PRACTICE?

It may seem premature to discuss the next point here, but it is an important part of an Exit Strategy. What will you do after you leave your practice? Here are some suggestions, just to keep your mind active (and perhaps pick up some pocket change).

Lecture in your field at professional colleges.

Rep or lecture for companies whose products you have used.

- Practice your profession in underserved areas, with or without pay.
- Substitute teach in science at a High School or Community College.
- Review medical/dental liability cases for insurers or attorneys. (Your expertise might serve to prevent frivolous claims from being pursued.)
- Work part-time for your purchaser (if she or he allows you to do so, since some new owners do not want the previous doctor to stay on more than just long enough to introduce the new owner, and then leave).
- Work part-time at hospitals, clinics, or for a colleague, being careful to avoid violating restrictive covenant clauses.

Keep attending Continuing Professional Education courses and lectures.

Become a professional practice broker. (You can do this with a phone and a modem from anywhere. In fact, if this appeals to you, call us at (516) 520-1000 for advice as to how to accomplish this.)

Don't lose your identity, but also start enjoying other interests.

19B BUYING A PROFESSIONAL PRACTICE

If you are buying a professional practice, you also have a lot of work to do before you even look at one. Some considerations:

Where do you want to live?

Do you want to practice nearby, or do you prefer to separate practice and home and be "the doc" at work, but remain anonymous in your home neighborhood?

If separate, how far are you willing to commute?

What can you afford to invest? (Notice! We did not say, "pay." This is an *investment* in your future.)

Will you be happy in that practice, based on location and patient population.

What income level are you expecting?

Can you deal with limitations and restrictions imposed by insurers or public assistance programs?

To quote hockey star Wayne Gretzky, the most important thing to remember on the ice is to keep your eyes on where the puck is going to be, not where it is. Buyers must keep their eyes on where they want to be, then, rather than staying in place, work on getting there. If you have the drive, personality and ambition, there is nothing like being your own boss—owning your own practice.

TO BUY OR NOT TO BUY?

You have spent many years (and a great deal of money) in education and training. You may already be in debt. Now you must decide whether to (a) work for someone else for a while on the potential promise of eventual partnership; (b) search for a location and "start cold;" or (c) search for and buy an established practice.

Professionals who are starting out differ in their needs. Some need the mentoring and companionship that can be found in working for an experienced professional, getting further "on the job" training while starting to repay debts. Some may be more adventurous or entrepreneurial, or more financially secure, and be able and willing to strike out on their own.

There is something to be said for a mentoring relationship. A young professional may be faced with a patient or a situation not seen while in training. Having an experienced practitioner on whom to rely is reassuring, to say the least. On the other hand, a new physician, dentist or other professional in an area is rarely alone. In these days of instantaneous communications, colleagues will nearly always be available, and willing to lend a hand or offer a "curb-side" consult to a younger colleague.

However, the experience alluded to above can also be accessed when buying a practice if a smooth transition is planned, and the selling doctor is willing and able to share his experience and expertise. There are many clinical and behavioral situations that occur in which years of experience and judgment can provide a simple solution. This is a very valuable, and not quantifiable, asset that is acquired in a buyout.

In view of the above, it should be clear that, in general, the professional who is starting out on his or her own may benefit from buying a practice, if only for the comfort gained by having a seller available for the transition. Of course, having a seller remain for a period of time to introduce the buyer to the patient and referral base is a most important asset.

When buying a practice, there is always the question of patient retention. How many patients will remain in the practice when a trusted professional leaves? Patient loyalty, such as it is in this new era of managed care, is often to the office as well as to the doctor. Inertia prevails. Studies constantly show that the loss will be less than 2 percent within six months of the practice sale. In fact, no buyer of any practice we have sold has ever failed to succeed. No seller has had to take back a practice because of buyer financial failure. Production by a new, usually younger and more energetic practitioner, one who takes less time off and is more interested in building a clientele, usually sees an increase of at least 25%!

Purchase of an existing practice will be much more profitable more rapidly every time!

The most important benefit to buying a practice would be the financial considerations. In general, the purchase of an established, viable, income-producing business will financially outperform a "cold start" every time. After considering the investment required in equipment, and the time and cost of building a practice from scratch, purchase of an existing practice will be much more profitable more rapidly every time for a dental or optometry practice, and nearly every time for a medical practice. In fact, if you have an experienced accountant or professional practice broker crunch the numbers for you, your earnings in buying an established practice may, after five years, total three to five times what you might earn through starting out on your own.

PRACTICE PHILOSOPHY

When you buy a practice, and are exposed to the seller's methodology in dealing with patients, you pick up a practice's philosophy. Patients are used to being greeted and treated in a certain way. Some are used to a significant amount of hand-holding and pampering by the seller. Patients in other practices may be accustomed to being treated professionally, with no intimacies tendered. If a new practitioner is unaware of how patients in this practice, over the years, have self-selected the office for that kind of care, he or she will fail to keep a significant number of patients who liked being treated that way. A "fuzzy" joke-teller will not inspire confidence in a patient who is used to a dignified, "keep your distance," professor (and vice versa). If most of the patients come from one area of social contact of the owner, can you duplicate the attraction? This appears superficial, but is a fact of life.

In fact, when contemplating purchase of a practice, you must determine whether the philosophy of that practice will dovetail with your own. If you don't fully agree with the philosophy, can it be changed? Will you lose patients? Can you estimate how many? Will you gain patients? In some occasions, through indifference, a seller may have neglected patients, who have only stayed out of a sense of loyalty. When a new and hopefully better approach is instituted, they will welcome the change, and refer other patients.

DEMOGRAPHY

There are major demographic shifts constantly occurring—urban, suburban, and rural. Demographic studies need to be done and reviewed so that, no matter whether you buy or start fresh, you're comfortable with the demographics of the area you'll serve.

QUESTIONS TO ASK WHEN CONSIDERING BUYING A PRACTICE

How long has the practice been in business?

A practice with a long track record will be well known in the area. Patients are used to visiting the practice, adding to the value of Goodwill. The longer the present owner has been in practice, the more likely it is, of course, that he or she has been successful.

Why is the present owner selling?

If the owner of the practice has been there for two years, is 45 years old, and tells you he wants to retire, be suspicious. The more valid the reason for the sale, the more realistic the seller will be in accepting your offer. Gauge the personality of the seller. Some people get restless, jump from practice to practice, or from location to location, because they are bored. But is something compelling the move? Are there misconduct or fraud charges pending that he has not disclosed? Are there liens against the seller, personal or professional? Is there a lease problem, or is there a major change in the neighborhood coming that has not been disclosed. Does the seller have huge personal debts, and, if so, why? If the practice is doing well, the seller should not be in debt. Due diligence is very important, and even more so when you sense a red flag. Why the seller is selling is an important question—you **must** get the answer.

What do the financial records look like?

The financial records of the practice are a good indication of how well the practice has been doing historically. However, they do not reflect the many perks taken by single proprietorships—family on the payroll, convention trips that are really vacations, trips to Costco or Sam's Club that involve home goods as well as office supplies, and so on. If you have not already done so, read the chapter on RECASTING to get a better idea as to the proper way to value a business. The problem is that recast earnings will not serve as bona fide credentials to possible lenders. They will rely on filed income tax returns, which are prepared in such a way as to minimize taxes. This may lead to your needing some owner financing when you buy. In the long run, financial records tell you what the history of the practice has done. Its future is up to you.

Is it better to be a boss or an employee?

Being in practice alone can be a daunting prospect. There are no guarantees. Running your own practice, as in any business, is not a nine to five job. You will have to work hard. But when you are running your own show, you are making your own decisions and building your future. And of course, you can never be fired! Nearly all professionals we know tell us they would never go back to working for someone else again.

TAX RAMIFICATIONS

If a practice is set up as a PC, it is crucial for all parties to agree on what kind of sale it will be. If it is to be in the form of stock in the corporation, the proceeds received would be treated as a long-term capital gain, which would be a distinct tax advantage for the seller. If, on the other hand, the sale is for the components of the practice—hard assets, such as furniture, and accounts receivable, for instance—that would not be to the seller's advantage. In such a case, the proceeds are treated as ordinary income on which the corporation would have to pay income tax.

To make matters worse, if the seller decides to withdraw this money as a dividend, there would be personal income tax on that withdrawal— the proverbial double whammy! In most instances, a seller should attempt to negotiate a deal that is for 100 percent of stock in the corporation. Needless to say, services of a highly qualified tax counselor are required here, and well worth the cost.

If the owners also own the property, another series of questions are raised. They would face the prospect of being the buyer's future landlords. They must negotiate the terms and duration of the lease, the amount of the rent, and who would be responsible for utilities and cleaning. Expert advice is, again, mandatory.

WHY DOES A GOOD PRACTICE NOT SELL?

We had a large dental practice listed with our firm, referred by a pleased client and accepted over the phone pending our visit. The practice was very busy. I was unable to find a spot in the decent sized lot adjacent to their office. I walked in and was appalled. The waiting area was filthy. The examining areas were not much better in appearance, though hopefully they were surgically clean. And, if I needed the rest room, I would have sooner gone to the gas station down the street than use theirs. The owner could not understand why a previous broker was unable to sell it during an entire year!

The first thing I did was take the owner outside, and have him walk in through the door the patients used. He had never entered that way, and was so busy in the back office, that he had ignored the front. He was not even aware of how disorganized and messy his front office staff had been. After he had invested a goodly sum in modernizing the office, cleaning the carpets, painting the operatories and sprucing up the waiting room, we were able to get some buyers involved.

Not every office that does not sell is as filthy as that one was. Some merely show signs of age and neglect—waiting room furniture from WalMart, magazines from the year of the flood, patient charts strewn across receptionists' desks. Pictures on walls should be pleasing to the eye, and not faded from years of hanging around.

One of our biggest headaches is selling offices that are not computerized. If a good recall system is in place, that has dollar value. Computers should be used, not just for billing, but for scheduling patients, keeping track of recall dates, and maintaining financial records. Paperless charts are not futuristic—they are here and now—and an office that is up-to-date will sell much more quickly that one that is mired in the dark ages.

I relate selling a practice to the advice given my children by a college admissions advisor years ago—"It's all in the packaging!" If the package is pleasing, and all else is equal, it is much more likely that what you are selling, a practice or yourself, will be accepted. The seller may be so accustomed to his practice environment, he does not see the obvious deficiencies and problems. An experienced professional practice broker can spot these problems, hopefully in time to correct them before they become major impediments to a sale.

SUMMARY

In short, buying a practice boils down to where you want to look, what you are willing to pay (since a degree after your name eases your way to financing when the purchased practice is deserving of the amount asked), and when you want to buy. Ideally, a broker, who often will have dozens of listings in all areas, will be your best choice. While some brokers get half their commission from the seller and half from the buyer, most buyers would do well to work with a broker who gets no commission from them. While the seller will be figuring in the commission in what he or she wants to receive, it usually works out best for the buyer if the negotiated price is all that the buyer pays.

A buyer will have to be pre-qualified. If you are buying a high-grossing practice, the seller may want a Dun and Bradstreet rating or credit score before even entertaining an offer. In general, your degree is enough to ensure your getting timely financing. If you have not checked your credit score, now would be a good time to do so, before you even think of applying for a loan to buy a practice.

There will come a time when you see a practice you like and want to make an offer. This is usually done through the broker. However, it would be a wise move at about this point to hire an accountant and an attorney to make sure the facts presented by the seller are accurate. In a recent deal involving an optical boutique, last minute discovery revealed that the seller was presenting inaccurate data. Among other problems, he showed net salaries rather than gross in calculating the bottom line. Based on recalculation, the buyer realized he would probably go bankrupt in the first year with such an increased outlay, and, the day before the closing, walked away from the sale. While the broker does the best he or she can to determine the accuracy of information presented, it is the buyer's responsibility to do due diligence to confirm it. If facts are found to have been grossly distorted, money spent for the legal and accounting advice will be money well spent, saving a buyer considerable grief. If data are not accurate, but the buyer still wants to proceed after correct figures are available, there may now be leverage in negotiating a lower price. A good broker can usually recommend an experienced lawyer and/or CPA to assist.

19C PROFESSIONAL MERGERS

Small practices can merge. If you are planning an Exit Strategy, and are unwilling to retire or unable to find a buyer, a practice merger might be to your advantage. By finding like-minded colleagues, you may discover that a merger may lead to less office time with better patient coverage, economies of scale, better contracts, and ancillary revenues. But a merger must receive expert consultation. A merger specialist may prevent a situation, all too common, wherein revenues may increase but individual partners see no increase in income. This usually occurs when the merger is composed of professionals who lack the willingness to operate as a group, rather than as a collection of separate practices.

If you do a merger correctly, it should produce a return on investment within a reasonable period of time. You need a proper business plan, and it must be well executed. Merger costs are a one-time event. Aside from legal, accounting, and consulting fees, there may be hidden costs. These include replacement of computer systems, marketing, setting up a central office, or relocating practices to a central site. A new practice management system alone may cost a medium-sized group $100,000 or more. Even if the merger allows the practitioners to stay in separate offices, it's important to have a single billing and scheduling system. Individual offices gather billing data and feed it into a central office which can lead to major inefficiencies in collections. Hiring an administrator may be necessary for large groups, adding to outlay but usually increasing the bottom line.

Once again, there is no substitute for expert advice, especially when it comes to mergers. Large professional practice brokerages have in-house merger and acquisition specialists. Our firm has experienced physicians, dentists, chiropractors and optometrists on staff. If you are looking at this alternative to selling a professional practice, be certain you look for a firm such as ours in your area. It will be well worth the search. If you need assistance, you may call (516) 478-0752 for access to the professional practice brokerage division of our firm.

CHAPTER TWENTY
AFTER THE SALE

 **KEY POINTS**

Think Ahead
Do Something
Do Not Vegetate!

CHAPTER TWENTY
AFTER THE SALE

What do you do with yourself after you sell your business? Too many people who have been active all their lives stop working and, because they have no other interests, start dying. That is NOT what you want for yourself.

Certainly, if you have handled your *Exit Strategy* correctly you, feel free to buy cars, buy houses, buy boats, buy horses or buy any other toys, to your heart's desire!

Ideally, you will have not been an all work and no play type of person, and will already have other interests. Some adventures and ventures you can look forward to in your after-work years include:

- Remain as employee or consultant to the buyer of your business.
- Playing with your grandchildren.
- Travel
- Taking courses at a local college (often free).
- Teaching people who would like to do what you have done in business on a college level.
- Substitute teaching in a high school or business school.
- Attend conferences within your field to keep on top of things.
- Serve on social or professional organization committees.
- Lecture for, or represent, some of the companies whose services you have used in business.

- Become a Business Broker specializing in the business field you know best.
- And, of course, golf, tennis and bridge.

Whatever you do, do something!

PLAN YOUR EXIT STRATEGY WELL!

APPENDIX I
BUSINESS BROKER TRAINING MANUAL

(Author's note: While this book is written to help business owners rapidly and profitably sell their businesses, and, in select chapters, to enable buyers to obtain a suitable business for the right price, you will have noted that we often suggest that both buyer and seller utilize the services of experts. The one expert to pull this all together must be a competent and caring Business Broker. My firm has over 60 brokers in the New York metropolitan area, as well as affiliated brokers all over the country. In fact, we are always looking for brokers in areas that are either new to us or underserved. If you have any desire to utilize your business knowledge to help others buy or sell practices, we would be happy to advise or to welcome you to our company. Please call me at (516) 520-0000, and I will guide you in how to best do so. At the present time, with so much downsizing and so many layoffs, Business Brokerage is an incredible opportunity because tens of thousands of people lost their jobs and are seeking to buy businesses.

In fact, one of the great things about Business Brokerage is that it is not affected by bad economic times: In bad times people want to sell because they are not making as much money as they used to. In good times people want to sell to make a large profit and find a better business.

When new brokers come under my auspices, they are given a training manual. To give you an idea as to what Business Brokerage entails, as well as show you what a Business Broker can and should do for you, I have abstracted some portions of this manual. (Note: The information and advice provided below are written for a Business Broker, but are provided so you may understand what a Business broker can (and should) be doing for you.)

TRAINING MANUAL

Relationships

Relationships, between Broker and clients, and between Buyer and Seller, are incredibly important in Business Brokerage. The Seller needs the Buyer to stay in business to pay the Seller the notes. They both have a vested interest in the success of the business. This is very important for the deal to go through.

The Broker should let the Buyer know he is here to help the Buyer figure out how to earn a living and make money and achieve a desired lifestyle. The Buyer must know that though you work as agent for the Seller, your goal is to make both happy. The number one rule in closing deals is you need both to be happy or you have no deal.

THE BUSINESS OF BUSINESS BROKERAGE

In most instances, Business Brokerage focuses on small, "mom and pop," privately held businesses, not publicly traded companies.

Ninety-five percent of businesses have annual sales of $1 million or less and 20 employees or less.

Three percent of businesses have annual sales of $1 million to $20 million and 100 employees or less.

That means a total of 98% of existing businesses are small privately held businesses. This 98% is the market that Manheim Business Brokers specializes in.

There are approximately 35,000 businesses per 1 million people.

Twenty percent of them are for sale at any given moment in time, which means the opportunity for a Business Broker to earn a great deal of money is outstanding. *(Author's note: This also means the opportunity to purchase a quality business is great at any given time, and, conversely, the ability to sell a business on your own may be limited, hence the need for a good business broker.)*

As Manheim Business Brokers educate their Buyers, we help them to interpret and understand the financials of the business they are looking to buy. This is important because the financials normally show a loss or no profit for tax purposes. Because they are usually small businesses, an owner does not pay any taxes as a result of the financials. (See our Chapter on Recasting to see how this is handled.)

A Broker must educate the Buyer to understand the Banks will not lend money (SBA loan) on a purchase of a business with no collateral. A Bank does not have the skill to come in and run the business should they take it as collateral. Hence the need, often, for owner financing The owner surely has the skill, if not the desire, to take the business as collateral and take it back and run it should the Buyer default on its notes. In a tight money market, it is often a better idea for a seller, if willing, to lend the money (Purchase Money Mortgage) to the buyer.

The Buyer may need some hand holding since a business purchase is a big financial and emotional investment. You must educate the Buyer that financials are filed, not for paying the most in taxes, and explain Recasting to determine the true cash flow. He must be reassured that a Seller would not offer owner financing unless he expects the Buyer to stay in business and pay his notes.

Documentation

Brokers must document everything that occurs in a deal. Brokers must keep records of all documents (i.e., notice of showings, any signed forms, etc.). Brokers must keep records and write down everything that happens, for example, the date and time of each meeting with a buyer or seller and what was discussed. It is vitally important to maintain accurate records. This way, at a time in the future, days, weeks, or years, you will have a written account of all that occurred. It protects all parties, especially, for the broker, in a commission dispute.

Confidentiality

It is very important for the Broker give no information about a business to a potential Buyer until an NDA (Non-Disclosure Agreement) is signed, and preferably until the Broker and the Buyer meet in person.

Bits and Pieces

The three most important considerations in evaluating the potential for sale of a business, as a Business Broker, are:

1. Location
2. Track Record (length of time in business, sales, etc.).
3. Management (Although, if a company has been run badly, it might be a great opportunity for the buyer who can run it well.)

Ten percent rule: People are happy making 10% decisions, so most decisions they make in their lives are 10% decisions. These are decisions that are just not all that important, so that ramifications, should the decisions be incorrect, are rectifiable. Decisions that should not be 10% decisions, but 100% decisions, are 1) Marriage, and 2) Buying a Business. These decisions require "research" and then commitment. The point is that a Broker must understand how big and scary the decision to buy a business is for most people. It can be almost as life altering as marriage. A Buyer is putting at risk a substantial amount of time, effort and money to invest in a business, and such a decision must be treated with consideration and respect.

Seventy-two hour rule: If Buyers see a business and do not make some sort of a decision within 72 hours, they are likely to be gone after 72 hours.

Who gets the money? Generally, Accounts Receivable and Accounts Payable both go along with the business when it is sold. Cash usually stays with the Seller. This does not, however, usually apply to professional practices.

Help Sellers plan for the future: Keep Sellers focused on what they are going to do after the sale. Not only is this the decent thing to do; it may benefit the Broker. This is an excellent way to pick up a motivated new buyer. After all, with all that money you just got him for his old business, why not buy a new business?

Help Buyers plan for the future: Keep Buyers focused on what they will do with the business once they buy it.

Lower Risk: *(this can be explained to Buyer if Buyer is deciding between the following)*
The Buyer has three choices:
1. Job: The Buyer can get a job. An entrepreneurial buyer will not be happy working for someone else. There is the insecurity of working for a company that may not succeed, or may downsize by firing employees. But if you own your own business, you are more secure because you are in charge of your own security.
2. Start Up: 65% to 90% of all startups fail within 5 years.
3. Buy an Existing Business or Franchise: The Buyer must be convinced that this is the more secure choice because of reduced risk in buying a business that has a track record of success. In some cases it is much cheaper to buy a business then to start one. Example: To build a new 1,800 sq. ft. pizza store would take 3 to 4 months to build and at a cost of about $120,000. To buy an existing pizza store in a great location would cost about $50,000 to $80,000.

Advantages in Buying an Existing Business:
- Actual results rather than pro-forma.
- Immediate cash flow: you can use cash flow to pay the notes and have some for yourself immediately.
- Trained employees in place.
- Established suppliers and credit.
- Established customers and referral business.
- Existing licenses and permits.
- Training by the Seller.
- The availability of owner financing.
- You can take everything they are doing and improve on it.

Advantages in Buying a Franchise:
- Known name means instant recognition.
- Proven product or service.
- Ongoing support means you are in business for yourself but not by yourself.
- More than 90% of new franchises are successful.
- Operating system in place—mistakes already made have been rectified.
- Opportunity to add additional units within the franchise system.
- Training by the seller and the franchise company.
- The availability of owner financing.

Note: Remember, ultimately the success or failure of the business is the owner's responsibility.

Three Areas of Focus:
1. Business (not financials): Do not focus on the financials because they are for tax purposes only. Rather focus on the actual business. Get the Buyer excited and emotional about the actual business.
2. Top Line (not Bottom Line): Do not focus on the bottom line of the financials. Rather get the Buyer to focus on the top line, the Gross Sales; look at the Gross Sales because a Buyer will keep 10% to 20% of this (including cash not accounted for in the financials).
3. 70% after the sale (not 30% before the sale): 30% importance should be given to how the Seller has run the business and what the Seller has done with the business. Do not focus on this 30%. Rather, focus on what has 70% of the importance in the decision to buy, which is how the Buyer will run the business.

The Broker must excite the Buyers about how they can run the business much better than the Sellers and give them examples and reasons how they can do it better. They will thus make more money than the Sellers have earned. You should have the Buyer list things that he would keep and what he likes about the business, and also list things he would change about the business and what he would do to improve it.

Owner's Actual Take Home: (same as EBITDA—Earnings Before Interest and Taxes and Depreciation and Amortization).

Following is an example of what an owner will actually earn for the year:

Gross Sales	$100,000 = 100%
-Cost of Goods Sold	-$50,000 = -50%
Gross Profit	$50,000
-Business Expenses	-$30/$40,000 (and taxes too)
Owner's Actual Take Home 10% to 20%	

Example to explain that cash is ok:
Farmers take the wheat they grow and milk from their cows and live off that. In the same way, business owners take cash from their businesses. When you are calculating the amount a new buyer will be receiving, it is important to remember that there is usually not a mortgage on the balance sheet of the seller. However, when a buyer purchases the business, there will be a mortgage. A broker should point that out to a buyer, who may not realize the importance thereof. That cost must be added. It is always better to be honest, and to be certain the buyer knows everything in advance. Not only is honesty the best policy, but failure to inform and lack of understanding can be deal breakers.

Financial Relationship between Buyer and Seller

Selling Price	$100,000
Down Payment	40,000
Note back to Seller	60,000
(Owner Financing)	
"This Note Subject to Offset"	

Educate the Buyer about the above clause in the contract regarding material misrepresentation. This should make the Buyer feel more confident about the truth of the Seller's information. In the contract, normally, the above clause will mean that the note is subject to offset for 1) Material Misrepresentation, and 2) Liens. Hence, if the Seller misrepresented any of the information in a material way, then the Buyer will have a way out. This is very important.

What holds a deal together is the shared risk between the Seller and the Buyer: the Buyer has to do well because it's his life, and the Seller is at risk because he is financing the buyer and depends on the Buyer to do well.

Negotiations

Negotiations are a path to terms and conditions that make the deal work for both the Buyer and Seller—that is what is needed to make the deal go through. The Broker must be creative in figuring out how to structure the deal so it goes through, thus making both the Buyer and Seller happy. This structure may differ considerably depending on the individual set of Buyer and Seller for each deal.

A Buyer ordinarily has some money to put down to buy the business. But that money, set aside for the down payment, is dwindling away as he hesitates. This is a great motivation. It is the Broker's responsibility to a buyer to encourage him to make a decision before all his savings are gone.

A deal is a good deal if both the Buyer and Seller are happy.

The 90% Rule—Facts About Buyers:

1. 90% of all buyers are first-time buyers. They have never been in business before.
2. 90% of all buyers will finance their purchase.
3. 90% of all buyers do not know what kind of business they really want, or what type of business best serves their needs.
4. 90% of all buyers are terrified and/or uneducated in the business buying process.
5. 90% of all sales will be financed by the Seller, especially in a tight market.
6. 90% (or more) will buy a business other than that which was advertised or the one about which they inquired.

7. 90% of all buyers have from $25,000 to $100,000 that they are willing to risk as a down payment.
8. 90% of all buyers are used to making, and are comfortable with, 10% decisions.

Business Valuation—Rules of Thumb:
1. Always suggest that the Seller get a 3rd party appraisal. (We will supply you with a list of appraisal companies.)
2. Field Formulas: *(Franchises may differ the formulas below, but those differences are usually small.)*
   a. **Retail:**
   Asking Price: 70% of Gross Sales (for most recent year).
   Selling Price: 70% of the asking price, probably.
   b. **Food Service:**
   Asking Price: 60% of Gross Sales (for most recent year).
   Selling Price: 60% of the asking price, probably.
   c. **Service:**[3]
   Asking Price: 50% of Gross Sales (for most recent year).
   Selling Price: 50% of the asking price, probably.
   d. **Professional Practices:**[4]
   Asking Price: 60-75% of Gross Sales (for most recent year).
   Selling Price: 50-70% of the asking price, probably.
   Rather than use the most recent year, some businesses and professional practices may wish to use an average of the preceding three years. If you do this, make sure you note whether sales are increasing, decreasing, or remaining about the same. Sales that are decreasing are a red flag. Look for reasons, and be ready to explain them to a buyer.
   e. **Coin Op/Dry Cleaning, Printing:**
   Asking Price: 100% of Gross Sales (for most recent year).
   Selling Price: 70% of the asking price, probably.
   Equipment intensive businesses demand higher sales prices.

3, 4 *Service industries involve many personal relationships which may or may not continue with a change of owners.*

APPENDIX I

    f. **Manufacturing:**
    Asking Price = **Sales Price** = 100% or more of Gross Sales. *Metal Manufacturing, not wood manufacturing.*

    g. **Liquor Store:**
    Sells for inventory cost + 2 years of Owner's actual take home (what the owner actually makes from the business including cash, "perks," etc.).

    h. **Convenience Store:** (retail store with gas—inside sales is what matters)
    Asking Price: 70% of Gross Sales (inside sales, not gas sales) (for most recent year) + gas in ground at time of sale.
    Selling Price: 70% of the asking price, probably.

3. Higher volume businesses or businesses grossing over 1 million dollars—Lehman Method = 5% of 1st million, 4% of 2nd million, 3% of 3rd million, 2% of 4th million, and 1% of each million thereafter. (Bottom Line Approach)

    a. **A multiple of 3 to 5 Years earnings (EBIT—Earnings Before Interest and Taxes, EBITDA—Earnings Before Interest and Taxes and Depreciation and Amortization).**

    b. **Adjust this for the living expenses of the Seller that are taken out of the business.**

Another method of valuation:

Restaurants

Bagel	20 times weekly gross sales
Bar	20 times weekly gross sales
Deli	16 times weekly gross sales
Pizza	20 times weekly gross sales
Restaurant	½ annual gross sales

In Restaurant sales: Owners ask for 50% down, but usually get one-third down.

Other Businesses

Alarm Company	40 times monthly income on recurring sales; must be based on 5 year average exclusive

Auto-Transmissions	2 times yearly net income
Cards	60% of yearly gross sales
Beverage	1/3 of yearly gross sales, plus inventory
Convenience	15 times weekly gross sales
Dry Cleaner	80% of yearly gross sales
Laundromat	70 times weekly gross sales
Limo	50% of yearly gross sales
Liquor	25% of yearly gross sales, plus inventory
Supermarkets	7 times weekly gross sales, plus inventory
HVAC Business	3 to 5 times yearly gross income, before taxes
Ice Cream	2 times yearly net income
Accounting Firms	1½ yearly volume, dollar for dollar. (Sometimes commission is paid by buyer at 15%, usually paid over 3 years, with 20% down, and the remainder paid over 36 equal monthly payments. IMPORTANT: 1 year RETAINAGE—any account that leaves during 1st year will have its yearly fee deducted from total amount of the sales price.

In Business sales (other than restaurants), Owners usually get 50% down. Selling prices throughout the country are essentially the same with a mean of 50.1% to 54.3% of Gross Sales.

In a small business (under $1 million), there is a greater correlation between Gross Sales and Sale Price than between Earnings and Sales Price. In businesses over $1 million, we are more likely to use Earnings to determine the sales price.

For small businesses, you must look at Gross Sales (Top Line) to determine how much a Buyer can make, not Bottom Line.

APPENDIX I

If the Seller asks you what you think you can get for the Seller's business, then you can explain, "Normally, in your type of business …"—then explain the appropriate rule as outlined above, indicating that that is a usual "ball park" figure. Indicate that much depends on supply and demand, location, physical condition of the business, possibility of retention versus attrition of clients or customers, etc. You can suggest an independent appraisal.

If the Seller says, "I want $xxx for my business," and you believe it is unrealistic, the Broker can indicate that, although you do not think it will go for that high a price, you will push hard for it. Most sellers will want to ask for a much higher price than they really think they are going to receive. While this may work out well, more often too high an asking price will dissuade buyers from even seeing the business, much less making an offer. In point of fact, later, when you have an interested buyer, the seller usually lowers the price., but may have missed out on others who would have, creating an "auction" or bidding war, may have led to a higher sale price.

THE PROCESS OF BUSINESS BROKERAGE: FROM BEGINNING TO END

THE LISTING

Listing Agreement (signed) (*Exclusive* **Listing Agreements only)**
Office Approval
Copy of Lease and Related Assignments
Financial Statements
Tax returns
Evaluation
Franchise Agreement

Often, people buy a business, run it for a few years, then, for personal reasons, want to sell (e.g., "burn out," lack of enjoyment, divorce, illness, relocating, etc.).

Whatever the asking price, the Broker should suggest half of the asking price to be the down payment—this cements the deal, and has the side benefit of educating the Seller to the possibility that he will have to finance the Buyer.

Inform the Buyer as to any problems with the business, so they do not discover them later and think you withheld information. When buyers find out detrimental information later, it is much more likely to break the deal.

After getting the Seller's listing and educating the Seller and Buyer, the Broker puts the Buyer and Seller together to form a relationship. Hopefully, the Seller then excites the Buyer about the business. The

APPENDIX I

Seller tells his story about the business, and the Buyer tells the Seller about himself, to make the Seller comfortable with possibly taking notes from the Buyer. *NEVER LET THE BUYER AND SELLER MEET OR SPEAK WITHOUT YOU BEING THERE.* Try to stay between the buyer and seller as much as possible. This is for 2 reasons: 1) it shows that you are doing your job, and at closing you do not want the Seller saying to you "You did nothing on this deal, the buyer and I did all the work," and 2) the less the Buyer and Seller are together, the less likely it would be for one of them to say something which may inadvertently break the deal.

1. Getting a Listing

In order to be successful as a Business Broker, each individual Broker must have a huge, and continually growing, inventory of Listings.

THIS IS THE MOST IMPORTANT ASPECT OF BUSINESS BROKERAGE. WITHOUT QUESTION, THE NAME OF THE GAME—FOR YOU TO MAKE MONEY—IS "LISTINGS, LISTINGS, LISTINGS." AS A BUSINESS BROKER, YOU CANNOT BE SUCCESSFUL WITHOUT CONSTANTLY FOLLOWING THE METHODS DESCRIBED IN THIS MANUAL TO GET LISTINGS.

Example of the importance of inventory: Home Depot is the #1 home improvement retailer in the world. To attain and maintain that status, and earn a lot of money as a result, Home Depot must always maintain a huge inventory of products, e.g.: from a manual hand lawn mower, to a gas powered automatic lawn mower, to a tractor size lawn mower; from a hand stapler to an electric powered staple gun. Home Depot maintains an inventory from the smallest to the largest type of product for all their products. Had they not done this, they would not have survived, much less become #1.

In the exact same way, each business broker MUST maintain a huge inventory. That is why working for a company like Manheim Business Brokers is so important: with many salespeople putting all their listings together, it gives all of us a greater chance of making a buyer happy. That means you must follow all the methods as described in this manual, and work hard to constantly build your inventory of listings. It must be a daily routine that never stops. Why? Because this is how you will be a successful Business Broker. If you do not follow these methods, you will not be successful as a Business Broker. It's really as simple as that!

Just as we need a large selection of "pots," we need appropriate "lids" for these "pots." This means we must attract Buyers for our listings. The key to finding buyers is to build your inventory of listings. If you build a huge constantly growing inventory of listings, then you will attract proportionately more buyers, and therefore close proportionately more deals, and earn more commissions.

Just as Home Depot has many types of products, a Broker must have different types of Listings: Retail, Restaurants, Services, Manufacturers, Catering, Lounges, Dry Cleaners, Coin-Operated Laundromats, Convenience Stores, Distributorships, etc. Also, for each there must be some that would sell for a down payment of $30,000 to $60,000, some for $60,000 to $100,000, some for several million dollars, and, from a geographical point of view, some in Town A, some in Town B, some in New York, Texas, California, etc.

Actively getting listings is crucial. You have to let people know we exist. You must let everyone you know and meet that you are from Manheim Business Brokers, and that you can help them sell a business or buy a business. You truly never know where you may find a Buyer or Seller of a business, and unless you market yourself by speaking directly to people and letting them know what you do, you are likely to be missing valuable opportunities to make a deal and collect a commission. You will be pleasantly surprised by how much people like to talk about themselves and their businesses. In all personal contacts, the two initial introductory comments involve a name and "what do you do for a living?"

***Always carry all the documents and tools (e.g., 5 Step Plan, Brochure, etc.) necessary to get a listing (e.g., in your car, brief case, etc.), because you never know when you will find a potential Seller to get a Listing.**

APPENDIX I

Methods of Getting Listings:

Always start off communications with a compliment as it makes it easier for you to speak to the owner. For example, "This is a beautiful store, I love it, is the owner in, I would love to tell him how happy I am shopping here."

1. Direct Mail

There is a 1% to 3% return (2% to 6% return if you follow up with a call).

2. Cold Calling (In Person)

Walk into stores and talk to the owner about selling that business, as follows:

- If you do not know who the owner is, speak to an employee, and first give them a compliment, like "This is a great store, I love the store, is the owner in today, I would like to tell him how happy I am shopping here?" or "You know, this is a great restaurant, it was a great meal, is the owner available to speak to?"

- If they ask why you want the owner, just say that you like the store and just wanted to meet the owner, or depending on the situation, you might just say "It's personal."

- You must then take the owner to a place where NO ONE IS AROUND—confidentiality is your most important weapon at the first meeting. Then say to the owner, "Hi, you have a nice business." It is important to hand him your business card at this time. He might be unwilling to say he wants to sell if he does not know you are a **REAL BUSINESS BROKER**. "I am Joe Smith, I'm from Manheim Business Brokers, and we have a lot of Buyers looking to buy a business like yours. I was wondering if you are planning on selling your business now or within the next few months." If you cannot get the owner alone, and he has read your business card, then say, "I have something I would love to talk to you about. Can I call you when you're free to talk." Ask for his business card.

- Another approach might be to indicate that you are a business broker, and are wondering if the owner has any plans to expand. If not, tell him you have many businesses like his, and would appreciate leads if he knows anyone who is ready to sell. Many owners will call you later, when no employees are in earshot, and say, "Hey, you got me thinking. How much can I get for my business?"

3. Cold Calling (Telemarketing)

You will be spending a lot of time on the phone, calling businesses to see if they want to sell. Ask for the owner, indicating, if asked, that "It is personal." When you speak to the owner, say "Hi, my name is John Smith, I am calling from Manheim Business Brokers, and we have a lot of people looking to buy a business like yours. I was wondering if you were looking to sell your business now or in the next few months."

When the owner says that they are interested, you then set a time for you to go to their business and meet with them. When you meet with them, you bring all the necessary forms for the owner to sign for the Listing.

If the owner is not interested in selling right now, and you have a pleasant conversation going, ask if he knows any other possible seller.

4. Specialized Cold Calling

If you have a buyer who wants a specific business, e.g., a Laundromat, and you do not have any Laundromat listings, use the Yellow Pages or the Internet and call all the Laundromats you can. Persistence works.

5. Networking

Networking presents amazing opportunities where you may not expect them. Become part of whatever organizations or groups you can, e.g., Kiwanis, Masons, Better Business Bureau, Small Business Associations, church, temple, etc.—let everyone know you are a Business Broker from Manheim Business Brokers and to contact you if they or anyone they know ever wants to Buy or Sell a business. It is very important to speak to every lawyer and accountant you can find, because they are the people that owners often speak to before they sell their businesses. Lawyers and accountants will refer you to people seeking to buy or sell a business.

Make a point to go to different restaurants, dry cleaners, etc., and then it is easier to talk to the owner.

APPENDIX I

4. Drop Notes
(11% to 15% return) *The number One way to get listings and buyers*
Write on a card in blue ink (and put it in an envelope), "We represent many people who are seeking to buy a business like yours. My name is Joe Smith and I am from Manheim Business Brokers. If you are interested, I would love to speak with you to assist you in the sale of your business. Manheim Business Brokers is the most experienced and largest Business Brokerage in New York State. Please contact me at (516) 520-2000. I look forward to meeting you. Sincerely, Joe Smith, Manheim Business Brokers."

On the outside of the envelope, write "Confidential for Owner." Slip this under the door of the store after hours.

Each Broker should do 100 drop notes per day.

Convincing the Seller to give you an *Exclusive Listing:*
When you have an opportunity to get an exclusive listing, move on it quickly. Things happen very fast; the seller may find his own buyer, or an accountant or lawyer may present a buyer to the Seller. Go to the store or office and meet the seller. Do not waste time! Have your documents with you, show them the 6 Step Plan, and get the listing signed. If you need additional help, ask a manager to attend the presentation with you.

When trying to get a Listing, be prepared, and have ALL of the tools listed below with you at the meeting with the Seller *(YOU MUST USE ALL THESE TOOLS EVERY TIME YOU MEET A SELLER TO GET AN EXCLUSIVE LISTING):*

1. An Exclusive Listing Agreement.

2. The 6 Step Plan Presentation (specific to the business you are trying to list—for example, if it is a pizza store, then use the 6 Step Plan that says "6 Step Plan to Sell Your Pizza Store" on top.)

3. A Color Brochure—this includes a picture of the exact business text about the exact business that you are trying to list. This is a very valuable tool that Sellers become very excited about, because it shows them that our company has spent a lot of money and time to develop this brochure to sell their business.

4. A copy of the Sunday Newsday Business Opportunity section that shows how dominant our Manheim Business Brokers advertising is. (Note to Brokers from other areas reading this—select the dominant newspaper in your area and work on getting volume and placement.)

5. A laptop computer that will be used to show the main Manheim Business Brokers site and our specific web site for their type of business. For example, www.DeliBroker.com for a deli, or www.PizzaStoreBroker.com for a pizza store. Even Professional sellers like physicians and dentists will be impressed by the number of listings featured on our web sites, www.professionalpracticebrokers.com and www.MedicalDentalhealthCare.com.

6. A copy of our confidentiality agreement.

To get an Exclusive Listing you must follow these procedures in your presentation:

First, tell the Seller that you would like to talk in a room where none of his employees will hear you. (*This is important because it sets a tone that you keep the sale of his business confidential and secret from his employees.*)

Second, you take control of his desk. Open up the 6 step plan right in front of the Seller so he has to look at it. You then have all the rest of your tools ready for him to see as you speak.

Third, follow the instructions below in using the 6 Step Plan:

1. **EXPERIENCE:**
Point to Step 1, and start reading the words: "EXPERIENCE—We are the largest Mergers and Acquisitions firm in New York with over 60 brokers at your service to sell your business." **Then, explain that our company has been selling businesses for nearly 40 years.**

2. **NETWORKING:**
Then, point to Step 2, and start reading the words: "NETWORKING—Manheim Business Brokers will invite real estate and business brokers to actually view your business." **Then, explain that we will co-broke with other reputable business brokers, mergers & acquisitions firms, and real estate brokers,**

which means that you will have many more individuals working on selling your business. (We do not co-broke our buyers, however.)

3. ADVERTISING:

Then, point to Step 3, and start reading the words: "ADVERTISING—We will advertise your business for sale in the Wall Street Journal, New York Times, Newsday, Daily News, local papers, the Internet, radio and/or television." **Then show the Seller the copy of the Sunday Newsday Business Opportunity section, and tell them that you can see that the Manheim Business Brokers advertisements dominate the section. Point specifically to our ads.**

4. COLOR BROCHURE:

Then, point to Step 4 and start reading the words: "COLOR BROCHURE—Our graphic design department will design and produce a magnificent color brochure of your business or building at no cost to you." **Show the Seller the brochure. Explain that we show this only to pre-qualified purchasers. Then say, "You can see how professional our presentation of your business is to potential purchasers—and this is one of the important steps that enable Manheim Business Brokers to sell your business for the highest price and faster than anyone else." If you wish, our graphic design department will work with you and me to modify the brochure.**

5. THE INTERNET:

Then, point to Step 5 and start reading the words: "THE INTERNET—We will contact national, international, and local buyers through an Internet, direct mail, & telephone marketing campaign." **Manheim Business Brokers has one of the largest networks of business Internet sites in the world. Your business will be listed in our main site, which has tremendous visibility and has hundreds of thousands of companies and individuals to view your business. Of course, all the information about your business that is listed on our Internet sites is general, so there is no way anyone reading it would know it was your specific business for sale. You now open up your laptop (which should** have been turned on prior to the meeting and set up to show the sites) and show the Seller the specific site to their type of business (i.e., www.DeliBroker.com, www.CosmeticsBroker.com, www.PizzaStoreBroker.com, etc.). Explain to the Seller that Manheim Business Brokers has a division and web site that specializes in selling only their type of business (i.e., restaurant, card store, distributorship, etc.—MENTION THE ONE SITE SPECIFIC TO THEIR TYPE OF BUSINESS). In fact, we are one of very few, if not the only, companies in the United States that specializes in business brokerage of (MENTION ONLY THEIR SPECIFIC BUSINESS HERE, i.e., delis, pizza stores). Explain that we get a large number of people who call us and visit the site seeking to buy your type of business from around the country. Then, click the link to the main Manheim Business Brokers site to show the Seller that site. Then click on the link to "view the office live" to show them our office. (This will work even if you are not connected to the Internet—it will be on the disk we give you).

6. **CONFIDENTIALITY:**
Then, point to Step 6 and start reading the words: "CONFIDENTIALITY—No information is given to potential purchasers without first assessing their financial strength and retaining a signed confidentiality agreement from them." **Then show the Seller the copy of the confidentiality agreement and tell them "this is an example of the confidentiality agreement we use."**

If a Seller asks how long it will take to sell their business, then answer with the following explanation: " It all depends on how much you want for your business. It could take one month to sell or it could take up to a year to sell. Most of our businesses sell between two and six months. We will put together a package that will make your business very attractive to a purchaser, but if you are trying to sell your business for over the market, it will take longer to sell. Whatever you want to ask for your business, we will push for that number."

***Manheim Business Brokers is an "Exclusive Listing House." We only take exclusive listings of businesses for sale.*

APPENDIX I

Explain the following to the Sellers if they do not want to sign with the exclusive arrangement:

1. It is the best way to get the highest price in the fastest time for your business. Our office and sales agents want to know that a client is a motivated seller, and by signing an exclusive, that is achieved. Since all our listings are exclusives, the brokers in the office will not sell your business unless it is exclusive because their commission is not protected without an exclusive.

2. The reason brokers do not sell businesses if there is no exclusive is because of the following: A buyer may go to you behind our back and say that they are interested in buying your business, and never mention Manheim Business Brokers. We are not saying that you will try to go behind our back, but rather, the buyer will go to you and you will not even know that it was Manheim Business Brokers that did its job and got the buyer interested in your business. For example, we will introduce your business to a potential purchaser, then that buyer will have his brother or friend go directly to you, and you would never have known that it was Manheim Business Brokers that did its job in introducing the buyer to your business. By protecting our brokers, we can have them working even harder to sell your business.

3. We do not charge you any fee up front or at any time unless a sale of your business actually goes through. Other companies charge upfront fees of $10,000, $25,000 or $40,000, depending on the size or your business. We do not do that because we are confident we will sell your business. But, for us to not charge you an upfront fee, we have to know that you are really interested in selling, so we can effectively do our job and get you the best price in the fastest time.

4. A third party, Manheim Business Brokers, in this case, can always negotiate a better deal for a seller than the seller directly. The reason for this is that Manheim can say anything and not seem desperate or emotional. This enables us to negotiate more effectively in attaining the highest price for a Seller's business, and doing so in the fastest time. So, I would suggest always letting us handle the negotiations with a potential purchaser.

The Broker should always get a one year exclusive. If you cannot get that, then in special circumstances, with management permission, management may allow the broker to take less, perhaps 9 months.

If the business has not yet sold at the time the exclusive expires, then at that point, you can say to the Seller that you have explored the market and the inability to sell the business is because the asking price was too high. If the seller reduces the asking price to what we believe is an appropriate amount, and gives us a little additional time, we can now sell the business in a much shorter time.

Writing up the Listings
***DO NOT ask for the below mentioned items until after the Seller has signed the listing agreement.

Learn as much as you can about the Listing:
- Get a copy of the Lease. Read it. (More deals have been squelched at the last minute because of landlords and lease problems than for any other reason.)
- Get copies of the seller's brochures, menus, web sites, and anything that represents their company to their customer.
- Get the Seller's permission to contact the Landlord, but DO NOT yet contact the Landlord, yourself. The lease is often going to be a problem, so DO NOT contact the Landlord until you must as part of the negotiation process.
- Get a copy of the financial statements.
- Learn the Seller's story behind their business—as much as you can: how they got started, what they love about it, etc., and why they are selling.
- Make yourself knowledgeable about the lease, the listing, financial statements, and other documents in the file. The more knowledgeable and professional you sound about the business, the better chance you will have of selling it.
- Go to the actual business and see how it runs.
- In the Listing Agreement, normally charge 10%, and also, that 10% will not be lower than $10,000. If a seller says to you, "Why are you 10% and this other Business Broker is only asking 8%,

your answer is as follows: "Manheim Business Brokers sells more businesses than anyone else; we will get you the highest price your business is worth in the shortest amount of time. These other companies can tell you they will charge 1%, but they will not be able to get you your best deal, and it will take them much longer to sell your business if they sell it at all, because we have so many more resources and higher quality resources and operate in a much more professional manner. If you want to waste your time, have unprofessional people sell your business or worse than that, lose potential buyers because the presentation of your company was done incorrectly, then go to these other business brokers. If you want your business represented by professionals and you want the greatest amount of money for your sale, then use Manheim Business Brokers."

- In many cases, the Seller's lease requires the Seller to get permission from the Landlord to assign the lease or sub-lease. Do not worry about this until the end of the Buying process. Take it step by step. **But it is very important to get a copy of the lease in advance.** Tell them we have an attorney on staff that will read it and help with any problems free of charge.
- Ask what the Seller wants for the business. If Seller does not know what Seller wants for the business, then use the formulas above to determine the price. Then if Seller asks you, explain the formulas, and throw it back to the Seller and say I think based on xxx that you should ask $xxx, what do you think? If you cannot determine a price, then ask your manager for assistance.
- **In the case of a small business, around $150,000 or smaller, ONLY IF the Seller questions the $10,000 minimum commission, then explain the following:** You say it is important to sell a smaller business with a minimum commission (i.e., $10,000) because this way the other brokers in the office will put forth maximum effort to sell your business, and this is absolutely important for you. Brokers would not work hard to sell your business as they would for a larger business, unless they know they are going to earn at least $10,000 (that really motivates them).

- A Listing is very saleable if 3 things occur:
    1. **The amount of the** down payment is small.
    2. **Management**—can a family run it, etc. is little experience needed.
    3. **10% commission, exclusive**—this will entice Brokers to sell it more quickly, and it also means there is a motivated seller.

Marketing a Listing:
"Listings" is where the money is. If you get a lot of Listings constantly, then the buyers will come to you.

Three places to market your listings:

1. **Sunday Newspaper**

    Headings for the ad:
    - Something about the fact that this is a GOOD BUSINESS! Don't put price in the ad.
    - Small Down Payment.
    - Include reason for why it is for sale: for example, "Selling because of divorce," "Selling because owner relocating."

    Examples of Ads:
    - TRAVEL AGENCY—Est. for 20 yrs. Very active clientele. Top location. Well known in town. Real $$ maker. Owners retiring. Small down payment. Come check it! Call (516) 520-2000 for details.
    - ICE CREAM STORE—Emergency sale! Illness forces immediate sale. Very attractive shopping center location (plenty of parking). Lots of stainless steel equipment. Perfect for husband and wife (or working family). Don't miss it! Small down payment. For details call (516) 520-2000.

2. **Internet**

We market Listings on our Internet site as well as other sites that list businesses for sale.

3. **Other Brokers in the Office**

During the weekly office meetings, Brokers should show their Listings to other Brokers in the office. Explain what is good about this Listing: for example, "This is a great location, easy for a family to run, etc."

You should make a one page summary of the listing to show at the weekly meetings to the other Brokers in the office including:
- What the business does.
- History
- Financial History
- Assets
- Location
- Price & Terms
- Owner Motivation

Dealing with the Buyer

Never forget: 90% of Buyers to whom you speak will buy a business other than that which they came to you to buy. This means the Broker must find out what the Buyer likes, and then suggest businesses to the Buyer that fit what those desires. This is key to the success of a Business Broker.

1. First build an honest relationship.
2. We must meet face to face.
3. We must manage the relationship to accomplish four very important things to help the Buyer get to his goal.
   - You MUST get to know the Buyer.
   - The Buyer MUST get to know you.
   - You MUST educate the Buyer about the Business Brokerage Rules (i.e., cash business, Seller financing, etc.).
   - You MUST get the Buyer to sign a confidentiality agreement.

Think of yourself as a" "Doctor of Selling Businesses" (DSB). If you are in pain, you will call the doctor when you are really uncomfortable. By the same token, a person will only call a Business Broker when he really wants to buy a business. A doctor has an exact sequence of events, which he must follow in order to help people (and succeed). As a DSB, your plan is the same: make an appointment, meet, diagnose, then, as needed, get medicine or whatever else is needed to remedy the situation. Business brokers must do exactly the same, according to the sequence in this manual, in order to diagnose your client's needs, guide the Buyer to completing a purchase, and succeed. Your reward: You may not save a life, but you do link up a happy seller with a happy buyer, and you earn a commission.

Suggestion: When you interview any prospective Buyer, suggest, in an offhand way, a few franchises as well near the end of your meeting. Do not try to sell the buyer on owning a franchise. Just put out the possibility, and if appropriate, have franchisors contact the buyer from franchises you think he might like. Just say to the Buyer, "In addition to the businesses we have listed, I would like to have a few franchises send you information on their opportunities. Is that OK with you?"

You will then contact the franchisor with the Buyer's info, and they will do the rest. Your work as far as the franchise is complete from here on in, except for following up to see if the Buyer is comfortable with the communications from the franchise or has any questions related to them.

> *You sell 7% to 10% of Buyers who come in your office. 30% of the Buyers who come in are never going to buy a business. Many of the rest of the people who come in the office would more easily buy a franchise because there is a system in place, a known name. They probably did not think of a franchise and do not realize it at first, but they may more easily succeed by owning a franchise.*

Ad Call Format

This is the conversation a Broker should have when the Broker answers the phone when a potential Buyer is calling about an ad.

Ring, Ring …

BROKER: "Manheim Business Brokers, John Smith, may I help you?"

CALLER: "I'm calling about the ad (e.g., Restaurant, coin op, convenience store) you had in the paper Sunday."

APPENDIX I

BROKER: "Have you been in that kind of business before?"

You should ask this one question to put yourself in the driver's seat of the conversation.

CALLER: "Yes, for 12 years," or "No, but we're thinking about it."

BROKER: "Well, the employees of that business don't know it's for sale, so because of the confidentiality of a business sale, I really can't give you much information over the phone."

"What I would like to do is meet with you for a few minutes and then I could tell you where it is, give you the financial information about the business and let you go by, on your own, to take a look at it and, if you're interested after that, we'll get back together."

"Let me tell you where we're located:" (Give the address and, if necessary, instructions to the office.) "I could meet with you this afternoon at 4:00 or would tomorrow morning, about 11:00 be better?" Always give two options of a time to meet.

CALLER: "Well, I need to talk with my husband (or wife) and he (she) doesn't even get home until 7pm."

BROKER: "Well, I could meet you next Wednesday at 8pm if that would be more convenient."

CALLER: "Yes, I believe we could come in at 8pm Wednesday."

BROKER: "Fine, I look forward to seeing you and your husband (wife) this Wednesday at 8pm. By the way, my name again is John Smith. May I have your name please?"

CALLER: "My name is Francis Johnson."

BROKER: "Alright Ms. Johnson, I'll see you Wednesday at 8pm, oh, by the way may I have your phone number please, in case something comes up?"

*****AT THIS POINT, GET OFF THE PHONE IMMEDIATELY, POLITELY, BUT AS FAST AS YOU CAN*****

You have to get off the phone immediately because you have one very focused goal in this conversation: to get the buyer into the office. If you do not get off the phone immediately, then you may say something to make the buyer decide not to come in. For example, if they call about a business that happens to be in Town A and you tell them that it is in Town A, you will lose them if they are only interested in Town B. Had you gotten them in to the office, although they called about a business that happened to be in Town A, you could have shown them all the businesses in the town they wanted and kept them as a Buyer.

Any more questions that you answer will just be chances for you to say something they do not want to hear. If you get them in the office, you can then show them businesses based upon what you have learned about them.

Do not ask them if they have dealt with someone in the office before. This just gives them one more opportunity not to want to come in to the office. If they have dealt with someone in the office before, they will tell you.

If, on the phone, they push and ask where the business is, just tell them, "I have several businesses listed, and I'll show you all of them when you come in."

If they ask how much it is, then say, "Actually, we have several, many of which have small down payments and we may find some where the Seller will finance it for you."

If they get very pushy, you can say, "We have a written contract with the Seller not to give any specific information without meeting with the prospective buyer."

Do not worry about qualifying the Buyer because the Buyer has qualified himself by calling you to begin with. The full qualification questions come during the actual meeting.

In business brokerage, there are more Buyers than Sellers, which is why it is important to constantly get more Listings.

Reminder About Buyers
Only 2% have owned businesses before, so the Broker must educate the Buyer.

The average small business Buyer is willing to invest $25,000 to $100,000 (as down payment).

They do not know about Owner Financing, so the Broker must educate them, and they must know they are not going to get an SBA load unless they put up collateral, like their house.

Many Buyers are numbers oriented, so the Broker must show them the Business before the numbers, to get them excited about the business. Get the romance of a business to catch the eye of the buyer.

What do we offer at Manheim Business Brokers?

This should be explained to Buyer.

Security
A big advantage in buying an ongoing business is that you as the new owner have an immediate cash flow and an established customer base. You don't have to build a business; you simply take over an existing successful business with the present owner's assistance.

Financing
We assist you in obtaining financing. Banks are reluctant to finance business purchases for several reasons. One is that all small businesses attempt to minimize profits shown on financial statements to reduce tax liability. In addition, a bank cannot come in to manage a business if foreclosure becomes necessary. Therefore, over 90% of business purchases are financed by the owner himself, which demonstrates his confidence in the business. Most successful Business Brokerages, like ours, have alternate methods of financing available to share with their Buyers.

Confidentiality
Unlike the sale of real estate or franchises, the sale of an ongoing business is very confidential for both the Seller and the prospective Buyer. All inquiries are held in strict confidence. Meetings are confidential, and we are available after hours and on weekends.

Things a Buyer Should Know
We at Manheim Business Brokers are advocates of finding a business that you like and feel comfortable managing. You, like every other

prospective buyer, have a vision of being your own boss and calling your own shots. An old saying in the real estate industry is "the three most important things a buyer should look for are location, location, and location." While location is important to a business buyer, be aware that track record and management round out the three components of a successful business. Let's assume that you find a business that you like and its location in fine. But because of poor management, the business may not show the greatest track record. Purchased for the right price and terms, this business could become more successful with proper management making it a good way to achieve your vision of being in business for yourself. And finally, be aware that many businesses sell for much less than they are originally listed. So, if it's a business that you like, don't be afraid to make what you consider to be a low offer.

Help and Technical Support

Help and support continues from Manheim Business Brokers even after the Buyer purchases a business. We know that quite often, the new Buyer of a business will become a Seller. We want to maintain and help all Buyers and develop a great relationship, so when they decide to sell, they will call us.

The Buying Process

This is for the Buyer to make him feel comfortable about the process. Explain this to Buyer.

Evaluate the basic information on alternative businesses that sound interesting to you.

Visit the business without announcing yourself as a buyer (incognito) to get a "feel" for the business. (Note—This is NOT done with professional practices.)

Your Broker will introduce you to the Seller, and you will then ask the Seller from general to probing questions on anything and everything, **except** actual price negotiations.

Do your preliminary evaluation, based on the information provided by the Seller to Manheim Business Brokers and to you. While Manheim does everything possible to check the reliability of information given by the Seller, we can not guarantee its accuracy. It is the job of the Buyer and his advisors, legal and financial, to do due diligence before completing an important transaction such as this.

When you make an offer, include contingencies, which allow you to confirm that the information you have been provided is correct. Manheim Business Brokers will show you how to write an offer to protect you as the Buyer, subject to your legal advisor's input.

Once a sales price is agreed upon, make an even closer investigation into the business, confirming, to your satisfaction, the validity of your offer.

Close the purchase, and begin your first day as the owner of your own business. The Seller will assist in an orderly transition because most of his money is coming from your success.

You are part of the American Dream—You and your family own your own business!!

The Broker MUST educate the Buyer about the following:

In Real Estate Brokerage, confidentiality does not matter as much. But in Business Brokerage we do not want employees, customers or competitors to know the business is for sale. This is so the business is not affected, and it is important for the Seller as well as the Buyer.

The most important thing is to find a business that you like and can manage.

Three components of a successful business:
- Location
- Track Record
- Management

Explain that in Real Estate, Location is the single most important thing, but for a business, all three as listed above are just as important.

There is usually a human, personal reason for selling: i.e., retirement, poor health, divorce, relocating, etc. Tell the Buyer, "I always want to know why someone is selling. In my experience, I have found that, most of the time, the reason is simply a human personal reason."

As mentioned above, banks may not finance the purchase of a business, normally, because, if the Buyer fails, the Bank can not take over and run the business. In addition, small business financials are done so as not to pay taxes, thus showing a loss or no profit. This makes the purchase of even a terrific business appear more risky to a bank finance officer, especially during periods of credit tightness. Banks have normally made SBA (Small Business Administration) loans to existing businesses with a track record. They are reluctant to lend money to buy a business because of the 2 reasons above. Prepare your Buyer to realize he will likely have to put up his home or other collateral for a bank loan.

We usually suggest that the Seller finance the purchase, at least in part, taking notes from the Buyer. While the bank cannot come in to run the business if it does not succeed, the Seller can. His willingness to do so tells you a lot about the Seller's business, since he knows what the cash flow is better than anyone else. Seller financing means that the Seller is "putting his money where his mouth is." A Seller reluctant to do Seller financing may be a "red flag" that needs examining as to motive for not wishing to assume some risk.

It is not unusual for an accountant, examining the financials alone, to tell a Buyer not to buy the business. The financials, prepared in such a way as to allow the Seller to reduce or even avoid tax liability, may cause a conservative accountant to steer clear of even a great business investment. The accountant has to advise you based on the financials, not based on what really happens in almost 100% of small businesses, which are cash businesses. This may that a lot of what an owner earns is taken as cash from the store, allowing the financials to show no profit or a loss. The seller must also realize, however, that income that can not be clearly proven cannot be included in the evaluation of the business' selling price. The same is true of "perks' taken by an Owner, hence the need for recasting financials. (See chapter on Recasting for a full explanation of the subject.)

Owner Financing (also raises Buyer's comfort level) tells more about a business than financials.

Give Divorce Court Example: Say to the Buyer that someone once told you a great example that explains how a small business runs as far as cash and the money that the owner can really make. "Imagine a husband and wife in divorce court. The husband is on the stand," then Pick up paper and say, "You honor this is my tax return; we lost money last year" and point at bottom of the paper, "and then the wife says this is actually a very valuable business, it has supported our lifestyle the past 8 years. Actually, you have to look at the top line (and explain that top line is more important than bottom line in a small business, and explain why…if you bring in $xxx, then you can make $yyy).

The following basics hold true regardless of financial statements:
Owner's Actual Take Home (what the owner truly earns for the year) = 10% to 20% of Gross Sales
Cost of Goods Sold = 50% of Gross Sales (in retail business)
Other expenses (rent, wages, etc.) = 30% to 40% of Gross Sales

Explain this to Buyer: When the seller explains how much he is really making from the business, if he explains his number and essentially his numbers work out that he is earning 10% to 20% of his Gross Sales, then I would believe him because that is in accord with the number above.

Americans are not used to negotiating, so it is important to make an offer. You can tell the buyer that most often, businesses sell for less than the asking price, he should not be afraid to make an offer, if you like the business. By the same token, explain to sellers that they should not be offended by a low ball offer—that is what negotiation is all about.

Ask the following (their answers to this should go with the Buyer Registration form to manager):

"Are you married?" "Do you have a husband (or wife) who will be working the business with you?"

"Why do you want to be in business for yourself?"

"What type of business do you desire: Retail, Service, Manufacturing, Distribution, Restaurant, Lounge, Coin-operated Laundromat, or Liquor Store, etc." (These are all the top level categories of businesses.)

Then ask them what type of business specifically do they want (i.e., convenience store, card store, etc.). *If they do not know, then narrow it down for them.*

"Do you plan to operate the business 1) Full Time, 2) Part Time, 3) Absentee Management?"

"What are your monetary expectations?"

"What would you feel comfortable with as a down payment?" They almost always will say "it depends on the business." Then you say, "I know it does, but if you found a business you really liked, what would you feel comfortable with writing a check for, $15,000, $20,000, $100,000 down?" Then see what they say.

Qualifying the Buyer

A key factor in generating deals is to qualify a perspective buyer. Do not be afraid to ask important questions:

1. How much cash do you have to invest? Where are you getting the funds from? (Don't ever qualify a Buyer solely by how much money they have because if they are hot Buyer, they will get the money they need.

2. Are you ready now to buy a business, or is there a date when you will be able to buy?

3. You must always meet in person and get a copy of the Buyer's Driver's License. If he does not want to give it to you, END IT right there, he is hiding for some reason, probably to try and go behind your back to make the deal. Be nice but call a manager over to handle the problem immediately. But most of all, if a person does not want to give you his proper information, then he is not really an interested buyer and you are wasting your time.

4. Do you have to sell a business that you own now? If he has to sell something else, now is the time to tell him we can sell it and find you a new business better than any other firm. You then make a double commission, the one for selling the Buyers business and the one for selling him another business.

5. Ask for his attorney's number that he is going to use. This is

APPENDIX I

important because if you find a business for him, it will move much faster. If he needs an attorney, you can only recommend attorneys qualified and certified by Manheim Realty. There are legal issues and we want everything to be legally done correctly.

6. Can you purchase this business by yourself or do you need a partner?

List the businesses or franchises you have shown the Buyer.

Confidentiality Agreement
At the first meeting with the Buyer, have the Buyer read and sign the confidentiality agreement.

After the First meeting between the Buyer and the Seller:

NEVER LET THE BUYER AND SELLER MEET WITHOUT THE BROKER BEING THERE.

Meetings between the Buyer and Seller should always be held at the business because it helps get the Buyer more emotional and the Seller has more to talk about to increase the Buyers emotion.

When meeting with the Buyer and Seller, don't be with the Seller when the Buyer arrives to the meeting. Wait for the Buyer and walk in together, then leave with the Buyer. This is important because the ball is in the Buyer's court. Remember, you need both parties happy with the deal, so you must be helpful and friendly with both parties.

After the first meeting with the Buyer and the Seller together, you must do an exit interview. Don't give the financials at this point to the Buyer. You want to go as long as you possibly can without giving the financials to the Buyer. Do not be afraid to ask the question: "Do you like the business and would you be interested in buying it if we can get to a price that you and the seller can agree on?" We always like to make them understand that it is a give and take and the Buyer and Seller have to agree.

Let the Buyer know beforehand that they should never make an offer directly to the Seller. Rather, the Buyer should always make the offer through you, the Broker. The Buyer should communicate his/her offer to the Broker, then the Broker communicates the offer to the Seller. A Broker can always negotiate a better deal for a Buyer than the Buyer directly.

Making an Offer and Completing the Deal

After the first meeting between the Buyer and Seller, the Broker should keep asking the Buyer if the Buyer "wants the business." And when the Buyer says, "I have to look at the Lease, etc." just say "but if that is all good, the lease, the financials, etc, then do you want this business?"

At this point, the Broker should discuss with the Buyer what he wants to offer for the business. After establishing what the Buyer wants to offer, the Broker then orally communicates that offer to the Seller. At this point, the Seller will either accept the offer, or more likely reject the offer and from this point on, the negotiation process continues. The Broker then goes back and forth talking *separately* to the Buyer and the Seller, with different offers, until the Buyer and Seller agree on the terms.

Once the Buyer and Seller agree on the terms, the Broker then fills out the "Sales Agreement" form with the terms and has the Buyer and Seller sign it. Also, at the same time, the Broker fills out the "Commission Agreement" form, and has the Buyer and Seller sign it.

Once the "Commission Agreement" and the "Sales Agreement" have both been signed by the Buyer and Seller, the Broker then contacts the Seller's attorney and the Buyer's attorney to set a time for the two attorneys to talk on the phone and complete the contract. This is why the Broker must already have the name and phone number of the attorney for the Buyer and the attorney for the Seller.

After the Broker sets a time for the two attorneys to speak to each other, the Broker then must continue to follow the progress of the deal to ensure that it is completed. If problems arise in the contract, then the Broker must come up with a way to resolve any problems in order for the deal to go through. Do not hesitate to go to Mr. Manheim or a manager for assistance.

APPENDIX I

Financial Statements

You want to delay as long as possible before showing the Buyer the financial papers.

Before the Buyer ever sees the financial papers, the Buyer must know the whole story of the business, and Broker must "recast" the numbers and show what is really going on (based on what Seller has told you). Recasting the numbers means the Broker explains how the business works in terms of cash and how the owner truly makes a living from the business. This is VERY IMPORTANT because the financial papers have one purpose, and that is to show no profit or a loss. Therefore, for tax purposes, they will not have to pay any taxes.

The following example shows how a small business owner really lives off his business, and how a Broker must re-explain or recast the number to the Buyer to illustrate that, although the financial statements say there is no profit, the Seller in fact is completely supporting his lifestyle through the business:

This owner of a liquor store often throws personal parties at home and the drinks come from the owner's store, so the Cost of Goods Sold is really lower than it is reported. The owner and his family's salaries are incorporated in the financials. Thus, Seller is making much more money than is shown in his financial documents.

Explain how the cash and other income Seller takes are after tax because it is either taken in cash or expensed out to the business. So the 10% to 20% that Seller is making of Gross Sales is really after tax. So for example, a Seller who says a Buyer could make $100,000 per year, it is $100,000 after tax—which means it is really about $130,000.00 a year, not $100,000.00 a year.

Making Sales—Overview

1. PREPARATION
   Educating the Seller at the time of the Listing.
   Educating the Buyer at the time of the first interview.
   Find a willing Buyer and Seller.

2. CREATIVE FINANCING
   Down Payment driven business.

Get financing from other sources like the Small Business Administration. This is important, because if the buyer has all cash, the price of the business will be less.
Explore alternate financing sources.

3. THE OFFER ITSELF
   Interest signs versus buy signs and the "comfort level."
   Taking the offer.
   Re-educating the buyer.
   Presenting the offer.
   The counter offer.
   Re-educating the Seller.

4. THE SALE—PROBLEMS
   Buyers
   Sellers
   Attorneys and Accountants
   Relatives and friends
   Landlords

5. CLOSING
   Bulk Sale
   UCC
   Inventory

APPENDIX II
FORMS

Appendix includes sample Confidentiality Agreements, letters to buyers for different situations, Letters of Intent, a sample outline of a Purchase Agreement, a Selling Memorandum and other documents important to the sale of your business.

SAMPLE FORMS

1. COMMISSION AGREEMENT FOR A PROFESSIONAL PRACTICE

Commission Agreement

Re: Sale of _____ Practice ("The Practice"), identified as _____, located at _____. The undersigned (Seller) hereby retains _insert Broker's name here_ as its sole and exclusive broker and representative to obtain a buyer for The Practice for the period to expire _____ ("Agreement Term") subject to the terms set forth below.

Upon the sale of The Practice, _insert Broker's name here_ shall be paid a commission ("The Commission") in the amount of 10% of the aggregate consideration paid or payable for the sale. The Commission shall be not less than $10,000. The Commission shall be due and payable in full at the closing of the sale of The Practice. The consideration for the sale shall include all moneys and other consideration paid or payable with respect to the sale, including but not limited to the purchase price for equipment, restrictive covenant, good will and consulting or similar fees (other than moneys payable for actual time to be devoted by Seller at The Practice after the closing).

The Commission shall be paid upon the closing of the transaction, or upon any other act tantamount directly or indirectly to a sale, consolidation, transfer of assets or transfer of a shareholder, membership or other equity interest, merger, reorganization, employment, partnership, corporation, company, trade, transfer, or other related conveyance or transaction, whether for the whole or any part of The Practice. Any of the foregoing shall constitute a sale of the Practice. The Commission shall be paid either by certified or bank check. The Commission shall be payable upon _insert Broker's name here_ demand in the event that the sale does not close due to the default of the Seller.

A Commission with respect to the sale of The Practice to any person or entity introduced to the Seller by _insert Broker's name here_ shall be payable to _insert Broker's name here_ by the Seller in accordance with the above terms, provided that a sale take place not later than 30 months after said purchaser is introduced to the Seller during the Agreement Term to a prospective purchaser.

Should the purchaser sell The Practice to a purchaser not introduced by _insert Broker's name here_ during the Agreement Term, the commission payable to _insert Broker's name here_ shall be 5% of the aggregate consideration but not less than $5,000.

Seller hereby grants _insert Broker's name here_ and its agents the right to deliver any relevant information pertaining to The Practice during the Agreement Term. This Agreement may not be modified except in writing signed by Seller and _insert Broker's name here_. This Agreement shall be binding upon the heirs, successors or assigns of the parties hereto.

The foregoing is accepted and agreed to:
Signed: _____ Date: _____
Print Name: _____
Address: _____
Social Security # _____ or EIN # _____
Agreement accepted by:
_____Date: _____
for _insert Broker's name here_ .

APPENDIX II

2. SAMPLE CONFIDENTIALITY AGREEMENT

Confidentiality Agreement

This Confidentiality Agreement will confirm our mutual understanding in connection with our providing, and your receipt of, information regarding the _____(Practice for Sale)_____ in _____ (Location)_____ ("The Company").

"Information" means all written or oral data, reports, records or materials obtained from us or the Company, including the name, address, and type of business of the Company, the knowledge that the Company might be considering a sale, or even the fact that information has been provided. Information shall not include, and all obligations as to non-disclosure by the undersigned shall cease to be a part of, such information to the extent that such information: (i) is or becomes public as a result of acts by the undersigned: (ii) can be shown to be already known by the undersigned at the time of its disclosure hereunder: (iii) is independently obtained by the undersigned from a third party having no duty of confidentiality to the Company; (iv) is independently developed by the undersigned without the use of any Information supplied hereunder; or (v) is obligated to be disclosed pursuant to applicable law, regulation or legal process.

The undersigned agrees that Information is being furnished solely in connection with the undersigned's consideration of the acquisition of the Company and shall be treated as "secret" and "confidential" and no portion of it shall be disclosed to others, except those of employees and agents whose knowledge of the information is required to evaluate the Company as a potential acquisition and who shall assume the same obligations as under this Agreement. The undersigned hereby assumes full responsibility for the compliance of such employees or agents to the terms of this Agreement.

It is understood that the company is the intended party and beneficiary whose rights are being protected and may enforce the terms of this Confidentiality Agreement as if it were a party to this Agreement. In the event of a dispute, the venue shall be _County_, _State_. The prevailing party shall be entitled to recovery of all reasonable costs including attorney's fees, court costs, costs on appeal, and interest from date of breach. Any and all disputes shall be resolved binding arbitration in accordance with the rules of the American Arbitration Association.

No visits, no employee, supplier or customer contacts without express permission. The undersigned agrees that it will not hire any of the Company's employees, nor interfere in any of its business acquired under this Confidentiality Agreement nor use any such Information in a manner harmful to the Company. All communication shall be directed through _____ or attorney _____ unless otherwise specified in writing.

All information shall be promptly returned or destroyed, as directed by _____.

It is understood that (a) no representation or warranties are being made as to the completeness or accuracy of any Information and (b) any and all representations shall be made in a signed acquisition agreement or purchase contract and then be subject to the provisions thereof.

The undersigned acknowledges the responsibility to perform a due diligence review at its own cost and expense prior to any acquisition. The respective obligations of the parties to this Agreement shall survive for a period of two years following the date hereof.

SIGNATURE: _____ Date: _____
Name of Individual: _____Title: _____
Organization: _____ E-mail Address: _____
License Number: _____ State: _____
Telephone: _____ Cell phone _____ Fax: _____
Address:
    Street _____
    City _____ State_____ Zip Code _____

APPENDIX II

3. BUYER REGISTRATION

insert Broker's name here
insert Broker's address here
insert Broker's phone number here
insert Broker's fax number here

Buyer Registration NOTICE: You are instructed not to introduce yourself to sellers or their employees. Look at the location, then contact us for an appointment with the owners. This contract made and entered into by and between the undersigned and _insert Broker's name here_ , I, the undersigned, for and in consideration of _insert Broker's name here_ , furnishing me with special and confidential information pertaining to the particulars, location, price and other detailed information of each of the businesses, properties, including but not limited to real estate and buildings on/in which the business is located, or stores (hereinafter collectively referred to as "Listing" or "Listings") listed below, which information I have requested and received from _insert Broker's name here_ , and in further consideration of the brokers agreeing to render any additional services that may be necessary to effectuate the sale of the Listing listed below, in whole or any interest therein, either to me or to any of my assignees, nominees, administrators, agents, designees, heirs, affiliates, successors, assigns, dummy companies, or any person, entity, subsidiary or parent related to me (hereinafter collectively referred to as "Buyer" or the "undersigned"), agree: 1. That I hereby grant to _insert Broker's name here_ , for a period of three (3) years from the date hereof, the sole and exclusive right to negotiate and obtain for me any of the Listings listed below, which I might desire to purchase in whole or part. 2. That the information, details and particulars set forth below and received by me were heretofore unknown to me. 3. With respect to the Listings listed below, I will not enter into any negotiations for the purchase thereof in whole or part except by communicating my offer or negotiation through a representative of my exclusive agent, _insert Broker's name here_ . Further, I will not conclude or close any transaction or sale or take title or possession of the premises or Listings listed directly or indirectly unless _insert Broker's name here_ has received payment of their commission of 10%

of the total purchase price from the seller or unless I have received authorization in writing from _insert Broker's name here_, to do so. I agree that if I do not comply fully with this clause that I will pay _insert Broker's name here_, full commission of 10% of the total purchase price upon closing (minimum commission to _insert Broker's name here_ is ten thousand dollars). 4. That I will not accept the services of any other broker or intermediary with respect to any of the Listings mentioned below. 5. That the information given to me is confidential and that I will not furnish to any other person any of the information that I receive with respect to any of said Listings, and will not act, directly or indirectly, as mediator, intermediary broker, co-broker, or in any other capacity with respect to the purchase or sale of the Listings listed below. 6. That the commission due to _insert Broker's name here_, is 10% of the entire purchase price paid for the Listings listed below. Should Buyer purchase, in whole or part, any of the Listings listed herein, said commission shall be paid by the seller, unless I breach this contract in any way in which event I agree to pay to _insert Broker's name here_ an amount equal to 10% of the price listed below. Minimum commission ten thousand dollars. 7. Purchase price shall include, but not be limited to, the cash down payment and any other cash, any equity transactions, any transfer of securities, stock, stock options or stock warrants, purchase money mortgage and the balance of all security agreements, accrued interest, debts, or other obligations remaining outstanding at the time of closing or any other act tantamount to a sale, partnership, merger or employment contract. 8. That if the undersigned is introduced to another party by _insert Broker's name here_, and the undersigned and such other party purchase or exchange a business or property, including but not limited to real estate and buildings, or any interest in such business or property, or a lease or leasehold interest or enter into a lease for the purpose of constructing a business, whether or not such business or location is listed below, and such transaction is consummated either in the individual names or through the medium of a corporation or the purchase of stock in a corporation, or through some agency or person other than _insert Broker's name here_, then and in that event, the undersigned agrees to pay to _insert Broker's name here_, as and for compensation for procuring a business associate a sum representing Ten percent of the total sales

APPENDIX II

price or a commission of 10% of the total rent payable under the lease. 9. The undersigned expressly acknowledges that the agency created by this agreement shall not preclude _insert Broker's name here_ from acting as agent for any seller or prospective purchaser, or from giving the below listed information to other prospective purchasers. 10. If _insert Broker's name here_, is required to engage counsel in order to enforce this agreement, the undersigned agrees to pay _insert Broker's name here_ reasonable expenses including attorney's fees in the amount of 35% of the selling price as stated below. 11. The validity of this agreement shall not be diminished by virtue of the fact that the owner of any business listed herein has sold this business, been foreclosed, or that the seller conveying title to the undersigned is not presently the owner. If any provision of this Agreement is found to be legally unenforceable, such unenforceability shall not prevent enforcement of any other provision of the Agreement. 12. The monies to be paid under this agreement shall be based on the "gross selling price," which price shall include, but not be limited to the balance of all security agreements, accrued interest, debts or other obligations remaining outstanding at the time of the sale. Same shall apply in the event of the sale of stock of a corporation. 13. In the event that I lease any of the locations listed below from the business owner, the landlord or any other person who controls the location, then _insert Broker's name here_ shall be entitled to a leasing commission (Minimum leasing commission to _insert Broker's name here_ is ten thousand dollars). 14. The statements, facts and figures contained herein were obtained from the seller and sources deemed reliable, however, no guarantee is made as to their accuracy. I will not hold the broker responsible for any misrepresentation made.

Signed_____

Date _____

Name: _____

Address: _____

Cell phone: _____

Home phone: _____

Office phone: _____

E-Mail: _____

4. MEDICAL PRACTICE QUESTIONNAIRE

Full Name: _____

Name of Practice: _____
Address: _____ Zip: _____
Phone: _____ Fax: _____
Home Phone: _____ Cell Phone: _____
E-mail: _____
Last Year Gross Income: $ _____ Net Income: $_____
Prior Year Gross: $_____ Net: $_____
Location: Prof. Bldg._____ Shop Ctr. _____ Free Standing _____
Size of Office: _____ Sq. Ft.   # of Rooms Equipped: _____
Rent $____/month   Own Office? __ Lease? __ Lease Expires ____
Leases Assignable? Yes/No   Conditions _____
Makeup of Practice: FFS __% PPO __% HMO __% Medicaid __%
Value and Age of Equipment: _____
(major office equipment, leasehold improvements—not supplies & instruments)
Years in Practice _____ Number of Days Worked _____
Full Time Receptionist? _____ Number of Assistants _____
Will Staff Stay On? _____
Of Professional Employees?   DRs _____   NPs _____   PAs _____
Do Employees Have Non-Competes? _____
Salaries: Professional Staff $_____ Non-Professional $_____
Number of New Patients Per Month _____
Insurance Plans Accepted: _____
_____
_____

Zip Codes Most Served _____
Pending Litigation, Disciplinary or Board Actions? ___*(explain below)*
Reason for Leaving and Time Frame Expected: _____
_____

Please Fax this questionnaire to *provide Fax number*. If you are unsure about some numbers, please estimate. This is for me to help you come up with a fair and appropriate asking price.

5. SAMPLE LETTER TO PATIENTS

Dear _____:

It has been an honor to serve your family's needs, and I am writing now to let you know of my plans to retire. I have selected Dr. _____, a highly qualified _____ whose background includes _____, to take over my practice. I am sure you will find Dr. _____ as caring and concerned for your health needs as I. I will be in the office for the next __ months to ease the transition, and my receptionists and nurses, _____ and _____ will remain to work with Dr. _____. Please feel free to call us with any questions.

Thank you again for allowing me to care for your medical needs. I am certain you will feel comfortable and secure in the future with Dr. _____.

6. PRACTICE APPRAISALS

The following information is among that which will be required in order to create a professional business appraisal:

- Financial Statement Input and Adjustments (up to 6 years of historic input; includes annualization by last 12 months or percentages)
- Financial Statement Analysis (5 schedules and 30 charts)
- General Schedules (premiums and discounts, excess/non-operating assets, working capital analysis, capital expenditure analysis, and long term debt analysis)
- Valuation Methods (use up to 22 valuation methods)
- Income Approaches (4 methods)
- Market Approaches (12 methods)
- Cost Approaches (3 methods)
- Custom Methods (up to 3 methods)
- Deal Structure and What-if Analysis (includes sanity check, deal scenarios, pay back analysis, IRR and what-if scenarios)

GLOSSARY OF TERMS

Accounting Period
The period of time over which a business's income and expense statement summarizes changes (usually based on a fiscal year).

Accounts Payable
An obligation by a business to pay an amount to a vendor or other creditor for goods and services purchased on credit.
Amount owing on open accounts to suppliers, vendors and other creditors for goods and services.

Accounts Receivable
A financial claim by a business against a customer arising from a sale of goods or services on credit. One measure of the health of a business is how fast customers pay off their accounts. Less that 30 days is good, 30 to 60 days may be okay, and over 60 days could be a problem.

Accrued Interest
Unpaid interest to date on a note or mortgage.

Accumulated Depreciation
The total depreciation of an asset that has been charged as an expense to date.

Acknowledge
A declaration by someone that something is true.

Addendum
Anything added to a document, letter, agreement, or legal instrument—similar to an amendment. For instance, there may be several addendums that accompany an offer to purchase a business or real estate, such as a contingency addendum.

Adjusted EBITDA
Adjusted EBITDA (Adj. EBITDA is often the abbreviation) is generally the net profit showing on the bottom line of a tax return or profit and loss statement; plus interest expenses on items which will be paid off at closing or items which a Buyer would not have, such as vehicles which are excluded from a sale, or bank loans which will not be assumed; plus federal and state income taxes expensed; plus depreciation and amortization; plus Seller's salary which is expensed (where there is a W-2 or 1099…) plus Seller's personal perks which could be considered superlative to the operation of the business, such as Seller's life insurance, Seller's health insurance (perhaps the Buyer's spouse has other insurance which would cover the Buyer,); plus section 179 expenses; plus tax loss carry-forwards (again, non-cash in current year;) plus any one-time non-recurring costs (as in a new air conditioning system which won't need replacement for years;) plus any automobile expenses not necessary for the efficient operation of the business. (Note that there are certain items some Sellers will attempt to add back to cash flow which may or may not be legitimate add-backs to cash flow, but which lenders certainly will not consider as legitimate add-backs since the lender will not be auditing every invoice expensed. A Buyer could do so, but only if no is lender necessary.)

Adjusted Net Income
This figure is equivalent to a real world estimate of income. ANI includes an adjustment for the inevitable depreciation (and occasional appreciation) of assets.

Affidavit
A sworn statement; written oath such as acknowledgment.

Affirmation
A solemn declaration; a non-religious oath.

Agency
The legal relationship between a principal and his agent arising from a contract in which the principal engages the agent to perform certain acts on the principals behalf.

Agency Disclosure

Written explanation to be signed by a prospective buyer or seller. It is an explanation to the client the role that the broker plays in a transaction. The purpose of disclosure is to explain whether the broker represents the buyer or seller or is a dual agent, (i.e. representing both) or a subagent (an agent of the sellers broker). This allows the customer to understand to which party the broker owes loyalty.

Agent

A person (natural), corporation, society, association or partnership (legal persons) acting by authority of a principal in a realty transaction for compensation.

Agreement of Sale

A bilateral contract whereby buyer promises to buy and seller promises to sell by execution and delivery of deed; also know as Purchase and Sale Agreement (P&S). Agreement means the same as Contract.

Agreement in Principle

A preliminary agreement reached between the buyer and seller of a business that outlines the general terms under which more detailed negotiations will be undertaken.

Allocation of Purchase Price

In an asset sale, the purchase price must be allocated to certain assets; the balance is goodwill.

Generally, when a Buyer and Seller assign a specific number of dollars to various components of a business purchase or business and real estate purchase. For example, the allocation might assign a certain dollar value to the furniture, fixtures and equipment; another portion of the purchase price to a non-compete agreement; another dollar amount to the inventory at cost; another dollar amount to leasehold improvements; another to goodwill (or the intrinsic value of a going concern); a portion to training and consultation and possibly the balance to the building and land if it is part of the sale.

Amortization

A spreading out of costs over a period of time similar to depreciation. For example, it can be a reduction in a debt or fund by periodic payments covering interest and part of the principal over a period of time. It is different from depreciation in that depreciation usually refers to physical things where amortization applies to things that expire (mortgages, patents, etc.). Act of liquidating an indebtedness by equal and periodic payments usually monthly; this direct reduction method means each payment remains constant but ratio of principal and interest changes with an increasing larger portion credited to reducing debt; savings and loan associations popularized method.

Amortization Schedule
A tabular presentation of the reduction in value of something being amortized.

Arms-Length Buyer
Any person, corporation, or other entity with whom you deal regarding the sale of your business and who has no prior financial or family involvement with you.

Asking Price
The total amount for which a business or an ownership interest is offered for sale; Seller's asking price for the business.

Angel Money
Money obtained from wealthy individuals or groups who ordinarily believe in the investment potential of the business. A Venture Capitalist, a person or firm investing funds in a business venture, expecting financial returns, is, to the buyer, an Angel.

Annual Receipts
Gross sales in dollars for last full fiscal year.

Appraisal
An estimate of value.

Appreciation
Increase in value resulting from market forces such as demand stronger than supply.

Asking Price
The total amount for which a business or an ownership interest is offered for sale.

Asset Sale
Purchase of certain assets and/or liabilities, leaving the seller the remainder as well as the corporate entity. The term has two definitions. The proper definition depends on its usage:
1. The means by which a business owner transfers ownership of tangible and intangible assets to another owner without transferring the ownership structure.
2. The sale of a business enterprise at a price based solely upon the value of the tangible assets.

Asset-Based Lenders
Commercial lenders who are willing to take on more risk than commercial banks, lending against accounts receivable and inventory and being subordinate to commercial banks.

Assumed Name
Sometimes referred to as "Fictitious Name," it is the name of the business. In most areas, the name is filed with the County Records Department and/or at the State Level. (See DBA)

Attachment
A writ issued, beginning or during a legal action, commanding sheriff to attach (seize) property, rights and effects of defendant to satisfy possible credit demands of plaintiff if judgment comes out in plaintiffs favor.

Attorney-in-Fact
Anyone who is authorized in writing to perform certain acts for another under written power of attorney; valid only during lifetime of party giving this power.

Auction
When the seller and/or its intermediary orchestrates the selling process by encouraging buyers to bid and rebid until the highest and best offer is received.

Balance Sheet
A statement showing the nature and amount of a business's assets, liabilities, and equity on a given date. In dollar amounts, the balance sheet shows what the business owned, what it owed, and the ownership interest in the company of its owners.

Base Rent
The minimum rent in a retail, office building or warehouse lease, before any lease provisions for common area maintenance, tenant's pro-rata share of real estate taxes and insurance, or any special advertising expenses as one might find in a major retail shopping mall. Most leases will have a base (beginning) year, after which the lease will call for tenant's pro-rata share of any increases in the extra expenses. Other building leases may contain a provision for a percentage of additional rent above the base rent if the business hits a certain dollar value of annual gross income (often termed a "percentage clause" or "percentage lease").

Bill of Sale
A written instrument which is the evidence of transfer of one persons right in personal property to another. It is a legal document or instrument used to transfer personal property. A "business" is considered personal property. The Bill of Sale is signed by the Seller of the business at Closing. It is generally a document prepared by the escrow or Title Company as the case may be.

Blue-Sky
That portion of a requested price that cannot be supported through the application of established valuation methodology and which generates no economic benefit.

Board Certified Business Evaluation
A document that shows financial market value for a business entity. It will be prepared by a third party firm certified to perform valuations and will show substantiation for the value stated.

Book Value
Also known as net worth, the figure derived by deducting all the liabilities from all the assets. It signifies the value of the equipment and fixtures after depreciation has been taken on the balance sheet of

a business. There are more concise and in depth definitions of this, but for the purpose of this glossary, this is a number that accountants will generally want to see. It may differ from the actual fair market value of the assets.

Book Value (of a Business)
The book value of a business is determined from the financial records, by adding the current value of all assets (generally excluding such intangibles as goodwill), then deducting all debts and other liabilities. Book value of the business may have little or no significant to relationship to actual market value due to depreciation and lack of consideration for goodwill (intangible assets).

Book Value (of an Asset)
The accounting value of an asset shown on the balance sheet that is the original cost of the asset less its accumulated depreciation. Keep in mind that this value may have little or no relationship to the real market value of the asset. Frequently, depreciation expenses are charged much faster that the actual decline in the asset's value.

Bridge Loan
A temporary loan to cover the financing shortfall of the acquisition until permanent funding is available.

Bulk Sale
A transfer in a whole or substantially all of the inventory and fixtures of a business, which is not in the ordinary course of business, such as the entire business.

Bulk Sales Act
State laws, which are to protect creditors against undisclosed sales of all or substantially all of a business's goods prior to receiving payables due creditors or vendors. In these cases, there will most likely be no financing. It requires certain notices prior to the sale and sets forth ways of voiding the sale (see Uniform Commercial Code.) Some states, such as Texas, have repealed the Bulk Sales Act. In this case, in lieu of the Bulk Sales laws, the escrow or title company will generally prepare an "Affidavit of No Debts and Liens" for the Seller to execute at Closing.

Bulk Transfer

Article 6 of the Uniform Commercial Code regulates the bulk transfer through the sale or ownership change of a large portion (usually greater than 50%) of a business's inventory, material, supplies, merchandise, and equipment. Requirements include the advance notification of creditors of the impending sale of a business and its assets listed above to prevent fraud. Provisions in each state are somewhat different so check your local statutes.

Business Broker

A Business Broker is an intermediary dedicated to serving clients and customers who desire to sell or acquire businesses. A business broker is committed to providing professional services in a knowledgeable, ethical and timely fashion. Typically, a Business Broker provides information and business advice to sellers and buyer's, maintains communications between the parties and coordinates the negotiations and closing processes to complete desired transactions. Other common names are business transfer specialist, business intermediary, merger & acquisition agent and business consultant.

Business Potential

What a business owner wants to base his business sale price off of. In actuality, it is one of the main reasons a buyer chooses a particular business.

Business Valuation

Determination of the fair market value of a business. A valuation differs from a business appraisal in many ways—primarily the cost and the fact that in an actual appraisal, the value of the equipment is researched to determine more exact fair market values.

Business Plan

A written plan detailing a business's sales projections, expenses, marketing strategy, and objectives. A business plan is of great importance to anyone in business, but of paramount importance to anyone buying or starting a business. You will never get there if you don't know where you are going.

C Corporation

Entity or organization created by operation of law with rights of doing business essentially the same as those of an individual. The entity has continuous existence regardless of that of its owners and generally limits liability of owners to the amount invested in the organization. The entity ceases to exist only if dissolved according to proper legal process. It is easily transferred and has an unlimited life.

Capital Assets

Permanent assets such as machinery, buildings, land, fixtures, equipment, etc. Inventory is not included as a capital asset. Often used interchangeably with FFE (Furniture, fixtures and equipment) when there is no real property involved.

Capital Expenditures

Investments of cash for improvements to remain competitive in a business.

Capitalized Items

Have an economic life of one year or more and the cost is moved to the balance sheet, and then these costs can be written down by depreciation or amortization over time.

Capitalization Rate

The conversion of income into value as part of the valuation process by the application of a capitalization factor (any multiplies or divisor used to convert income to value). A rate of return utilized to derive the capital value of an income stream, generally expressed as a percentage. It is merely one quick indicator of real estate value or business value, as it is basically a function of supply and demand—a reflection of the current market conditions. Annual income or adjusted EBITDA divided by the cap rate equals value. Generally accepted cap rates may vary greatly within different geographical areas, within different business industries, and within sub-areas, such as different neighborhoods of a particular city. In the business service sector, there are countless types of service companies, which could all have differing accepted cap rates for their specific company type. In addition, the generally accepted cap rates for one type of business may be one rate in Dallas, and a totally different rate in New York. The market cap rates are also in a continual state of flux, affected not only by all of the above, but also by changes in local, national and world economics, political and other conditions.

Cash Cow
A business that has a steady cash flow, but whose earnings have remained nearly the same for the past five years, showing little growth.

Cash Flow
The amount of money left over after the cost of goods sold and general, selling, and administrative expenses, but before interest depreciation, taxes, and amortization. All cash (and cash equivalent) that flows to the benefit of the Owner including the net profit declared on tax returns. Dollars available to business owner from operations of company (business earnings before interest, taxes, depreciation and owners compensation assuming it's an owner operated business).

Cashier's Check
Generally required as earnest money deposit on a purchase offer for a business. The Buyer will exchange actual cash, wired funds, or other good funds with the bank for a small fee. The bank will then give the Buyer a check, which is almost like cash. If the offer is not signed both ways, the Buyer can usually take the same check back to the bank for exchange for cash. In business purchases, it is generally not deposited until the offer is accepted. It is often not deposited with an escrow agency until the Brokers have been given the authority to open escrow, meaning the parties wish the escrow or title company to begin preparation of the closing documents and all of the contingencies are generally removed. (In pure real estate transactions the earnest money is generally deposited with the title company upon acceptance of the offer.)

Caveat Emptor
Latin for "Let the Buyer beware."

Certified Lender Program
This process is for the more sophisticated and experienced lenders who have graduated beyond GP status. Typically, the lender now

submits a complete package to the SBA and as a CLP Lender they are guaranteed a 3-day turnaround from the SBA.

Client
An entity with which a Business Broker has a fiduciary relationship.

Closing
The process of legally completing the purchase. When all of the lien searches have been performed, the final documents prepared by the escrow company, the proofs of those documents have passed muster with the attorneys for all parties, the contingencies of closing have all been approved, the lease has been transferred, any legal incorporation work has been completed by the purchaser, and when the purchaser brings the balance of the down payment or total purchase price to the escrow company or title company in the form of a cashier's check, wire-transferred funds, or via funds from a third party lender. In short, this is usually when the business is transferred from the Seller to the Buyer. If there is no third party lender, then this is also when the Seller is paid his/her proceeds, and the Buyer takes possession of the business. If a third party loan is involved, the loan generally takes two to three business days to actually fund.

Closing Costs
Costs of seller and buyer at conveyance of realty.

Closing Statement
A written accounting of funds to seller and buyer at passing of papers. It is a statement that spells out the financial settlements of debits and credits between the business or real estate Buyer and Seller. The Buyer and Seller will generally have separate statements.

Co-Brokerage
An agreement between two or more business brokers for sharing services, responsibility and compensation on behalf of a client.

Co-Business Broker
A Business Broker who shares services, responsibility, and compensation on behalf of a client.

Confidentiality Agreement
A pact that forbids buyers, sellers, and their agents in a given business deal from disclosing information about the transaction to others.

Contingency
A clause in an agreement or contract that is only binding upon the occurrence of a stated event. For example, the sale of the business is contingent upon the Buyer obtaining an SBA Loan, or that the Buyer is satisfied with the books and records. These contingencies (sometimes termed "conditions") generally have an expiration date in the agreement or contract, beyond which the contingency is considered to be removed or satisfied.

Covenant
A promise in an agreement or contract agreeing to performance or nonperformance of certain acts, or requiring or preventing certain acts or uses.

Cooperating Business Brokers
Business brokers who share their knowledge, expertise, and skills for the benefit of the business brokerage profession, clients, customers and the public good.

Collateral
Property pledged by a borrower to protect the interests of the lender. A security, such as a mortgage, given to protect debt, and sale of a business by exchanging asset titles. Stock certificates, cash, promissory notes and bank loans are often collateralized or secured by the company's accounts receivables, inventory, and/or equipment.

Commingling
The mixing of funds held for the benefit of others with the broker's personal or business funds.

Commission
The negotiated fee, usually a percentage of the purchase and sale price of the total business cost, earned by a business broker for facilitating the sale of a business. Usually, the value of the inventory and other non capitalized assets are excluded from the calculation of the commission.

Confidentiality
The provision of proprietary information by one party to another for that party's exclusive use, with a prohibition against passing it on to others.

Conditional Sales Contract
A contract in which owner retains title until buyer has met all terms and conditions; a familiar device in land sales; also called land contract or installment contract. Buyer acquires equitable title until final payment; after delivery of deed, buyer has legal title.

Consideration
Something of value exchanged between parties of a contract; money, services, goods or promises.

Contract
A legal instrument between two parties to do or not to do something; in reality, it must be in writing to be enforceable.

Counter Offer
Voids first offer and creates new offer.

Contingent
Dependent on or conditioned by something else. For example, the price established for the business may vary depending on some future event.

Contingent Payments
Future financial obligations that are dependent on contractual events taking place.

Conventional Bank Financing
In the realm of small business transfer, it is financing provided to a buyer based on a company's assets and the buyer's collateral.

Cost of Goods Sold
The price paid for the merchandise which has been sold by a business; beginning inventory plus net purchases minus ending inventory equals cost of goods sold.

Covenant Not To Compete
An agreement given by the seller of a business to the business buyer to not compete in that or a similar business for a specified period of time, and within a specified geographic area.

Covenants
Binding agreements between the buyer and the seller that restrict each party from taking certain actions, particularly during the letter of intent period and closing.

CPA
Certified Public Accountant.

Current Assets
Also known as "liquid assets" which could easily be converted to cash. For instance, this would not include real estate, as real estate is not readily convertible within a few days.

Current Liabilities
Short-term debts or accounts payable to employees, vendors, etc.

Customer
An entity to a transaction that receives services and benefits but has no fiduciary relationship with the Business Broker.

DBA
"Doing Business As"—the assumed name and/or identification of ownership of the business. For instance, a corporation or an individual or partnership entity could have one name for the particular legal entity, but be doing business as another entirely different name, which is the name the public generally recognizes as the company name. Immediately following closing, the Buyer will file a notarized assumed name certificate with the county records department (and sometimes also with the state) taking with them in hand the signed and notarized "assumed name abandonment form" executed by the Seller.

Deal Flow
A stream of potential business acquisitions moving across your desk in a quantity that allows you to select the few that meet your criteria.

Debt Service
This is the payment of principal and interest required on a debt (usually a loan or mortgage) over a specified period of time and interest rate.

Deficiency Judgment
Court award to lender if sale at public auction does not equal mortgage debt.

Definitive Agreement
A document that settles or describes the terms of a business transfer in a final and conclusive form.

Depreciation
Charges against earnings to write off the cost, less salvage value, of an asset over its estimated useful life. It involves amortization of fixed assets, such as plant and equipment, so as to allocate the cost over their depreciable life. Depreciation decreases taxable income but does not reduce cash. It is a bookkeeping entry for accounting and tax purposes and does not represent cash outlay.

Disclaimer
A hold harmless statement that puts one party on notice that it is not liable for information which it does not investigate and which would be impractical to investigate, as when one cannot be an investigator into accounting information when one is not an accountant. Or when a Seller gives a Buyer information, or the Seller gives the Broker information, who in turn gives the same information to the Buyer and the Broker is disclaiming any liability or responsibility for the accuracy of said information.

Discretionary Earnings
The earnings of a business enterprise prior to the following items:
- Income taxes
- Non-operating income and expenses
- Nonrecurring income and expenses
- Depreciation and amortization
- Interest expense or income
- Owner's total compensation for those services, which could be provided by a sole owner/manager.

Downpayment
The amount of cash a qualified buyer needs to qualify for seller financing.

Draw, Owners
Sometime the owner of a small business (sole proprietorship or closely-held corporation) will take income as a draw as opposed to a salary. The terms are essentially the same except that generally a salary means that all withholding taxes, FICA, etc., are accounted for on the books of the business, whereas draw is straight cash to the owner who pays all tax obligations separately on a personal income tax return.

Due Diligence
The investigation of the other party's business practices in an attempt to uncover previously unknown information or verify given information. It is the research performed by a buyer on the company they have intent to purchase. Due diligence includes items such as review of financial statements, analyzing aging reports and speaking with vendors.

Earnest Money
Deposit or binder given with Agreement to Buy.

Earnout
A part of the purchase price that is dependent on a future performance variable, such as profits or sales. It is a method of a seller note that is based on the company's sales and/or earnings by the new buyer. The company's sales and/or earnings must meet a predefined level for the seller to receive full payment of the earn-out.

EBIT
Business earnings before interest and federal or state income taxes. (also see EBITDA and Adjusted EBITDA)

EBITDA
Business earnings before taking into consideration the interest expenses, federal and state income taxes, depreciation and amortization expenses (non-cash items.) Most business Sellers, Buyers and lenders accept the common practice of adding the non-cash expenses such as

depreciation and amortization back into the profit to derive the true cash flow available.

Employment Agreement
This is an agreement whereby key employees agree to remain with the business for a specified period of time under certain conditions.

Escrow
Money that is delivered to a third party and held on deposit until the party to receive it fulfills certain conditions. Also, money that is given by a prospective buyer with an Offer to Purchase or Letter of Intent to show good faith to a seller. If the company is sold, it also acts as a down payment.

Escrow Company
A company used as an intermediary to perform all the legal background checks, title and lien searches and other items. They are also responsible for housing the escrow deposit that is supplied with a Letter of Intent or Offer to Purchase. In addition, they act as the transfer agent for the monies that come from a buyer and/or loan source to the seller.

Equity
Value or interest an owner of realty has above any debt on property; difference between value and mortgage debt.

Escrow
The holding of something of value by a person (escrow agent) for the benefit of other parties.

Exclusive Right to Sell
An employment agreement and contract giving the broker the right to receive a Commission, if the property or business is sold by anyone including the seller during the term of the agreement.

Expense
Anything that a company buys that has an economic life of less than one year. It shows up immediately on the income statement.

Fair Market Value
What a willing Buyer is willing to pay and willing Seller is willing to sell for—neither party being under duress to buy or sell. What the assets would most likely sell for in the open market; this is often determined by a professional appraiser.

FF&E
Furniture, fixtures and equipment. Leasehold improvements are often loosely included in the FFE values.

Fiduciary
A position of trust (e.g. broker to principal).

Fictitious Name
A name frequently used by sole proprietors or partnerships to provide business name, other than those of the owners or partners, under which the business will operate. Also known as the trades name and that "doing business as" (d/b/a) name.

FIFO
The first-in/first-out method of inventory accounting that assumes that goods that enter the inventory first are the first to be sold.

Financing Statement
A recorded document filed generally in the Secretary of State's office, which puts the public on notice of a recorded lien against the fixtures and equipment of the business. This lien must be removed by the filing party prior to transfer of ownership of those assets or the business as a whole. (See UCC also)

Finders Fee
An amount paid to another party for locating and referring a client or customer (illegal in Hawaii).
Also, a fee to a broker for arranging a loan for a client; or can also mean a fee to a broker for locating a property for client.

Fiscal Year
The annual accounting period selected by a business to best correspond to its operations. A fiscal year can correspond to a normal calendar year or begin/end anywhere in between, e.g.; the federal government's fiscal year begins October 1 and ends September 30.

Fixed Assets

Items such as building structures, land, furniture, fixtures, and equipment, vehicles (or rolling stock.) Inventory and Supplies are in a separate category. Leasehold improvements are generally included in the fixed asset values. The leasehold improvements are especially important in businesses that require an extraordinary amount of plumbing, refrigeration, electrical lines, etc. For example, in a coin laundry purchase, the leasehold improvements could actually be a depreciable asset over a relatively short time. It depends on the tax laws at the time.

FMV (FF&E)

Fair market value of furniture, fixtures and equipment.

Form 4506

A form required by SBA from the seller, which is used to obtain a certified copy of the company's tax returns for verification purposes.

Franchise

A form of business organization in which the franchisor (the primary company) provides to a franchisee (the local business) a market tested business package involving a product or service. The franchisee operates under the franchiser's trade name and markets goods and/or services in accordance with a contractual agreement.

General Program

This is the lowest rating and is given to lenders who know little about the SBA process. These lenders must submit each loan application to the SBA for additional underwriting and ultimate approval. This process can take up to two weeks with multiple requests for additional information.

Going Concern

Any business that is operated in an active, for profit way that creates value beyond the company's assets.

Goodwill
The collection of intangible assets represented in dollars by the difference between the total purchase price for the business and the net value of the tangible assets being purchased.

Gross Lease
Owner receives rent and pays out expenses such as in apartment leasing; Net Lease: owner receives rent and tenant also pays out expenses normally paid by owner such as taxes, etc.

Gross Revenues
Any positive cash flow that enter a business. Gross revenues do not take expenses into account, and are therefore not the most highly recommended figure to extrapolate a business's value from which to extrapolate the value of a business.

Hard Assets
Furniture, equipment, property, fixtures owned by a company. This is everything that a buyer can feel, touch and see.

Highest Justifiable Price
The highest price that a willing and able buyer will pay for a company.

Hold Harmless Agreement
An agreement wherein one party agrees to repay another for any loss or damage suffered. Generally, a Broker's document will include multiple hold-harmless clauses, as a Broker does not investigate the accuracy, truthfulness or completeness of information it receives from a Buyer or Seller and therefore cannot be held liable for same.

Holdback Provision
In the purchase and sale agreement, a provision stating that if a buyer winds up having to pay a debt that the seller did not disclose, it will be paid from an amount that was held back at closing and placed in an escrow account.

Income and Expense Statement
A summary of a business's revenues, expenses, and profits for a specific period of time, usually for a full fiscal year.

Indemnification
Exemption for the buyer from incurred penalties or liabilities after the closing as a result of incomplete representations and warranties of the seller.

Intangibles
Assets that are not physical, such as licenses, franchises, trademarks, customer lists, unpatented technology, etc.

Intermediary
An agent who is a mergers and acquisitions consultant to the buyer or seller and is expected to facilitate the transaction.

Inventory (INV)
Items, which a business owner has purchased or manufactured available for sale to customers or clients.

Investment Banker
An intermediary who often provides additional services such as bridge loans or underwritings.

Irrevocable
Unchangeable.

Judgment
A court action describing indebtedness of one to another.

Lease
The agreement between parties for the rent of a particular asset (real estate, automobile, equipment, etc.). Contract between lessor (landlord) and lessee (tenant) for exclusive possession of realty for specified period under specific terms after which property reverts to lessor.

Leasehold
The interest, which a lessee has in realty.

Leaseback
The purchase of improved property and the leasing of it back to seller; creates capital and favored tax treatment for seller.

Lease Improvements
Usually refers to the improvements made by a lessee to a lessor's property. Generally, leasehold improvements may be capitalized by a business and depreciated against income, but ownership reverts to the lessor upon completion of the lease.

Lehman Formula
The industry standard commission rate, which is a sliding scale, i.e., 10-9-8-7 percent on each successive million dollars of the purchase price.

Letter of Intent
A preliminary offer to purchase a business, usually non binding, which if accepted by the seller leads to the drafting of a purchase and sale agreement. The letter of intent is an agreement between a buyer and a seller used in connection with the acquisition of a company. The letter of intent describes the basic terms and conditions of the transaction between the buyer and the seller, including price, due diligence periods, exclusivity or no-shops, and the basic conditions to closing the deal. Customarily presented before a definitive purchase agreement is entered into, the letter of intent provides a road map for the parties involved in the transaction. A letter of intent to purchase is generally non-binding and unacceptable on the purchase of a small business. However, it is quite common in the middle market arena. This is a preliminary agreement between two parties that intend to enter into a business transfer. This letter is often followed by an Offer to Purchase or Definitive Agreement.

L.I.
Leasehold Improvements, such as piping, built-in cabinetry, electrical, carpeting, or special built-in display components, etc. (synonymous with tenant improvements).

Lien
A charge or hold on assets, usually by a creditor until indebtedness is satisfied.

Liquidation Value
The market value of a business's tangible assets minus its liabilities under a forced sale. A debt; a claim against property for payment of some debt.

Lis Pendens
Notice filed in a registry of deeds warning all persons that title to certain property is in litigation.

Listing
A written engagement (contract) between a principal and an agent authorizing the agent to perform services for the principal involving the principal's property (business). Generally the services provided by the agent involve the proposed sale of the principal's property or business. Also, the property or business listed by the agent is called a Listing.

List
To obtain a Listing.

M & A
An acronym for mergers and acquisitions.

Market
Companies with sales between $2 million and $150 million.

Multiples
An abbreviated terminology for capitalization rates.

Master Lease
A lease that contains the authority to control subsequent leases generally referred to as subleases. The one who holds the master lease is, in effect, one of the landlords, whether he/she owns the property or not.

Middle Market
The lower end of M & A (Mergers and Acquisitions) where the company grosses between $5 and $50 million.

Month to Month ("M—M," "M to M" or Tenancy At Will)
A situation wherein there is no written lease, so the lessee can be evicted on short notice, generally thirty days or whatever is required in a particular state.

Monthly Payroll
Salaries and wages to employees.

Multiples
An abbreviated terminology for capitalization rates.

Net Income
The profit of a company that is calculated by subtracting the total expenses from the total sales. This is the amount that taxes are calculated from.

Net Present Value
Money paid out in the future discounted at the opportunity cost of capital for a similar risk over the specified period of time.

Non Disclosure Agreement (NDA) (Also called Confidentiality Agreement)
These are generally agreements, which the Sellers of businesses and often Sellers of commercial real estate and/or their brokers will require to be executed by potential Buyers prior to disclosure of the location and sensitive and confidential information.

Non-operating/Noncontributing Asset
An asset unnecessary to the operation of a business enterprise and the generation of its revenues.

Off-Balance Sheet Items
Unrecorded obligations such as repurchase agreements, pending lawsuits; and unfunded pensions.

Offer to Purchase Agreement

An agreement wherein the title to the inventory, fixtures and equipment of the business remain with the Seller, until the terms and conditions of the contract have been met, and all contingencies removed. Some Buyers will place a condition in this agreement specifying that once everything has been satisfied and the transaction is ready to occur, that all parties will execute a more definitive asset (or other) purchase agreement.

Open Listing

An employment agreement and contract given to any number of brokers without any liability to pay a commission to anyone except the one who first secures a buyer who is ready, willing and able to meet the terms of the listing or presents an offer acceptable to the seller. The sale of the property or business terminates all open listings, and in most cases, the seller may cancel an open listing at any time. In many states an open listing must have an expiration date.

Overhead

Method of allocation all non-labor costs to the various products manufactured or services performed.

Owner

A generic term used in business brokerage to represent the proprietor, general partner or controlling shareholder (singular or plural as appropriate) of a business enterprise.

Owner (Seller) Carry Back Note

The portion of the sale price that is not paid to the owner at closing. In essence, the seller is "loaning" the buyer that amount since the buyer will pay installments to the seller on that portion.

Owner's Discretionary Cash Flow (ODCF)

The current owner's true profit, excluding any discretionary expenses, personal expenses, owner's salary if a corporation, one-time non-recurring expenses, and/or non-cash items such as amortization or depreciation; or Seller's discretionary profit. When determining the market value of a small company ODCF is more commonly used than EBITDA, since most small businesses afford a monetary benefit to the owner, which can be limited to the EBITDA. (Has often been used synonymously with EBIT, EBITDA, Adjusted EBITDA, Seller's Discretionary Cash Flow, SDC, Seller's Discretionary Earnings, SDE, Normalized Adjusted Earnings.)

Owner's Salary
The salary or wages paid to the owner, including related payroll burden.

Owner's Total Compensation
Total of an owner's salary and perquisites, after the compensation of all other owners has been adjusted to market value.

Partnership
A legal business association of two or more persons co-owning a business and sharing in the profits and losses. Although there are several kinds of partnerships, the tow most common are, general and limited partnerships.

Perquisites (Perks)
"Owner perks" are elements of compensation in addition to a regular salary, such as the use of a company automobile, country club membership, entertainment allowance, etc. Expenses incurred at the discretion of the owner, which are unnecessary to the continued operation of the business.

Preferred Lender Program
This is the top designation and enables the respective lenders to approve their own loans with no additional underwriting by the SBA. Typically, this designation means that the lender has sufficient experience and track history to adhere to SBA standards and make quality loans.
Courtesy: Ed McCormick, Simple SBA.com

Prepaid Items
Expenses of the business that are paid in advance and agreed between the parties to be pro-rated at closing. Examples are rent and Personal Property Taxes.

Procuring Cause
A legal term that means the cause resulting in accomplishing a goal. Used in real estate (or business brokerage) to determine whether a broker is entitled to a commission.

Pro Forma
A set of projected financial statements which usually includes: income and expense statements, cash flow projections, and balance sheets. Generally, in a purchase and sale of a business, a seller prepares an optimistic pro forma statement. The buyer should ensure that a realistic pro forma is used as part of the business plan for the newly acquired business.

Profit
All positive cash flow, minus any direct expenses made to generate said revenue. In Europe, profit is not synonymous with income, although in the USA it is.

Profit and Loss Statement
The same as the income and expense statement, a profit and loss statement or income statement provides a summary of a company's sales, expenses and net income over a stated period of time.

Promissory Note
A written promise to pay a sum of money at a specified future date in accordance with a predetermined interest rate and payment schedule. A written promise to repay a loan. Usually a key part of a business sale. Normally written from the buyer to the seller for a defined period, often 5-10 years.

Pro-Rate
To divide taxes, rent, and possibly other prepaid items based on the percentage of time, whether of the current month of closing or the current year, by the Seller and Buyer.

Recasting
Reconstruction of the financials to reflect what the income statement would be without excessive salaries and perks.

Referring Business Broker
A Business Broker who provides introductory information, which leads to a client relationship.

Rent
Monthly current payment to landlord or seller for facility lease.

Representation
A statement or condition made that something is true or accurate.

Representations and Warranties
Indemnifications and covenants written into the purchase and sale agreement that provide factual information that is important to protect the buyer in the event of future problems.

Return on Investment (ROI)
The annual income that an investment earns. Rate of return of total capital invested for the purchase of a business or real estate (for our purposes here) relative to the profits or adjusted EBITDA returned or assumed to be returned to the Buyer over a period of time, and is generally stated as a percentage.

ROI, ROE
Return on investment and return on equity; they must be greater than the cost of capital in order to create shareholder value.

S Corporation
An unaffiliated corporation owned by thirty-five or fewer individuals in which the profits flow to the individuals without a corporate tax being imposed.

SBA (Small Business Administration)
The U.S. Federal Government entity (www.sba.gov).

SBA Loan Fees
Generally 3% of the total loan, which is paid by the Borrower and goes directly to SBA. This is in addition to any Lender closing fees such as fees for business valuations, real estate appraisals, surveys, title policy, environmental appraisal fees, Lender packaging fees, etc.

Seller Financing
A situation in which the seller extends his or her own notes to the buyer in lieu of paying all cash at closing or obtaining other debt financing, such as bank loans.

Seller's Discretionary Cash Flow (SDC)
See Adjusted EBITDA, EBIT, EBITDA, Owner's Discretionary Cash Flow (ODCF).

SIC Code
Abbreviation for Standard Industry Code, a numerical categorization of industries. Most business directories, manufacturing or service, are organized by geography and SIC code.

Simple Interest
Interest on principal only, as compared to compound interest which is interest on both principal and accumulated interest.

Skimming
The business owner's personally taking money "off the top" of company revenue stream.

Sole Proprietorship
A form of business owned by one person who is responsible for the entire business operations and liabilities.

Stipulation
To make a special demand for something as a condition of an agreement.

Stock Sale
Purchase of the company's shares of stock; the buyer then assumes all the assets and all the debt, both tangible and intangible.

Sub-Chapter S Corporation
The IRS designation for a small corporation that offers the same liability limitations as a C corporation, but does not pay corporate taxes. Taxes on company profits and losses are paid by the individual shareholders in proportion to their ownership.

Tombstones
The details of a business sale transaction brokered by investment bankers and other intermediaries.

Transaction Value
The total of all consideration passed at any time between the Buyer and Seller for an ownership interest in a business enterprise and may include, but not limited to, all remuneration for tangible and intangible assets such as furniture, equipment, supplies, inventory, working capital, non-competition agreements, employment and/or consultation agreements, licenses, customer lists, franchise fees, assumed liabilities, stock options, stock or stock redemptions, real estate, leases, royalties, earn-outs and future considerations.

Uniform Commercial Code (UCC)
The laws (each state has their own version), which regulate the transfer of personal property (a business.) For instance, in Texas, a UCC I is filed as a recorded lien against a business, which cannot be transferred until a UCC III is signed by the Lienor (or Lender.) This is generally handled at closing by the Escrow Company or Title Company out of the proceeds from the Buyer. (Also see Financing Statement)

Valid
Legally binding.

Valuation
The formal process of estimating the worth of a business.

Walk Away Price
The highest price that a buyer will offer.

Warranty
An expressed or implied statement that a situation or thing is as it appears to be or is represented to Buyer.

Working Capital

The readily convertible capital required in a business to permit the regular carrying forward of operations free from financial embarrassment. In accounting, the excess of current assets over current liabilities as of any date. Also, funds invested in a company's cash. Working capital finances the cash conversion cycle of a business—the time required to convert raw materials into finished goods, finished goods into sales, and accounts receivables into cash.

The author welcomes your comments!

If you are interested in calling him, he can be reached at (516) 520-2000.

Printed in the United States
209486BV00001B/145-171/P